HEALTH AND NATIONAL RECONSTRUCTION IN NATIONALIST CHINA

The Development of Modern Health Services, 1928–1937

to

R., F. Y., and F. A.

HEALTH AND NATIONAL RECONSTRUCTION IN NATIONALIST CHINA

The Development of Modern Health Services, 1928–1937

Ka-che Yip

Published by the Association for Asian Studies, Inc.
Monograph and Occasional Paper Series, Number 50

Published by:

Association for Asian Studies, Inc.
1 Lane Hall
The University of Michigan
Ann Arbor, Michigan 48109

Library of Congress Cataloging-in-Publication Data

Yip, Ka-che, 1944–
    Health and National Reconstruction in Nationalist China: The Development
    of Modern Health Services, 1928–1937/ Ka-che Yip.

    p. cm—(Association for Asian Studies Monograph and Occasional Papers
    Series, Number 50)
    Includes bibliographical references and index.
    ISBN 0–924304–28–6 (hard copy)

    1. Medical policy—China—History—20th Century. 2. Medicine, State—
    China—History—20th Century. 3. Public Health Administration—China—
    History—20th Century. 4. Medical Education—China—History—20th
    Century. I. Title. II. Series: Monograph and Occasional Papers Series
    (Association for Asian Studies); Number 50.

RA395.C53Y57 1995   95-32271
362.1'0951'09043—dc20   CIP

The publication of this volume has been financed from a revolving fund supported
in part by the Luce Foundation. A full listing of the AAS Monograph Series appears
at the end of this volume.

Printed in the United States of America on archival quality, acid-free paper.

Contents

Acknowledgments

This study originated as a research project on the careers of several prominent modern physicians in the Republican era. As my research progressed, it became evident that the historical context, as well as the way in which modern health services developed in China, have received little attention from scholars working in the Nationalist period. At the initial stage of the formulation of a focus for my study, I am profoundly indebted to my *laoshi*, C. Martin Wilbur, for his always incisive and thoughtful comments. I also benefited from the interest and encouragement of Barbara Starfield of the Johns Hopkins School of Hygiene and Public Health who made it possible for me to undertake a Postdoctoral Fellowship in the spring semester of 1979 in the Department of Health Services Administration. I have profited greatly from my association with the faculty of that department and their help and patience is much appreciated by this novice in the health sciences.

At various stages of the research and writing of this study, I received constructive criticism from numerous friends and colleagues who have read sections of my work or papers I presented in scholarly forums on the subject. I am particularly grateful to Mary Bullock, Gilbert Chan, Yuet-wah Cheung, Abe Hiroshi, Donald Jordan, David Pong, James Reardon-Anderson, Laurence Schneider, Nathan Sivin, John Watt, John Witek, and Odoric Wou. I had the good fortune to interview Dr. C. C. Chen twice and I thank him for sharing with me his views and the story of his career, which is so much a part of this study. I also wish to thank Dr. William Lowe for taking the time to discuss with me the career of his father, Dr. P. V. Loh at Shanghai Medical College, and Mrs. Irene L. Hou, daughter of Dr. J. Heng Liu, who graciously permitted me to quote a conversation I had with her regarding her father's career. A special appreciation must go to the late Peter New, son of Dr. New Way-sung, for his constant interest and support and for his tireless efforts in promoting the study of the history of modern medicine in China.

This study would not have been possible without access to several archives and manuscript collections. Li Yun-han and his staff at the Historical Commission of the Kuomintang, Taiwan, and the archivists and librarians of the United Church of Canada Archives, Toronto; the Rockefeller Archive Center, North Tarrytown; the Roger S. Greene Papers Collection, Harvard University; the Oral History Project Special Collections, Columbia University; and the libraries of the University of Hong Kong were most helpful in providing guidance in the location of research materials.

Financial support for research and writing was provided by the School of Hygiene and Public Health, the Johns Hopkins University; the University of Maryland, Baltimore County; the Rockefeller Archive Center; the American Philosophical Society; and the Pacific Cultural Foundation. To all these institutions, my sincerest gratitude.

Some of the material in this volume has appeared in my articles "Health and Society in China: Public Health Education for the Community, 1912–1937," *Social Science and Medicine* 16, no. 12 (1982); and "Health and Nationalist Reconstruction: Rural Health in Nationalist China, 1928–1937," *Modern Asian Studies* 26, pt. 2 (1992). I am grateful to copyright holders Pergamon Press and Cambridge University Press for permission to reuse this material. I would like to thank Jan Opdyke and Carol Kelingos whose skillful and constructive editorial work has greatly improved the final manuscript.

Finally, a heartfelt note of appreciation to my family for their support and encouragement during the long process of completing this study.

A Note on Romanization

This study employs the pinyin form of romanization throughout, except in cases of place names and personal names that are familiar in the West. Thus, in the text, Peking, Peiping, and Canton are used instead of Beijing, Beiping, and Guangzhou, and Chiang Kai-shek and Sun Yat-sen rather than Jiang Jieshi and Sun Yixian. The romanization of some personal names follows the form used by the individuals themselves in their published works: examples are J. Heng Liu for Liu Ruiheng, and P. Z. King for Jin Baoxian. In such cases, the pinyin romanization is provided in parentheses when the name first appears. Professional names, with their pinyin equivalents, also are included in the glossary.

Introduction

On 10 October, 1928, the National Government of the Republic of China was officially inaugurated in Nanjing. The establishment of the new government under the Nationalists marked the climax of a long struggle, led by Dr. Sun Yat-sen, to set up a government based on his ideals of constitutional republicanism. The republic, founded after the Revolution of 1911, had been transformed into a meaningless caricature by Yuan Shikai whose death in 1916 released centrifugal forces that splintered the country into competing fiefdoms controlled by regional militarists. Moreover, far from becoming an independent, sovereign nation, China continued to be dominated by imperialist powers that exploited the country's internal divisions to further their own ends. In 1919, modern Chinese intellectuals reacted to the double pressure of warlordism and foreign encroachment by inaugurating the May Fourth Movement, which promoted the idea of a cultural and intellectual revolution that would save China. The sense of urgency generated by the deteriorating internal and external situations reinforced social-Darwinian fears among Chinese nationalists—China must strengthen itself, they felt, or face national extinction. Most intellectuals came to believe in the efficacy of scientific values and the applicability of scientific laws to the evaluation of existing cultural and social institutions. Many also argued that democratic values must be developed among the people if a genuine republic was eventually to be established.

It was against this background of heightened nationalism that Sun's Guomindang (Nationalist party) and the newly formed Communist party entered into an antiwarlord, anti-imperialist alliance in the early 1920s intended to reunify the country. The collaboration was promoted by the Soviet government, which provided the parties with technical and military support. After Sun died in 1925, Chiang Kai-shek, with his control over the National Revolutionary Army, emerged as one of the major players in the struggle to control the Nationalist party. In mid-1926, the army embarked upon the Northern Expedition from its base in Canton, and by early 1927 Chiang had captured Nanjing and Shanghai. The Guomindang leaders,

1

however, split over the future of the revolution. The left wing sided with the Communists and remained in Wuhan in central China, while Chiang and his supporters established themselves in Nanjing. In April, Chiang launched a bloody purge of the Communists in Shanghai. In the meantime, a rift developed between the left-wing Guomindang and the Communists in Wuhan. After protracted negotiations, reconciliation between Guomindang leaders in Nanjing and Wuhan was finally achieved in September 1927. With the support of warlords Feng Yuxiang and Yan Xishan, Chiang resumed his march toward Peking. In June 1928, he captured the city and changed its name to Peiping. The new Manchurian warlord Zhang Xueliang, whose father had been assassinated that month by the Japanese, pledged his support of the Nationalists. The capital of the new regime remained in Nanjing and the Nationalist era began.

Despite the optimism that accompanied the founding of the new government, it was clear from the beginning that Chiang faced numerous obstacles in his attempt to build a modern, strong, and unified China. During the ten years between 1928 and 1937, when the Sino-Japanese War broke out, Nationalist leaders endeavored to establish the administrative structure of a central government, initiate economic measures intended to stimulate industrial and commercial development, encourage the expansion of the educational system and scientific research, and introduce reforms designed to improve the livelihood of the people. But the Nationalist decade was fraught with the problems of continual military separatism. As erstwhile allies became rivals, internecine wars between Chiang and the "new" warlords broke out in 1929, 1930, and 1931. Meanwhile, the Communists established strongholds in mountainous areas in the south. Between 1931 and 1934, Chiang launched five costly campaigns against them. The last one succeeded in forcing the Communists to evacuate their bases and begin the famous Long March, which ended in Yanan in north China. Not surprisingly, Chiang's reliance on armed force to resolve internal conflicts deflected much of the government's energy and resources into military concerns during this prolonged struggle to maintain central control.

Externally, although the foreign powers recognized the Nanjing regime as China's central government, they did not relinquish the treaty rights that they had enjoyed since the mid-nineteenth century. Japan emerged as a major imperial force competing for the exploitation of China's resources, and its control of Manchuria afforded the Japanese military a strong base from which to stage a full-scale invasion of China in 1937. From the early 1930s, China's internal crises were aggravated by Japanese aggression in the northeastern provinces.

These developments served as a backdrop to Nationalist efforts toward reconstruction during their decade in power. Any attempt to strengthen and modernize China also had to confront such deep-seated problems as a huge population, massive poverty, a high illiteracy rate, a high incidence of disease and widespread epidemics, rural discontent and social inequality, and a poor transportation system. Historians differ in their assessments of the Nationalist record during this time. While some point to economic growth, the expansion of modern transportation systems, the development of education, and the reassertion of control over customs and the salt revenue as signal accomplishments on the part of the Nationalist government, others stress Chiang's failure to solve China's social ills with far-reaching socioeconomic reforms. Political developments within the Guomindang and its relationship to the masses also have been scrutinized for clues leading to an understanding of the nature and consequences of the authoritarianism of the Nanjing regime.[1] James C. Thomson has termed this decade "a proper testing period for the Kuomintang government,"[2] but, given the fact that the first four years of the regime were largely consumed by military efforts to secure power, it is difficult to judge realistically its performance during a six-year period when new programs were introduced to deal with long-standing problems not given to rapid solution. This is not to excuse the incompetence and corruption that existed in the bureaucracy or the weaknesses of many of the programs. But the extraordinary circumstances under which the Nationalist leaders undertook the task of reconstruction should be taken into consideration in any evaluation of the Nationalist period.[3]

In recent years, academic writings on the Nationalist decade in fact have undergone significant revision, both in approaches and in subject matter. No longer are historians content merely to search for the seeds of eventual Guomindang collapse. The perspective resulting from examining the Nationalist regime from 1949 backward in time has tended to encourage a priori assumptions about Nationalist programs and activities as well as suggesting that there were sharp differences between the Guomindang regime and post-1949 Communist rule, in both style and content. Historians are now concerned with trying to understand the intentions of the Nationalist leadership, and the complexity of their programs, rather than dismissing them simply as inept attempts doomed to failure. Certainly the Nationalists were not successful in all areas of activity but their shortcomings, and even their failures, should not blind us to the value of their far-reaching efforts in the cause of national reconstruction during that crucial decade.[4] The attempt to build a modern health-care system was one of these efforts.

The content of the historian's inquiry also has broadened to include not only political developments, ideology, and institutions but Nationalist attempts at financial, social, educational, and scientific reform. Works by Parks M. Coble, Joseph Fewsmith, Prasenjit Duara, and Christian Henriot have focused on the Guomindang's social and financial programs and helped correct our understanding of its relationship with merchants, industrialists, and the local elites.[5] In the fields of science and medicine, historians have examined not only the transfer of western science and technology into China but the ways in which Chinese leaders adapted such knowledge and techniques to meet the country's needs. James Reardon-Anderson's study of the development of chemistry, and Mary Bullock's work on the Peking Union Medical College, have demonstrated the important progress made in the fields of science and medicine during the Nationalist era.[6] Nationalist efforts at scientific and technological modernization in fact foreshadow similar Communist programs, especially those included in the Four Modernizations initiated under Deng Xiaoping.

In many ways, there was actually no sharp break between Guomindang and Communist rule. Robert Bedeski has argued that the state-building efforts of the Nationalists laid the foundation for the Communists after 1949.[7] Many historians now view the warlord era, the Nationalist period, and Communist rule as constituting a continuum of efforts toward national reunification and state-building. Paul Cohen, for example, sees continuities, in both style and content, in the authoritarian reforms undertaken by the empress dowager Cixi in the late Qing period, by Yuan Shikai in the early Republic, by Chiang Kai-shek in the 1930s, and by Deng Xiaoping in the 1970s and 1980s. All four leaders were concerned with national strength, political centralization, bureaucratic reform, economic development, military might, and, despite their general distrust of the West, with the introduction of western capital and models.[8] An appreciation of these varied concerns is essential to an evaluation of China's protracted process of national reconstruction in the modern and contemporary periods.

The present study focuses on Nationalist efforts to build a modern health-care system in the context of national reconstruction. When the Guomindang took power in 1928, they formulated policies, established agencies, and initiated programs aimed at the political, economic, and social rebuilding of China. The provision of modern health care for all people was deemed an integral part of such national development. The Nationalist efforts marked the first time, after a lengthy period of national decline and political fragmentation, that a central government with some measure of control over the country was able to begin the construction of a modern, national, health system. This study examines the emergence, organization, development, and consequences of the Nationalist public-health administration and its services, as well as the infrastructure of medical and health education that emerged in 1928–37.

Several themes and lines of inquiry inform this study. First, we must ask, what were the political, economic, and social problems confronting Nationalist planners as they strove to build a modern health system? An effective health approach required clear commitment on the part of the central government and coordination with the other components of development. Political infighting in the Guomindang more often than not affected the establishment of central agencies, including the health administration, and efforts made in many areas tended to become fragmented and not well related to those of other sectors. In terms of financial support for a national health service, an important issue common to any modernizing country seeking effective development in the face of massive needs and scanty resources is the question of priority. What priority did the health sector receive in the allocation of funds during the Nationalist decade? The importance attached to a national health-care program depended to a significant extent on the Nationalist view of health's role in its reconstruction efforts. Inadequate budgetary support affected all parts of the health-care system but the impact was felt most strongly in the countryside where the overwhelming majority of the population resided. Rural areas also posed the most serious challenge to the introduction of modern medicine and health measures due to massive poverty, illiteracy, and poor communications, in addition to conflicts between traditional medicine and the biomedical system of the West. Social programs devised by Nationalist health planners therefore had to include proper and effective education programs as well as ameliorative measures that might help modern health systems to take hold.

A second theme of the study focuses on the role of foreign models and experts as well as on indigenous health experiments and the ways in which Chinese health planners tried to reconcile different approaches to health care. Medical missionaries had been the chief transmitters of western medicine before they were overshadowed at the turn of the century by other, mainly American, experts anxious to introduce "scientific medicine" into China. In the 1920s, two powerful influences helped to shape the philosophy and structure of the system that emerged in the Nationalist period. First, the Rockefeller Foundation supported the Peking Union Medical College, which exemplified the "Johns Hopkins Model," a model that combined clinical practices with sophisticated techniques and specialized laboratory research. With abundant funds for endowments and the sponsorship of advanced research fellowships, the foundation's impact on the training of medical personnel was far reaching. A second component of foreign influence was the League of Nations Health Organization with its complement of experts who provided guidance and support to Chinese planners in the building of a state medical service. Contrary to popular belief, Chinese health planners were concerned with introducing modern health care to the countryside, and independent experiments by Chinese rural reformers as well as the league's involvement actually encouraged the development of state medicine under the Nationalists.

The question of the appropriateness of foreign health-care models for China was and remains controversial. A central issue is whether it would be better for the Chinese government to adopt an approach that emphasizes the needs of the masses rather than promoting the research agenda of experts or trying to meet the expectations of other countries and the international science community. There is also the question of the role of traditional medicine. Supporters of the western biomedical model, "in which biological processes alone constitute the 'real world' and are the central focus of research interpretation and therapeutic manipulation,"[9] have tended to dismiss indigenous practitioners as quacks whose activities should be outlawed. They have failed to take into account, however, the fact that traditional medicine is an important part of Chinese culture and that the indigenous system has provided much needed, and often successful, relief to most of the population.[10] Such issues created tensions not only in the Nationalist health system in the 1930s but in the Communist efforts of the post-1949 period.

To work effectively, a modern health system requires an extensive educational infrastructure capable of training increasing numbers of medical personnel. A third major concern of this study is to examine how the Nationalist government tried to develop training institutions that could meet these demands. How successful were these and other institutions in producing both the quality and quantity of health personnel, and what were the patterns of their eventual distribution? It must be remembered that "health manpower" included not only college-level professionals but also intermediate and low-level workers, as well as the auxiliaries who in practice would be responsible for providing primary care to a large percentage of the population. Indeed, with college graduates still relatively few in number and a scarcity of all types of trained personnel, the role of laymen and practitioners of traditional medicine assumed great importance.

The Nationalist programs provided the foundation for medical and health initiatives undertaken by the Communists after 1949. As too often the concrete results of China's past experience in the building of a modern health system have been ignored, this study should lend a much needed historical perspective to our understanding of developments in the post-1949 period. In fact, there are substantial continuities in the philosophy, structure, programs, and personnel of health care in the Guomindang and Communist periods.

Although this study is concerned only with the programs of the Nationalist government, another source of influence that extended into the post-1949 period was the experience of the Communists in soviet areas during the 1930s and 1940s. Struggling for their survival, the Communists developed a medical system that emphasized preservation of the fighting capacity of their soldiers. Isolated from major urban centers, and with restricted access to medical supplies and trained personnel, their strategy in health care followed the mass-line approach, which they had developed for political, social, and economic campaigns, focusing on preventive medicine, mass mobilization, the training of paramedics, and the utilization of traditional drugs and medical personnel.[11] Certain features of this guerrilla medical tradition in fact paralleled some of the health measures introduced under the Nationalists. Communist planners later tried to synthesize the various legacies that constituted the baseline for their national health system in 1949.

This study does not pretend to be a comprehensive examination of medical developments in the Nationalist decade. It does try to illuminate one aspect of the social and institutional history of that crucial period: the evolution and development of a medical administration and public-health policies and services. Other important topics in the history of medicine during that period await future studies. These include the rise of the medical profession and the Chinese Medical Association, the development and practice of traditional medicine, especially at the local level, and the careers of prominent Chinese physicians.

1

Health Care in
Early Republican China

In 1912, Dr. W. W. Peter, an American medical missionary who had arrived in China the previous year, wrote that the recent revolution, which overthrew the Manchu dynasty and established the Republic under Dr. Sun Yat-sen, had led to a political change of attitude toward western medicine. He predicted that "the old standard will more and more be swept aside and be supplanted by those which obtain among the first rate powers. Nationally, China is on the eve of a transformation such as Japan passed through some years ago, when she took so eagerly to Western science."[1] During the next two and a half decades, China did move toward a western—primarily American—model of medicine and public health, and the years between the Revolution of 1911 and the founding of the Nationalist regime in 1928 saw the first steps in that direction. Nevertheless, political fragmentation of the country by warlord factions and a lack of understanding or concern for general health improvement on the part of those in power meant that efforts to deal with China's massive health problems were isolated and uncoordinated during most of this period.

The deplorable health conditions prevailing among China's 450 million people made the provision of health care a formidable task. Since there was little regular registration of disease, births, and deaths, health statistics in the early Republican period were meager. It has been estimated that the annual mortality rate was 25 to 30 per 1,000 persons, compared to approximately 18 for Japan and 12 for England in the same period. The leading causes of morbidity

9

and mortality were gastrointestinal diseases and tuberculosis. The former group included such common diseases as typhoid, dysentery, cholera, schistosomiasis, hookworm, and enteritis.[2] Other common diseases included smallpox, malaria, and kala-azar. The specific mortality of tuberculosis was conservatively estimated as 350 per 100,000 persons annually, compared to rates of 114 for the United States and 213 for Japan in 1921. Some of these diseases were endemic in certain areas: malaria in the southeast, hookworm in the provinces of Guangdong and Hunan, schistosomiasis in Jiangsu and Zhejiang, and kala-azar in Hubei and Jiangsu, to name a few. Tetanus neonatorum was primarily responsible for the high infant mortality rate of 250 per 1,000 live births.[3] This resulted largely from ignorance of obstetrics and sepsis on the part of old-style midwives. In certain parts of Fujian, for instance, cow dung was used as cord dressing with disastrous consequences.

The prevalence of many of these diseases was closely related to unsanitary conditions prevailing in both the cities and countryside. Knowledge of modern hygiene, in general, was very limited, although the situation was somewhat better in the cities. Yet, the following description of the nation's capital in 1925, taken from a report of the Peking Metropolitan Police Department, provides some clues to the most common problems.

> In dry weather, clouds of black dust are raised by wind and vehicles so that after a short time one's face is covered with a veil of filthy dust and the ears and nose are filled with it. The promiscuous street defecation practised widely in Peking means that much of the dust contains excremental material. . . . When it does rain in Peking, the absence of a modern sewage system results in water standing in the streets. . . . In the back streets, hutungs and one way lanes, one finds refuse, ashes and fecal matters piled up against walls in heaps, some of which can be measured by cubic yards. . . . Eighty percent of the water used by the people is secured from privately owned shallow wells [and these] are mostly uncovered. Many are located adjacent to the public latrines.[4]

China's early industrialization also created serious health problems for workers in factories, mines, and urban slums. According to an estimate made by the YMCA in the early 1920s, in Shanghai alone more than three hundred thousand workers lived in overcrowded and unsanitary quarters, often in neighborhoods without public utilities, roads, or drainage. Sometimes not even these accommodations were available, and many workers slept on the premises of the plants. As for working conditions in the factories, except for a few enterprises such as the Commercial Press and the British American Tobacco Company, which had introduced limited medical and social-welfare programs, most plants did little to alleviate the hardships of long working hours and unhealthy conditions. Most cotton plants, for example, made no effort to purify the air of cotton fluff held in suspension, and workers were crowded into rooms with insufficient light and ventilation. Toilet facilities often were absent. In 1923, a report of the Shanghai Child Labor Commission pointed to the prevalence of tuberculosis among workers and the lack of health measures to protect them. Most factories were not equipped to deal with accidents or sickness among their employees. The Peking government issued regulations in March 1923 in an attempt to regulate and improve working hours and conditions, but in the absence of a stable central government they were never enforced.[5]

Conditions in the countryside, where 80 percent of the population lived, were in most cases even worse. While some cities at least had introduced such sanitary measures as street cleaning, the vast countryside was virtually devoid of organized sanitation or public-health services. The nature of Chinese agriculture contributed to the prevalence of certain diseases. Human feces used as fertilizer usually were stored in uncovered pits that became breeding grounds for disease-causing organisms. Intensive fertilization in the rich, alluvial, agricultural areas of the Yangzi Valley helped to maintain the prevalence of helminthic diseases such as schistosomiasis. Standing water in the fields created ideal habitats for malaria-transmitting mosquitoes. Floods, a common occurrence, often were accompanied by epidemics of typhoid and cholera. Famines and general undernourishment contributed to a high incidence and widespread distribution of such deficiency diseases as beri-beri and pellagra.[6] Modern transportation, in fact, had resulted in the more effective spread of infectious diseases over large areas. In 1910–11, pneumonic plague ravaged Manchuria and parts of north China, exacting a toll of sixty thousand lives, thanks largely to the movement of people along the railways.[7]

The distressing consequences of such conditions were exacerbated by the lack of public-health knowledge among the population. Most people in rural China considered "cleanliness a luxury which only the rich farmers and city dwellers" could afford to enjoy.[8] The people's views of disease and health were closely intertwined with social and cultural concerns, and their patterns of belief about the causes of illness differed greatly from those inherent in the western biomedical approach. The efficacy of religious healing, for example, had always been an important component of popular culture. Within a radius of 3.5 miles in a rural district in Jiangxi, there were known to be fifty altars specially built to appease the "goddess of smallpox." In another district in Fujian, malaria epidemics occurred with such regularity that the local people expected to be visited by the spirit of the disease once every year (during the warm months). Local temples did a booming business during that time dispensing elixir to help victims survive that annual visitation.[9] The infant mortality rate was so high that the rural population referred to the delivery of newborns as "passing through Hell's gate," and the survival of babies a month after birth usually called for elaborate celebrations.[10] Even in areas where modern midwifery had been introduced, the majority of the rural population claimed that modern midwives could know nothing about birth, since most of them were "both young and unmarried."[11]

There was, in fact, a general lack of confidence in western medicine—except, perhaps, for surgery and the treatment of various communicable diseases. This attitude had changed little since the introduction of western medicine by medical missionaries in the second half of the nineteenth century. Nonetheless, one of them wrote that in cases of "injury or disease necessitating amputation or the removal of tumours," his work had "inspired a most encouraging confidence."[12] The effectiveness of western medicine in combating epidemic diseases such as eye ailments, smallpox, and cholera also added to its limited credibility. The failure of traditional physicians, who were generally untrained in the diagnosis and nomenclature of communicable diseases, to control the Manchurian plague epidemic of 1910–11 also helped change the attitudes of some Chinese toward western medicine.[13]

The fact remained, however, that to most laymen belief in the combined efficacy of traditional and scientific healing was a pragmatic matter that offered different treatment options. Appreciation of this attitude is important in explaining the persistence of indigenous medicine despite the dominance of modern treatment in the formal health-care system.[14] But plague prevention and modern control measures were not enough to convince everyone of their utility. Concerns such as fear of a foreign presence affected local reaction to the intrusion of modern medicine. When a plague epidemic occurred in Datong, Shanxi, in February 1918, local residents vilified the health workers, with their white robes and masks, as "foreign devil stock" who "stir up the hearts of the people making them feel uneasy and fearful." Indeed, local officials initially resisted strenuously attempts by Peking to dispatch modern medical teams to deal with the epidemic.[15]

Modern doctors were a rarity in the early Republic, especially in the countryside. In the early 1910s, except for about 450 medical missionaries and a few western physicians in private practice, there probably were not more than 45 to 55 Chinese who were trained in western medicine in Europe or the United States, and most of these worked in hospitals or medical schools. There also were a few modern-style physicians who had been trained in Chinese medical schools or in Japan.[16] By 1920, it was estimated that there were about 1,500 modern doctors in China, of whom 600 were either missionaries or foreigners in private practice.[17] In other words, there was roughly one modern doctor per 300,000 people. To make matters worse, these doctors resided almost entirely in urban centers. At the beginning of the Nationalist era in 1928, Shanghai and Nanjing alone had more than a third of the modern doctors in practice.[18] Although some medical missionaries operated out of isolated outposts in the interior, most worked in mission hospitals located in cities or towns. At the same time, in the mid-1920s, there were fewer than 2,000 nurses. By the end of the 1920s, there still were only about 500 hospitals in all of China, and unsanitary conditions made most of them far from desirable.[19] Thus, for the overwhelming majority of the Chinese population, traditional medicine was the only source of medical relief.

There are no accurate statistics concerning numbers of indigenous healers. These included traditional scholar-physicians, midwives, bone-setters, itinerant medicine peddlers, and mystic healers. In fact, since there were no licensing requirements, almost anyone, in theory, could set himself up as a practitioner. Many healers practiced demonic medicine, which was particularly influential among the rural population.[20] Most of these village practitioners were herbalists who, in addition to the primary treatment methods of plant and animal medicine, acupuncture, and moxibustion, often resorted to other therapeutic practices and religious routines. In the cities, the wealthy elite continued to patronize scholar-physicians whose classical education gave them not only more credibility but ample social status.

Whether it was demonic practices or the literate system based on ancient medical theories and classical texts, traditional medicine as a whole generally was dismissed by modern physicians as worthless superstition. In the early years of the century, intellectuals such as Chen Duxiu and Lu Xun, who saw science as the key to China's salvation, also attacked traditional medicine as part of the old culture to be rejected. In his article "Call to Youth," Chen chastised traditional doctors for their ignorance of human anatomy and bacteriology, and he ridiculed the ideas of the five elements and yin-yang as "nonsensical . . . and reasonless beliefs," which must "basically be cured by the support of science."[21] In 1914, the Minister of Education advocated the abolition of traditional medicine, and in 1915 the National Medical Association, a professional organization of modern doctors, urged the government to register all medical practitioners and dispensaries.[22] Proponents of the traditional system rose to defend what many considered to be part of the national culture. Some proclaimed Chinese medicine's superiority while others urged the scientification of traditional practices.[23] Attempts on the part of supporters of modern practices to regulate traditional medicine foreshadowed the long and often bitter feud that prevailed between the two camps during the next two decades. Despite repeated criticism and the growth of western medicine in the early Republic, the truth was that most people had confidence in, and access to, only traditional medicine. This would continue to be the case until western medicine—through government efforts and private initiatives—was able to penetrate into China's interior. Only then were people's attitudes sufficiently altered to accept its presence and utility.

Government Health Administration Before 1928

State-sponsored medical and public-health activities existed before the founding of the Republic in 1912. From the mid-Tang through the Mongol period, the imperial government had actively initiated and maintained public-health institutions throughout the empire. Tang authorities distributed free prescriptions and sponsored charity infirmaries for the needy. The Song continued these efforts, expanding them to include public dispensaries. The Mongol government established a medical bureau, which operated at all levels of local administration, to train and examine medical practitioners and to test drugs. Indeed, the Song and Yuan helped to establish the concept of state responsibility for promoting health among its citizens. This tradition of state activism in public health atrophied during the Ming, however, when official indifference was the rule except during epidemics. In the late Ming, and during the Qing, the state's role was gradually replaced by private organizations and efforts. Although the Qing government did establish the Sanitary Bureau in the Ministry of Civil Affairs, it generally encouraged private initiatives to fulfil public functions, including medical relief.[24]

After the founding of the Republic, a Sanitation Bureau was established in the Ministry of the Interior. Its main responsibilities were the prevention of communicable diseases, licensing and supervision of physicians and pharmacists, regulation of drugs, and control of hospitals and local health organizations. Other government agencies took charge of some aspects of national health administration: school hygiene was regulated by the Ministry of Education and industrial hygiene by the Ministry of Agriculture and Commerce.[25] Significantly, the list of qualifications for officials issued by the government in 1915 specified that candidates in medicine, pharmacy, and veterinary science must possess the "standards insisted upon by all progressive countries."[26] This implied the official recognition of modern medicine, and traditional medicine was not mentioned at all. The political fragmentation and instability of the early Republican era, however, precluded the possibility of any large-scale central initiative in health promotion. Moreover, with few qualified personnel and little funding, the Sanitation Bureau was "practically nonfunctioning." The government did approve a proposal to create a National Board of Health in 1921, but by 1926 it still had not been organized.[27]

The event that prompted the government to assume a more direct role in health matters was an epidemic of pneumonic plague that ravaged Manchuria in 1910–11. In 1912, the North Manchurian Plague Prevention Service, headed by Dr. Wu Lien-teh (Wu Liande), a Cambridge University graduate who had directed the fight against the plague, was established at Harbin. The success of Wu and other western-trained physicians in controlling the epidemic had changed the thinking of at least some Chinese officials. The jurisdiction of the North Manchurian Plague Prevention Service was confined to

Manchuria, and it was concerned primarily with combating epidemics, collecting epidemiological data on plague, and manufacturing vaccines and serum for plague, cholera, and other diseases. Despite its limitations, however, the founding of the service marked a genuine beginning in modern public-health work in China.[28]

In March 1916, the Ministry of the Interior promulgated regulations governing epidemic prevention and sanitation. Modeled after similar Japanese regulations, they identified cholera, dysentery, typhus exanthemata, diphtheria, and plague as communicable. They laid down provisions for official notification, as well as the segregation and treatment of patients.[29] Creation of a national agency to deal with epidemic prevention did not occur until 1919, following the successful control of another plague epidemic, which broke out in December 1917, affecting Mongolia and north China. The function of this new agency, the National Epidemic Prevention Bureau, included research in communicable diseases, manufacturing of serums and vaccines, collection of epidemiological data, and the promotion of vaccination campaigns and other public-health practices. In 1929, the bureau was placed under the Ministry of Health in the new Nationalist government.

In the provinces there were no special health departments, and provincial police departments usually took care of the basic sanitary functions. No municipal health departments existed before 1920 and sanitary administration was generally under the authority of city police departments.[30] Guangdong, however, created a Board of Health as early as 1912. It was headed by Dr. Li Shufen, a graduate of Edinburgh University.[31] In 1920, Canton established a Department of Health with elaborate administrative structures and regulations governing sanitation, communicable disease prevention, licensing of medical practitioners, and collection of vital statistics. Another western-trained physician, Dr. S. M. Woo (Hu Xuanming) became its first commissioner. Although enforcement of these regulations was not uniform, Canton's health organization provided a model for other modern municipal health departments after 1927.[32] Some cities also took initiatives in establishing and supporting hospitals and dispensaries. Peking, for example, maintained the Isolation Hospital and the Central Hospital, both modern institutions founded in 1915 and 1918, respectively.[33]

A notable development at the municipal level was the establishment of a demonstration health center in Peking in 1925. A joint effort on the part of the municipal police department and the Rockefeller-supported Peking Union Medical College (PUMC), the Peking First Health Station was set up in a ward of the city. Dr. John B. Grant, chairman of PUMC's Department of Public Health and Preventive Medicine and founder of the station, intended it to "serve as a controlled environment for teaching purposes," and as an "organized core of a regionalized system" of community health care.[34] Providing both curative and preventive services, the station maintained a health clinic and a school-health and public-health nursing service. It conducted vaccination and health education campaigns and introduced measures to improve environmental hygiene and communicable disease control. It also held conferences for local midwives and health-education classes for teachers and students.[35] Despite its limited scope, the station was the first major experiment in community health in Republican China and it served as a model for later health demonstrations. Moreover, since all PUMC students were required to serve a clerkship there after 1925, the station provided an invaluable training ground for many of the personnel who would staff the new municipal, provincial, and national health administrations after 1927. Finally, effective cooperation between the newly established PUMC and the Peking government underlined the important role that foreign philanthropic organizations would play in health developments during the Republican period.

As for the training of health manpower, there were little or no central planning and coordination. By 1921, the country's ten national and provincial medical schools were located in only six out of the eighteen provinces of China proper. Of these, two were coeducational, one was for women, and the rest were for men. Student enrollments were small, the average being one hundred per school. Despite government guidelines supposedly regulating the operation of medical schools, there was no uniformity in either admission requirements or the length of the course of study.[36] As there were virtually no systematic attempts to educate public-health workers, nurses, and midwives, most of the training was provided by individual hospitals. In fact, since the government had failed to provide leadership in the area of nursing, it was left to the Nurses' Association of China, founded in 1909, to establish standards for training through the standardization of curricula and examinations, and the imposition of minimum requirements on all schools desiring to register themselves with the association.[37]

Private Initiatives In The Countryside

It is clear that little progress was made before 1928 toward the establishment of a modern, national system to deal with the country's manifold health problems. What little was accomplished was rather rudimentary, the result of isolated efforts during a period of political turmoil. There was no coordination, nor was there sustained support in funds or authority for even these limited activities, which were concentrated almost entirely in urban centers. While there was still a low level of public awareness of health matters, Dr. Grant pointed out that "one of the most important, if not the greatest, of outstanding problems in China is the lack of perspective among those in authority who shape medical and public health affairs."[38]

The government's failure to address health problems in the countryside was offset, at least to a limited extent, by the efforts of a few individual reformers who attempted to improve conditions in rural China, including those related to health. These were the forerunners of the "rural reconstruction movement," which aimed at the comprehensive improvement of rural life and the economy. Tao Xingzhi, a noted educator, preached the importance of "life education," stressing the acquisition of knowledge and skills that could be applied to real-life situations. Rural education would bring about social and physical betterment, and begin the process of rural reconstruction. By early 1927, Tao's Rural Normal School Movement had set up a model school and a small hospital at Xiaozhuang, a small village near Nanjing. Tao hoped to organize a network of rural normal schools, with affiliated primary schools, to train teachers capable of dealing with the problems of illiteracy and the improvement of living conditions. He recruited a recent graduate of PUMC, Dr. C. C. Chen (Chen Zhiqian), to develop a rural health program at Xiaozhuang.[39] While Tao viewed rural education as the means of reconstructing rural life, another reformer, the Confucian scholar Liang Shuming deemed rural education and reconstruction to be the dual means of achieving the total reconstruction—intellectual and material—of China. His active involvement with the implementation of rural programs occurred in 1929.

Another attempt at organizing a rural health program was James Y. C. Yen's (Yan Yangchu) Mass Education Movement, founded in 1923, which became a pilot reconstruction program in Dingxian, Hebei, in 1926. Yen's prescription for rural development was based on education, economic amelioration, citizenship training, and public health. Nevertheless, before the founding of a special health department in 1929, the emphasis remained on literacy problems, and public-health activities were limited to sanitary improvements and occasional mass-vaccination campaigns.[40] All these initiatives underscored the importance of developing programs that took into consideration the actual socioeconomic conditions of the rural population. The health program of Dingxian, in particular, provided a model for rural-health programs during the Nationalist regime.

Besides individual Chinese reformers, western medical missionaries and philanthropic foundations were involved in promoting medical and public-health activities in the period prior to 1928. In fact, both groups continued to complement and collaborate with the Chinese government in health matters after the founding of the Nationalist regime.

Medical Missionaries

Since the second half of the nineteenth century, western missionaries had been the chief transmitter of western medical knowledge and practices to China. At first medical activities were seen primarily as an opening wedge that would lead to Christian proselytization. By the turn of the century, however, many missionaries began to see medical assistance not as a mere appendage to missionary evangelism but as an integral part of their work.[41] Nonetheless, while they were anxious to demonstrate to the Chinese that their medicine had a scientific basis, most also insisted that the low standard of medical science in China, and the readiness of the Chinese to accept "absurd" explanations of the causation of diseases, were due to the "absence of the liberalizing influence of Christianity."[42] Chinese medicine was, as one missionary put it, "thoroughly unorganized, unprogressive and unfit."[43]

Missionary medicine generally focused on curative work centered in dispensaries or hospitals, most of which were located in cities and towns. There also were attempts at medical education, initially undertaken through the apprenticeship method, with the aim of training native helpers. Later, a more formal institutional approach was adopted and mission medical schools were established. Public-health activities, however, did not receive much attention. The number of western medical missionaries in China increased steadily over the years, and by 1916 there were approximately 420 foreign doctors working in 265 hospitals run by Protestant missions. Protestant medical workers vastly outnumbered those of the Catholic societies, which supported only a small number of qualified western physicians.[44]

For the missionaries, the hospital was the center of their medical work. On one hand it was seen as a "model of hygiene and sanitation," which could "make a permanent contribution in teaching the people the principles by which disease can be prevented" and functioned as an "effectual training ground" for Chinese assistants and employees. On the other hand, the hospital was viewed as "a model of evangelistic effort," and "an object lesson in Christian love and mercy."[45] Thus, missionary hospitals usually conducted daily chapel services, sometimes in the hospital chapel, more commonly in one of the wards.

Most mission hospitals were relatively small. The average number of beds in a hospital was fifty, though the largest hospital in China did not contain more than three hundred. In a survey of conditions in 1919–20, 80 percent of the hospitals studied had only one foreign or foreign-trained doctor and 34 percent had no nurses, foreign or Chinese. Not only were the hospitals understaffed, but they were ill-equipped. Thirty-one percent did not have a laboratory of any kind, 87 percent lacked X-ray equipment, and 72 percent were unable to carry out pathological investigations to support medical and surgical work. Despite these shortcomings, mission hospitals maintained the majority of hospital beds in China in the 1910s and 1920s, and statistics from 1919 show that the Chinese themselves provided more then 50 percent of the cost of upkeep in the form of patient fees and government and local contributions.[46] As one Episcopalian bishop put it, the mission hospitals were helping to relieve "an immense amount of suffering while observing the best practice as far as possible."[47]

The impact of mission hospital work, however, was still largely confined to urban areas. Most hospitals were built near other centers of mission activity—schools, chapels, and compounds—but far from the real centers of population in the rural areas. In fact, as the cost of traveling to many hospitals often far exceeded the medical fees, low bed occupancy was common. Obviously, factors such as an unfamiliar environment, the curtailment of freedom, and the foreign routine also explained the unwillingness of some patients to enter hospitals. Yet in port cities bed occupancy was high.[48]

Since most of their resources were devoted to curative work performed in the hospitals, medical missionaries as a whole placed little
emphasis on promoting public-health education. Furthermore, since
mission hospitals catered only to a small percentage of the population, their value as a conduit of health information to the masses
was quite limited. One notable attempt at public-health education
was initiated by Dr. W. W. Peter, an American medical missionary
who in 1916 organized a Joint Council on Public Health with the
support of the YMCA, the Chinese Medical Missionary Association,
and the National Medical Association. The council's work included
the production and distribution of health materials, surveys of health
conditions in Christian schools, and special immunization campaigns. Nevertheless, their use of audio-visual devices to arouse interest was limited largely to the cities, and their posters and pamphlets
also failed to elicit much response in the countryside due to widespread illiteracy. Peter himself admitted that no successful public
health work could be undertaken at that time because "under our
prevailing organization and viewpoints, those who have an appreciation of the importance of public health are usually preoccupied
by their schools, hospitals, and other forms of regular work with no
time for other activities."[49]

The educational activities of the medical missionaries proved to
be far more successful and influential. Early on, missionaries had
begun training Chinese assistants, and by the turn of the century a
more institutionalized approach was adopted. Moreover, recognizing
the constraints on individual efforts, some mission groups cooperated to establish union medical schools. In 1906, the American Board
of Commissioners for Foreign Missions and the Board of Foreign
Missions of the Presbyterian Church, USA, jointly initiated, and later
maintained, the Union Medical College in Peking. Another union
school established in 1912 was the West China Union University in
Chengdu, Sichuan, which opened a medical college two years later.
By 1921, nine of the twenty-eight medical schools in China were
supported from mission sources. As in the case of hospitals and
dispensaries, American and British mission bodies dominated the
field of medical education.[50]

Conditions in these schools generally were poor, and most institutional staffs were small. The Union Medical College in Peking, with
a staff of fourteen, had the most personnel. Many instructors, who
previously had been full-time administrators of mission hospitals,

lacked the time to keep up with advances in the field. Facilities on the whole were inadequate and laboratory work for students was virtually nonexistent.[51] Roger S. Greene, resident director in China of the Rockefeller Foundation's China Medical Board, attributed the poor showing of the missionaries to their schizophrenic view of medical work. The old-fashioned ones, he noted, were not receptive to demands for better personnel and equipment because they considered education and medicine merely as "baits to catch the people so they can be preached to." Those more liberal in their views were often

> afraid that their constituencies at home are not ready for such strong meat as the theory that missionaries are justified in teaching school and healing the sick without any ulterior motive, however high, but merely because they want to help the people in that way.[52]

It must be remembered, however, that even this situation was an improvement over the early days, when Chinese medical helpers were trained by the apprenticeship method, and that these schools were instrumental in bringing western medical education to China, opening the way for the introduction of modern practices and ideas.

The Role of the Rockefeller Foundation

Health care in early Republican China also was shaped by the intervention of a powerful instrument of American philanthropy, the Rockefeller Foundation. Early in 1914, the foundation dispatched the First China Medical Commission, headed by Henry Pratt Judson, president of the University of Chicago, to study the conditions of medicine and medical education. The commission's report, *Medicine in China*, published later that year, was highly critical of the poor standards of missionary medical education. It recommended that the Rockefeller Foundation undertake medical work in China to be based on the most advanced scientific knowledge, and pointed out that in their present state mission medical institutions were not sufficiently equipped. In the United States, the accumulated impact of bacteriology, pathology, and developments in the basic sciences had begun influencing medical practice by the turn of the century, and private institutions such as the Rockefeller and Carnegie foundations, through their generous financial support, encouraged the application of biological and physical scientific research to medicine.

In 1914, the Rockefeller Foundation created the China Medical

Board to coordinate the planning and administration of medical education in China. A second commission visited China in the summer of 1915. Its members included Dr. William H. Welch, of the Johns Hopkins Medical School, and Dr. Simon Flexner, director of the Rockefeller Institute, whose brother, Abraham Flexner, had created through his books a revolution in American medical education. After further study based on the commission's findings, the foundation decided in 1915 to take over the Union Medical College in Peking—renaming it Peking Union Medical College—and develop it into a world-class institution comparable to the best in the United States and Europe.[53] American experts associated with the project, especially Welch and Flexner, considered the "Johns Hopkins model," which combined clinical practices, university and medical education, and scientific laboratory research, to be the ideal for PUMC. The college was to be a conduit for scientific medicine and a training ground for medical doctors capable of conducting advanced research. This model differed markedly from that of the mission medical schools, requiring the support of an extensive educational system and well-equipped facilities. As these conditions were lacking in early Republican China, the foundation found itself increasingly involved in the development and upgrading of science and premedical education in Chinese schools in order to produce qualified students for PUMC. The immediate need was met when the trustees of the college established its own premedical school in September 1917. Four years later, PUMC was formally dedicated.[54]

PUMC maintained rigorous standards with special emphasis placed on the teaching laboratory. In addition to course work, students were required to undertake clinical clerkships and internships in the fourth and fifth years, respectively. The students were drawn largely from relatively wealthy, westernized families. Dr. John Grant, of PUMC's Department of Public Health and Preventive Medicine, made note of the "upper class" background of the students, a situation resulting in part from high tuition fees.[55] Moreover, since English was used in the entrance examinations, and had been adopted as the medium of instruction, most successful applicants were from the missionary schools. Thus, PUMC students were drawn mainly from the westernized upper strata of urban China, thereby reinforcing the elitist nature of the institution.

The faculty of PUMC, graduates of leading universities all over the world, were both researchers and teachers. The research of the faculty and students yielded important findings in the understanding of such endemic diseases as schistosomiasis, kala-azar, and hookworm. The number of Chinese faculty members gradually increased, until by 1926–27 their total number was fifty-eight (compared to thirty-seven foreigners). Almost all the Chinese, however, were in the lower academic ranks of assistants and associates, while about half of the foreign staff were professors and associate professors.[56] After 1928, one Chinese faculty member in the Department of Surgery, Dr. J. Heng Liu (Liu Ruiheng), emerged as a key figure in the development of a national health system under the new Nationalist government.

PUMC also pioneered public-health education. In 1925, as already noted, Dr. John Grant founded the Peking First Health Station, with the help of the Peking municipal government, to provide curative services and public-health education for the population of one ward in the city. Grant's Department of Public Health at PUMC attracted a number of students. Many of these eventually would become top officials in the Nationalist government's health bureaucracy, thereby helping to spread the influence of PUMC in the development of a national health system.

The Peking First Health Station also provided an ideal site for the practical training of student nurses (PUMC's School of Nursing had been founded in 1920). In the health station, they were trained in areas such as industrial health, school health, and maternal care as part of their general nursing education. The school contributed greatly to the spread of public-health education; it also helped promote the respectability, and advance the course, of the nursing profession.

The influence of the China Medical Board on the development of medical education and health-manpower training extended beyond PUMC. From 1915 to 1919, the board provided financial and other support to encourage medical education in several other colleges. For example, in 1915, grants were dispensed to maintain additional teachers in the premedical and medical schools of the Hunan-Yale Medical College (Xiangya) at Changsha, a joint effort of the Yale-in-China Association and the provincial government of Hunan. The board also provided funding for a new premedical science building. In 1916, three classes of the Union Medical College, which was in the process of being taken over by the Rockefeller Foundation, were transferred to the Shandong Christian University (Cheeloo) Medical School. In addition, the China Medical Board contributed grants to Shandong Christian University for new buildings, equipment, and maintenance.[57]

The objective of the China Medical Board was to upgrade the facilities and curricula of various schools in accordance with its vision of promoting scientific medicine in China. To help develop the educational infrastructure necessary to support such a goal, the board provided grants to promising universities for the establishment of endowments, science buildings, equipment, research, and fellowships. Fujian Christian University, St. John's University, Ginling College, Yanjing University, and Lingnan University were recipients of the board's largess.[58] But the intervention of the Rockefeller Foundation functioned not only to help raise the standards of premedical and scientific education. More importantly, it served to promote American educational models and ideas in the development of Chinese medical education in the Republican period.

The activities of the Rockefeller Foundation and the introduction of scientific medicine significantly influenced China's health-care development. Since the foundation's intervention took place at a time when China's health-care system was largely undeveloped, and during a period when neither the government, private individuals, nor organizations were able—because of a lack of resources or interest—to develop coordinated health programs for China, the tremendous power and influence of the foundation and the prestige of scientific medicine made the ideas and practices of the American model particularly attractive to health planners. When the Nationalists took power in 1928, they were confronted with the task of properly integrating all the existing strands of medical development into their plans for building a modern health-care system, the objectives of which must be consistent with the imperatives of development under the Nationalist regime.

2

Health and National Reconstruction

When the Ministry of Health was inaugurated on 30 October 1928, the Nationalist government issued a mandate declaring that "the quality of health administration in a country not only directly concerns the health of the people but also the prosperity of the race." It was important, therefore, the mandate continued, to "develop healthy bodies, to train sound minds and to control and prevent epidemic diseases."[1] The proclamation reflected the nationalist nature of the new government's approach to health planning— that the future of China depended on the development of a sound health-care system. It is significant that the primary emphasis was placed on the people's need to maintain good health for the sake of the nation. By declaring that health was essential to the national welfare, the government was claiming medicine as a public function of the state. The logical consequence of this was to establish central control over health policy and priorities, to maintain supervisory control over the practice of medicine, and to provide medical care for the population. In short, health planning would be closely integrated into the broad goals of national planning and reconstruction.

Medical Modernization and National Strengthening

The belief that health and national reconstruction were closely related had been shared, in fact, by many intellectuals and reformers who were concerned about national strengthening and modernization in the late nineteenth and early twentieth centuries. China's domestic woes and the encroachment of Japan and the western powers had spurred them to clamor for immediate action to preserve

26

the race and ensure China's survival. That China's struggle was viewed in social-Darwinian terms is not surprising in view of the popularity of social Darwinism and other western ideas at that time. What is important is that, in addition to the need for new political and technological initiatives, the reformers also were raising the issue of health and medicine as a vital aspect of China's salvation. Generally they looked to the state to provide solutions to the manifold health problems that in their view had weakened China.

Two themes ran through the arguments of the advocates of medical modernization as a means of promoting national strengthening. One was medicine's potential contribution to improving the physical constitution of the Chinese people. The second was the ability of science, including modern medicine, to help realize the goals of social renewal and modernization. Writing in 1895, Yan Fu stressed the need to enhance the Chinese people's appreciation of physical fitness and improve their vigor as prerequisites for China's rejuvenation. He also pointed out that only healthy mothers could give birth to strong children.[2] In addition, both Kang Youwei and Liang Qichao urged the creation of a modern public-health system and the improvement of medicine in China so as to strengthen the race and, through it, the nation. As Liang put it, "there are two aspects to preserving the race: one is study in order to preserve its mental power; one is medicine in order to preserve its physical constitution."[3] He also identified government support of medical science and public health as a key factor contributing to the power and prosperity of western nations.

The efforts of reformers like Kang and Liang paved the way for a new generation of intellectuals. These men, frustrated by the failure of China to achieve independence and power after the Revolution of 1911, began to reevaluate China's traditional culture in light of what they perceived to be the key to the success of the West—modern science. A Descartian faith in the potential of science to solve mankind's problems led many intellectuals to welcome western medicine. At the same time, they denounced traditional practices as part of the old order impeding China's modernization. As noted earlier, Chen Duxiu, Lu Xun, and other intellectuals of the early twentieth century had, through the new literature, blasted traditional physicians as ignorant and irrational and the medicine they practiced as an amalgam of superstitions incompatible with scientific progress.[4]

Students in modern medical schools and western-trained physicians were promoting the development of medicine and public-health programs on the same grounds. To them there was no limit to the possibilities inherent in the application of science and modern medicine to national salvation and social betterment. They were even more explicit about the state's responsibility in health maintenance. In 1915, the National Medical Association of China was founded, a professional organization mainly composed of modern Chinese physicians. In its first conference, held the following year, the association urged the government to create a Central Medical Board and a national public-health service.[5] The association also published a journal with a view toward disseminating knowledge of modern medicine. This group, which changed its name to the Chinese Medical Association in 1932, actively promoted scientific medicine and helped to establish the social and professional standing of modern physicians.

Many medical and health journals, popular and technical, were published in the early 1920s by medical students, schools, individuals, and local health groups. Among others, the *Medical Journal of the Shanghai Christian University* commenced publication in 1921; the *Hygiene Journal* of the Zhejiang Health Association was founded in 1922; *Health Quarterly*, a popular monthly, was published by the Council on Health Education at Shanghai in 1924; and *Popular Medicine*, a monthly from PUMC, was launched in 1926.[6] While some of these were professional journals, others were concerned with the popular spread of knowledge and promotion of the benefits of health improvement through scientific medicine. An interesting development in the popularization of modern medicine and hygiene was the publication of special medical supplements by many newspapers in the larger cities. In the late 1920s and early 1930s, popular supplements were published by *Shen bao* (Shanghai), *Zhongyang ribao* (Nanjing), and *Chen bao* (Peiping). One of the more innovative and influential supplements of the time was the *Binying Weekly*, initially published in the widely read *Peking World Daily* in 1926 and then in the *Dagong bao* by a group of first-year PUMC medical students who had organized themselves into the Binying Society. The content of the weekly dealt not only with issues of raising the public's health awareness but also with medicine's role in national strengthening and the role of the state in the development of modern health care for the people.[7]

C. C. Chen, who later would join Tao Xingzhi, and then James Yen, in their rural health programs, was editor of the *Binying Weekly*. The aim of the publication was the education of the public about the scientific point of view and the immense potential of modern medicine to spur the process of social renewal. Worried about the public's conception of scientific medicine as being "foreign," one article in the *Weekly* insisted that modern medicine belonged to the world and that China, like Japan, could benefit from the application of modern knowledge.[8] While this assertion appears to have been an attempt to remove the onus of accepting something from the West at a time of heightened nationalism, there is little doubt that Chen and many of his fellow students were committed to the popularization of what they considered to be the most advanced medical practices in China. Unlike some of his colleagues, though, Chen and the editors of the weekly supplement did not dismiss traditional medicine outright, calling for the "equitable treatment" of both modern and traditional medicine and the application of uniform regulation to both types of practitioners.[9] The application of such regulation later would arouse the vigorous opposition of traditional practitioners who rightly pointed out that the "uniform" testing and registration of all physicians would affect them more than their modern counterparts. Besides the social benefit of modern medicine, the *Weekly* also raised the issue of health and its relationship to national economic growth. One article, for example, argued that public health was a national asset vital to the economic well-being and prosperity of the nation. "The economic value of health is enormous, and requires much study to elucidate its significance," it proclaimed.[10] The idea of health as an aid to productivity would become a central theme in health planning under the Nationalists.

Like many of their colleagues, the editors of the *Binying Weekly* stressed the government's responsibility in health planning and improvement. They called for the creation of an effective health administration, greater government control over both modern and traditional practitioners, the promulgation of appropriate laws regulating medication, the establishment of school health programs and education, and the organization of a rural health-care system.[11] In fact, these medical students were presenting an agenda that they hoped would form the basis of a modern health system in China.

Planning for Public Health in China

A more systematic plan for the building of a public-health organization was submitted to the British Boxer Indemnity Commission in 1926 by the Association for the Advancement of Public Health in

China, an organization composed of leading modern physicians and hospital administrators. Its executive committee included such notable medical leaders as Dr. J. Heng Liu, president of the National Medical Association and director of PUMC Hospital, who received his M.D. from Harvard and had done advanced research at Johns Hopkins University, and Dr. Wu Lien-teh, director of the Manchurian Plague Prevention Service. The association requested financial support out of Boxer Indemnity funds to launch a six-year program aimed at establishing a national public-health service. The explanation given by the association in its memorandum to the commission of the need for such a service in China provided an even more elaborate description of the current arguments for improved health care and planning.[12] First, pointing to the emphasis placed upon health care by British leaders who had accepted the principle that health was "the chief asset of a nation," the association argued that China's strengthening and modernization—the "transition from medieval-ism," as the authors of the request put it—could be completed only if public-health programs were established. Public health, therefore, was essential if China was to become a modern nation like Britain.

Public-health services also were necessary on economic grounds. Preventable illness contributed to the general poverty of the Chinese people, the association asserted. Public-health expenditures were jus-tified since they would help to maintain the people's health and productivity. In short, good health was an investment that should be supported not only by the government but by the community as a whole. Finally, the association stressed the humanitarian aspect of public-health work, pointing out that annual excess mortality in China was at least 15 per 1,000 persons—in other words, 6 million out of a population of 400 million people died unnecessarily each year. These figures, taken together with an estimated minimum an-nual excess of severe illness of more than 20 million, brought not only a substantial economic loss but tremendous suffering and mis-ery. The association maintained that a national effort to establish a health branch within the national government, on the scale of the movement that had brought about passage of the first Public Health Act in Britain in 1848, was urgently needed in China.

The proposal of the association consisted of a first-year prelimi-nary program to establish basic guidelines and institutions, followed by a five-year expansion program. Although the ideas put forth in the proposal were not acted upon at that time, they were significant in that they reflected the thinking of medical leaders at the time, and a number of association officers later served in the Nationalist health administration. Dr. J. Heng Liu became first the acting minister (and then minister) of health in the new Nationalist government, and was responsible for developing a modern health-care system until 1938. Some of the ideas originally submitted in the proposal were put into practice by Liu and his colleagues after 1928.

According to the proposed program, the first year's work would have consisted of the establishment of a Central Organization, a technical and administrative body with several divisions charged with overseeing the development of health programs. This body would be assisted by a Central Hygienic Institute, conceived as an expansion of the existing Laboratory of the National Epidemic Prevention Bureau. Experimental training demonstrations would be set up in Peking and two other locations (in central and south China, respectively) to provide sites for the development and demonstration of modern health measures and to train personnel. Also in the area of health manpower, qualified candidates would be sent to study abroad and would attend the training demonstrations, while chairs of hygiene would be endowed in selected medical schools. These initiatives would be expanded during the following five years. A second demonstration would be convened in the second year and the number of health personnel going abroad would gradually increase. In cooperation with local authorities, health centers and other local programs would also be established during this time. The association was confident that local health activities could be implemented if a functioning central organization were there to provide technical assistance and quality control. Finally, money would be allocated to endow departments of hygiene in the higher normal colleges and schools to train health inspectors. With the initial financial support of the commission, the association argued that the establishment of such programs would stimulate enough support from the central and local governments of China to support the programs in the future.

A central concern, which the proposal tried to address, was the issue of political instability. The association maintained that the initiation of successful public-health measures in China would depend not on stable national or provincial governments but on stable local authorities. Pointing to existing conditions under which local health administration was entrusted to the police—a model borrowed from Germany and Japan—the association asserted that, since the disorganization of the national and provincial governments did not extend to the local level, most police departments had been established and were functioning. There was no need, therefore, to create a new branch of government for the implementation of health programs. The argument assumed that the militarists controlling various parts of the country (and the local police departments of the 1920s) were equally interested in initiating and implementing modern health programs, and that local jurisdictions had access to funds with which to support these activities. Yet local police departments were still dependent on regional warlords for their existence. And, even if local administrations were stable, despite the national and provincial turmoil, there would be no guarantee that local leaders would accept health programs initiated by regional or national leaders. Such efforts could easily be construed as attempts to expand central control over the lower levels of government.

Another argument in the proposal, one that reflected current thinking about health planning, was the assertion that the "normal course" of the evolution of public health in China would follow four stages of development. First, initial health efforts would be undertaken in the cities; second, such efforts would be extended to various provincial centers; third, the emergence of provincial health administrations would form the basis of a national administration; and, finally, rural health administrations would be established. The proposal defended this course on the grounds of lack of funds and the backwardness of the population, especially people in the countryside. The proposal also recognized that control of disease was as important an issue as was the improvement of the standard of living. Its authors, however, did not deem a comprehensive attack on the massive health problems of the countryside feasible at that time because of the immense cost that would be involved in the introduction of modern sanitary and hygienic measures and the general amelioration of poor socioeconomic conditions. To many of the writers, the logical conclusion was to focus on the cities, where living standards were relatively high and some sanitary measures existed, while trying to develop rural health programs in a limited number of areas.

National Reconstruction under the Nationalists

It was against this background of heightened awareness that the Nationalist government established the Ministry of Health in 1928.

As indicated above, the government's mandate laid claim to the protection and promotion of the health and welfare of the Chinese people as both a function and a responsibility of the state. For the new Nationalist government, the process of state building had just begun. Public-health promotion therefore became part of the larger effort of national reconstruction, which included ambitious efforts in the administrative, constitutional, legal, social, economic, educational, and diplomatic realms. The Nationalists implemented a system of government in 1928, consisting essentially of five branches, or yuan—executive, legislative, judicial, control, and examination—which, it was hoped, would lay the foundations for a constitutional government during a period of tutelage under the Guomindang. In theory, the period of tutelage would end by 1935 with all the plans for reconstruction completed.[13]

In the socioeconomic sphere, the government attempted to improve the people's livelihood, solve the problems of agrarian decline and disintegration, and promote economic growth through the development of urban industries, water conservancy, electrical power projects, various other government enterprises, and railroad and highway construction. Ideologically, the Nationalists hoped to create legitimacy and national unity by applying Sun Yat-sen's Three Principles of the People. It must be remembered, however, that the Nationalist government was never able to unify the country and its authority remained partial at best. In fact, during the Nationalist period, provincial governments often carried out their own "reconstruction" work under various bureaus and ministries without direction from the central government.[14] The failure to exercise overall control and coordination seriously handicapped the central government's attempts to create a modern, national, economic infrastructure and to establish a stable social order with accompanying institutions.

Many of the Nationalists' initial efforts were concentrated on economic and material reconstruction. A National Reconstruction Commission was created in 1928 to develop various projects involving manufacturing, mining, water conservancy, and electrification,[15] though most of the plans were never implemented. In April 1929, the Guomindang Party Central approved a priority list of material reconstruction projects. These included, at the national level, railroads, highways, and other transportation networks, mining and basic industries, river conservancy and harbor construction; and, at the local level, highways and transportation, agriculture, husbandry, water conservancy, urban renewal, public works, and public health.[16] To coordinate these programs, T. V. Soong (Song Ziwen), the finance minister and vice president of the Executive Yuan, proposed the creation of a central planning commission in March 1931. In the spring of that year, several experts from the League of Nations visited China at the invitation of the government to discuss the possibility of technical cooperation in economic reconstruction. The League's experts, including Sir Arthur Salter, director of the Financial and Economic Section, and Robert Haas, director of the Transit and Communications Section, supported the idea of a "central organ for the elaboration, coordination and application of a comprehensive economic programme . . . to facilitate the performance of an urgent task of reconstruction and transformation."[17]

The Chinese government began organizing such an agency—the National Economic Council (*quan guo jingji weiyuanhui*)—in April. In November it was formally launched. The chairman of the council was Chiang Kai-shek, president of the Executive Yuan. The vice-chairman was T. V. Soong. Its Standing Committee included Wang Jingwei, the prime minister; Sun Fo, president of the Legislative Yuan; and Soong. When Soong resigned as finance minister in late 1933, the committee was enlarged from three to five members with the addition of H. H. Kung (Kong Xiangxi), the new minister of finance; and Chiang.[18] Although technically the council's role was advisory in nature, it assumed tremendous power because all the major ministries were represented on it and it was empowered to "plan, examine and approve projects" and "investigate and consider" funding requests for all state-proposed economic reconstruction or development projects. It thus became the primary agent of the government in determining the direction and policy of reconstruction.[19]

Under the council were five technical committees concerned with different aspects of reconstruction: roads, hydraulic engineering, public health, education, and rural reconstruction. To expedite implementation of the policies of these committees, three administrative organs—the Bureau of Public Roads, the Hydraulic Engineering Bureau, and the Central Field Health Station (*weisheng shiyan chu*)—were placed directly under the appropriate committees in 1933. Despite continued Japanese aggression in the northeast, the council announced in November 1931 a three-year plan of national reconstruction, which would focus initially on a few activities undertaken in selected regions. These included public works projects such as river

and harbor improvements, as well as construction of highways, educational reforms, land reform and agricultural improvements, industrial
development, financial policy, and public health and medicine. The
council's primary involvement in public health involved an attempt
to establish central technical institutions in the capital and to provide for the organization of selected areas for field application. In
these areas the Central Field Health Station would play a vital role.
It should be noted that some of these programs were strategic in
nature, designed to facilitate the movement of troops (although civil-
ians certainly benefited from improved transportation) and aimed
at securing popular support. While it provided direction and policy
control, the council left the details to be worked out by the technical committees, expert commissions, and ministries. Significantly,
the League of Nations was to provide some guarantee of the projects'
continuation through its participation. It began a period of technical collaboration with the Chinese government in 1931, working
through the National Economic Council and to a lesser extent with
other agencies of the Chinese government.[20]

Health and National Reconstruction

While economic planning remained a prominent feature of the reconstruction programs, with the founding of the Ministry of Health
in 1928 the government had also declared health improvement to be
an important component. The central questions were finding its
place in the larger effort toward reconstruction and determining the
philosophy that would underlie health promotion. Echoing views
expressed by contemporary medical leaders, official Nationalist policy
pronouncements generally asserted that health improvement was
part of the social planning that aimed to transform "the medieval
society of China into a modern society" through a "correlated application of modern science to the community life of China."[21] This
process was to be applied on both the regional and national levels.
In the area of rural reconstruction, for instance, scientific knowledge could be applied in the regional social fields of agriculture, rural
industries, rural cooperation, rural health, rural education, social
administration, and local government. National social fields included
community statistics, land tenure, irrigation, frontier settlement, transportation, currency, and tariffs.[22] A major function of the state, therefore, was to initiate and coordinate "interested and duly constituted

organizations and institutions [dedicated] to the joint solution of social-economic problems."[23]

The philosophical underpinnings that informed health-care policies in this social- reconstruction schema during the Nationalist decade revealed some continuity with the concept of health planning as it developed in the early Republican period. First, most leaders who staffed the new health bureaucracy shared the enthusiasm of their western counterparts at the end of the nineteenth century in believing that scientific advances, especially the advent of bacteriology and major developments in sanitary engineering, would open the door to the eradication of communicable disease and other social evils.[24] The emphasis was on the reformist nature of modern medicine and health care as a part of national reconstruction. Indeed, the larger objective of social reform was one of the goals of the Nationalist regime. Second, the development of modern health care was considered to be essential to the success of economic development, which itself was deemed vital. Poverty, it was claimed, resulted partly from sickness, and at the same time it was often a direct cause of sickness. Thus, the physical well-being of the population was closely related to increased economic productivity and general prosperity.[25] Health was not an end in itself but a means by which individual and social well-being could be achieved in conjunction with the strengthening of the nation. One official health publication compared a citizen to a cell in the body politic, and argued that unhealthy cells would lead to a weak nation. It called on every citizen to strengthen himself so that China could rid itself of the epithet "the sick man of East Asia."[26] Health protection and conservation were seen as part of the effort to implement Dr. Sun's ideals of nationalism, for a physically strong people would not be conquered or face national extinction.[27] This theme recurred in the health propaganda issued by the Guomindang. "The struggle for survival of the nation has reached the most critical stage," proclaimed the author of a popular handbook on health education, "and the health movement is the basic work which will liberate the nation!"[28] The social-Darwinian idea of health remained prominent in national-reconstruction planning throughout in the Nationalist era.

In addition to these broadly defined objectives, Chiang Kai-shek believed that the spiritual regeneration of the Chinese people should accompany material construction. Spiritual renewal would be accomplished through, among other things, healthful living. People were urged to revolutionize their lives through self-improvement in all arenas, including that of personal hygiene. This and other ideas were crystallized in the New Life Movement, launched by Chiang in February 1934 in Nanchang, the capital of Jiangxi Province, where the Nationalists had recently recovered some territory from the Communists. The New Life Movement combined traditional Confucian doctrines, Christian character-building ethics, and military ideals into a system of thought that was viewed as a viable alternative to Marxism-Leninism and other foreign ideologies. These ideas, properly inculcated and practiced, would create, according to Chiang, a revitalized, socially conscious, and disciplined population ready to build a new nation. In the speech inaugurating the movement, he proclaimed that

nowadays, the Chinese people generally live a barbaric life of filthiness, romanticism, laziness, and listlessness. We have to eradicate the life of filthiness, romanticism, laziness, and listlessness and live a civilized life which is orderly, clean, simple, efficient, and practical, and which conforms to the virtues of *li* [propriety], *yi* [righteousness], *lian* [integrity], and *qi* [a sense of shame].[29]

In the realm of health improvement, the movement advocated observance of a strict hygienic code. Personal hygiene, physical fitness, and cleanliness were paramount. Everyone should brush his teeth regularly, wash his body and his clothing, exercise daily, and abstain from alcohol, opium, and tobacco. The government initiated health-education and propaganda programs, clean-up campaigns and regular inspections of bathhouses and restaurants. It was expected that these attempts to improve personal and environmental hygiene would complement the efforts of medical leaders in the construction of a modern health system.[30] What is most significant, however, is that the movement reflected the role of the state in regulating individual behavior. Specifically, the movement stipulated ninety-six rules meant to direct individual actions that ranged from refraining from spitting in public, observing certain standards of orderliness, and maintaining personal hygiene and decorum to eating quietly and lacing one's shoes. Under the Nationalists, health matters became part of the larger effort to achieve national rejuvenation; the health of the individual was important because it impinged on the health of the nation.

To achieve these objectives, the state attempted to consolidate its control over medical and health matters while expanding its capacity to extract sufficient resources to support its reconstruction programs. Moreover, to ensure that the society at large would become more responsive to the state's demands for the acceptance of health programs, which in theory would provide protection for all classes of people, the state also wished to promote social cohesion. The latter, according to many Nationalist leaders, would be realized through widening political participation over a range of self-government initiatives. This would lead to a closer bond between the people and the state.[31] Health and socioeconomic improvements and the creation a close relationship between the people and the state would ultimately strengthen the nation in its struggle to survive in the midst of a hostile international environment.

According to Sun Yat-sen's *Fundamentals of National Reconstruction*, the rebuilding of the Chinese nation would depend to a large extent on the successful development of local self-government based on *xian* (county) reconstruction.[32] In October 1928, the Central Executive Committee of the Guomindang launched the "seven campaigns" at the *xian* level to lay the groundwork for local self-government. These campaigns addressed the areas of public health, *baojia* (a system of security and surveillance), cooperatives, road construction, reforestation, mass literacy, and the promotion of Chinese goods.[33] Taken together, these efforts were intended to improve socioeconomic conditions at the most basic levels and provide the foundation for national reconstruction. The Ministry of Health was made responsible for public-health work aimed at advancing the physical well-being of the Chinese people.

Another aspect of the seven campaigns, one that reflected the underlying concerns of national reconstruction, was rejuvenation of the rural economy. We have seen that Nationalist leaders viewed the people's physical well-being as vital to the success of China's economic reconstruction, and the countryside was the weakest component in this reconstruction strategy. The poor health of peasants often had been cited as a major cause of depressed conditions in the countryside, along with such factors as chronic disorder, political instability, the collapse of the rural economy, and natural disasters. Thus, while many still believed that the development of health services would begin in the cities, they also recognized the chronic need to improve conditions in the countryside. Dr. J. Heng Liu, health minister from 1929 to 1937, described the promotion of rural health work as an "urgent task," vital to the success of national reconstruction.[34] One of the major concerns in the National Economic Council's 1931 Three Year Plan on health was incorporation of the countryside into the new state health service that had been conceived as an instrument of rural reconstruction.[35]

The belief of the Guomindang was that the seven campaigns would ultimately foster social cohesion, cementing the bonds between the party, the government, and the common people. This, in turn, would facilitate the extraction of resources from the lower levels of society to support reconstruction efforts, as well as introducing these programs to the people and gaining their acceptance. In fact, the Guomindang considered the seven campaigns essential to the success of party-sponsored mass movements because they would create a "constructive" relationship between the party and the masses and secure the loyalty of the people.[36]

State Medicine

All these concerns encouraged active state involvement in health matters at every level. The state would consolidate control over public health and medical activities, and would provide health care and medical relief to the largest possible number of people. In order to accomplish these objectives, some medical leaders called for adoption of a system of state medicine. Practical considerations, apart from political ones, were important in promoting this idea among the health planners. The high cost of modern medicine and the general poverty of the people (both of which would result in large government financial contributions); widespread illiteracy and the lack of modern health knowledge, especially in the countryside; the predominance of communicable diseases, which would call for active official intervention; not to mention potential opposition, which might necessitate political protection—all these factors pointed to the desirability of some form of state-directed and supported medical system.

As early as the mid-1920s, Dr. C. C. Chen and some of his fellow students at PUMC had begun publicizing the idea of "state medicine" (*gong yi*) in articles published in the *Binying Weekly* and other Peking newspapers. State medicine generally meant "the rendering available to every member of the community, irrespective of any necessary relationship to the conditions of individual payment of all the potentialities of preventive and curative medicine."[37] As Chen explained it, if the government provided health care for the entire population, then it would be able to "promote public health improvements in the countryside as well as in the cities, regardless of individual background and income."[38] Chen and other medical leaders such as Li Tingan, a PUMC and Harvard School of Public Health graduate, and Robert Lim (Lin Kesheng), president of the National Medical Association of China in 1928–30, were aware of socialized health programs existing in other countries. They often discussed the concept of state medicine among themselves and in popular publications, especially its implementation in Britain and in Eastern European countries such as Yugoslavia and Czechoslovakia.[39] "To implement a system of state medicine," according to one of them, "is the best policy to actively improve the national economy and the people's livelihood."[40]

Proponents of state medicine generally envisioned a prominent state role in several areas of health planning. A central national health administration would have to be established, they believed, to organize and supervise medical and health efforts throughout the country. This administration would sponsor and encourage medical research, establish the infrastructure needed to produce health and medical personnel, promote hygiene and public health, and supervise the practice of medicine. At the provincial level, medical and health institutions would include a provincial health bureau, a provincial hygienic laboratory, and a provincial hospital and medical school. The *xian* level would be served by a county health station, hospital, and laboratory, and sub-*xian* levels by a rural health center, dispensary, and mobile unit. In order to supply the required personnel, medical schools would train not only doctors but health officers, nurses, midwives, pharmacists, and technicians. The better medical schools also would serve as normal schools responsible for training teachers. Since China would be faced with the problem of eradicating common communicable diseases for a long time, much planning would be focused on the use of health personnel in preventive and public-health measures. The state, therefore, should encourage the integration of curative and preventive functions in the medical system, and the rank and file of doctors would be charged with both curative and preventive work in the community. Only senior physicians would specialize as clinical consultants in hospitals or as preventive officers in charge of specific aspects of health conservation.

Such a system, it was claimed, would ensure the provision of adequate health care to all.[41]

A Conflict of Models

Health planners in the Nationalist government felt that gradual development of a state medical system would be the most appropriate course of action. The first step, according to J. Heng Liu, was "the development of administrative principles best adapted to local means and conditions,"[42] and establishment of a centralized administration of medicine and health. Chinese leaders vigorously pursued the first objective after the founding of the Nationalist regime in 1928. The extension of health care and medical relief to progressively larger numbers of persons, on the other hand, would require the establishment of facilities for training different types of personnel as well as a new organizational structure of medical practice. A problem arose when Chinese health leaders, attempting to meet these needs of state medicine, tended to allow, at least before 1936, the American model to dominate the development of medicine and medical education. Standardized medical degrees, private practitioners, and the separation of scientific and social welfare in public health were the main features of the American structure, and most Chinese medical administrators adopted them. The Rockefeller Foundation, through its support of PUMC and the development of science education in China, exerted a tremendous influence on the development of scientific medicine in China, both in the medical educational curricula and in the approach to public health.

The rise of the New Public Health Movement in the United States at the turn of the century was viewed by public-health experts largely as the result of the effective application of new scientific methods that led to a greater understanding of the underlying causes and processes of disease. The germ theory of medicine—the idea that diseases are caused by a specific, identifiable, etiological agent for which cures can be manufactured, either biologically through vaccines or chemically through drugs—became the underpinning of scientific medicine.[43] Developments in bacteriology and immunology enabled public-health physicians to deal directly with the causes of disease, and by the early 1920s the leadership of the American Public Health Association had cast aside "regressive notions of the relationship between filth and disease in favor of 'specific measures directed against specific diseases.'" The New Public Health Movement, therefore, reduced the importance of the social and physical environment in the control of communicable disease and redefined diseases in bio-scientific terms. Attention was focused now more on the disease process than on the diseased person. In place of nonmedical volunteers, who hitherto had been active in public health, physicians and nurses became the chief agents of the public-health movement.[44]

This emphasis on the training of medical experts and the pure-science ideal was duplicated by and large in the best medical schools in China. The success of PUMC and other modern medical schools in producing graduates to staff the fledgling health administrations or new medical schools and research institutions strengthened the hold of the supporters of scientific medicine. The adoption of the scientific medical model proved controversial, however, because it diverted resources away from the demands of state medicine—the other model that Chinese health administrators were trying to implement—which were intended to meet the immediate needs of the majority of the population. Implementation of the state system would entail aggressive efforts in the areas of sanitary engineering, control of communicable diseases, prevention, and general socioeconomic improvement. Adoption of the scientific model also raised the question of the role of indigenous medical practitioners in the delivery of health care. In the face of massive needs, how should the government allocate resources and address these concerns? These questions were especially pressing in view of huge demands made on the budget by military and political programs during the Nationalist decade. Where should a modern health-care system be placed in the hierarchy of national priorities?

Nationalist health planners also faced the dilemma of trying to define the quantitative-qualitative balance of personnel appropriate to the country's needs. A basic issue was whether to use limited resources to produce a few highly trained professionals or larger numbers of middle- or lower-level auxiliaries devoted to the health problems of the masses. Before the introduction of scientific medicine, the people had been served by indigenous practitioners. But with the advent of scientific medicine a small segment of the population, mostly residing in urban areas, tended to control the usage and resources of modern medicine, which also claimed a larger share of the limited funds assigned to the health sector. In terms of health manpower development, the prestige and power of modern medicine resulted in a manpower bulge of doctors in urban areas and a much greater bulge of indigenous healers in the lower segment of the man-power hourglass.[45] What approach, then, should health planners adopt in developing the national health system? The attempt by Chinese health leaders to combine the two approaches of massive public-health programs and the encouragement of clinical practices and sophisticated laboratory research created tensions in the system centering around urban-versus-rural issues and quality-versus-quantity dilemmas. As the following chapters will show, many of these issues would bedevil Chinese planners in the Nationalist decade.

3

The Organization and Administration of Health Services under the Nationalists

A 1932 article discussing public-health reconstruction under the Nationalist government described the founding of the Ministry of Health as follows: "The new National Government in its plan of reconstruction recognized the importance of public health and included in its organization in 1928 a new Ministry of Health."[1] While Nationalist leaders might be concerned with the role of health in national development, and the founding of the ministry was a major step in dealing with the enormous health problems of the Chinese population, it was not certain in the beginning that a health ministry would be established at all. The circumstances surrounding its creation clearly illustrate the close relationship between politics and health developments in the Republican period and provide vital clues to our understanding of the fortunes of the ministry during the Nationalist decade. Nevertheless, once it was founded the ministry managed to remain fairly stable—despite a change in name and modifications in its administrative structure—and it was led by only two ministers between 1928 and 1937. In fact, Dr. J. Heng Liu, who took over in 1929, was able to retain his position as head of the health administration until early 1938. This compares favorably with the record of other ministries, which, due to factionalism and political infighting, suffered from high turnover among key personnel.[2] The longevity of Dr. Liu's tenure facilitated the planning and development of health programs and ensured a relative stable organization amid much political uncertainty.

The Founding of the Ministry of Health

As a result of the success of the Nationalist army in gaining control over the central Yangzi Valley in late 1926, the Nationalist government had moved its capital from Canton to Wuhan. It began functioning officially in its new site on 1 January 1927. It was dominated by members of the left-wing Guomindang, including Mme. Sun Yat-sen. Anxious to secure the support of the new government for the creation of a health ministry, Dr. John Grant of PUMC and Dr. F. C. Yen (Yan Fuqing), a Yale Medical School graduate and dean of Xiangya Medical College at Changsha, conferred with some of the new leaders in Hankou. On 17 March, Dr. J. Heng Liu received a telegram from "the sister of Mrs. Sun Yat-sen," asking him to go to Hankou immediately. That afternoon, Grant also received a telegram from Dr. T. F. Huang (Huang Zifang), a member of the Health Section of the League of Nations Secretariat who was in Hankou, informing him that Mme. Sun Yat-sen had "unexpectedly" nominated Dr. Liu to head a new ministry of health.[3] But before Liu, Grant, and Dr. Henry S. Houghton, director of PUMC, could clarify the rather confusing situation at Hankou, political infighting between the Guomindang left and Chiang Kai-shek's rightist faction came to a head. In April, Chiang attacked Communist elements in Shanghai, organizing a new government in Nanjing on the eighteenth. Grant was disheartened by the political turmoil, which he feared would prevent the creation of a modern health administration. He was pessimistic about the "outlook for public health measures on the part of the Nationalist government" because the "Nationalists have very little money" and "a great deal of politics of a low order [is] carried on."[4]

Political developments in 1928, however, provided new opportunities for the medical reformers. In the initial establishment of the Nationalist government, Xue Dubi, a protégé of the warlord Feng Yuxiang, who had recently come to terms with the Guomindang, was awarded the directorship of the Ministry of the Interior. Xue, a former mayor of Peking, was a friend of Grant and had been associated with him in his work at the Peking First Health Station. Hoping that Xue would use his influence to found a Ministry of Health under Feng, Grant and Dr. Fang Shishan, the first director of the Health Station, went to Nanjing that summer and presented Xue with a formal proposal that they and J. Heng Liu had prepared. Xue, however, rejected the proposal as premature.[5] Despite apparent extensive lobbying on the part of such prominent medical leaders as Wu Lien-teh, New Way-sung (Niu Huisheng), and P. Z. King (Jin Baoshan),[6] as late as August, Liu was still expressing doubts about the feasibility of a new ministry because, as he put it, "our friends in the government lacked the interest to take the initiative."[7] But about eight weeks after Grant's meeting with Xue, he received a telegram informing him that Xue would be heading a newly created health ministry. This apparently occurred because Chiang Kai-shek, in an attempt to ac-commodate his new ally Yan Xishan in his coalition cabinet, gave Yan the Ministry of the Interior. Xue, Feng's protégé, was rewarded instead with a separate Ministry of Health.[8]

Thus, politics and personal relationships helped to give birth to the agency that would direct China's health developments for the next two decades. The way in which the ministry was initially staffed reinforced the importance of personal ties and the influence of a relatively small circle of modern medical leaders who, because of their small numbers in a country embarking upon medical modernization, exerted a disproportionate influence on medical developments at that time. Further, their similar backgrounds, close friendships, and working relationships tended to strengthen their impact. After the ministry was founded, Grant and these medical leaders once again intervened to ensure that the top personnel under Xue, the political appointee, would be competent people with modern training and backgrounds—preferably faculty, associates, or graduates of PUMC and the Peking First Health Station or graduates of well-known medi-cal schools who supported scientific medicine. Grant and Dr. George Y. Char (Xie Yuanfu), a urologist at PUMC who had treated Feng, went to see Feng's wife, herself a social worker well known to the PUMC community. They suggested that she submit to her husband a list drawn up by Grant and Char of nominees for the key positions in the health ministry. J. Heng Liu was recommended for the most important post, that of technical vice-minister, with P. Z. King as his assistant. Mrs. Feng complied with Grant and Char's request and subsequently the candidates on the list were appointed to the posi-tions. Liu was on a study tour of Europe at that time but he returned upon notification of this sudden turn of events.[9] The government officially appointed him administrative vice-minister of the health ministry on 31 October 1928. Liu took a leave of absence from his posts at PUMC—director of the college and superintendent of the hospital—and on 8 November left Peiping to assume his new position in Nanjing.[10] When Xue resigned ten months later, Liu became acting minister (in August 1929) and then minister in April 1930.[11]

In filling positions in the health bureaucracy, Liu relied heavily upon the faculty and graduates of PUMC, so much so that he provoked the ire of Roger S. Greene, acting director of PUMC from 1929 to 1934 and a member of the Board of Trustees, who accused Liu in 1934 of raiding the college for "supplying at short notice staff for every enterprise." He also chided Grant for wrecking his department by "giving up personnel for work outside and by neglecting PUMC in favor of outside enterprises."[12] But such acts simply confirmed the tremendous influence that PUMC, and through it the Rockefeller Foundation, wielded over health developments in the Republican period. The fact remains that the close friendship between Liu and Grant and their ties to the PUMC community, as well as to other modern medical leaders, enabled this group to dominate the newly established health agencies at both the national and local levels and to shape the policies of the ministry.

Organization of the Ministry of Health

Organization of the Ministry of Health was the first step in bringing under the central government the medical and public-health functions of the state. Under Liu, the administrative function was divided into four major components: two advisory boards, five administrative departments, special boards and committees, and health organizations under the direct supervision of the ministry.[13] The advisory boards included a Central Board of Health, which discussed and advised the leadership on national health policies, and an International Advisory Council of foreign experts. The names of the seventeen members of the Central Board read like a who's who of prominent modern medical leaders of the time, including, among others, Wu Lien-teh; W. S. New; F. C. Yen; Robert K. S. Lim, professor and head of the Department of Physiology at PUMC from 1924 to 1938 and president of the National Medical Association from 1928 to 1930; and Dr. S. M. Woo, secretary of the Joint Council on Public Health and first commissioner of Canton's health administration in 1920–21. Most of them were friends or colleagues acquainted with Liu or Grant, or had ties to PUMC. Several of them, including Liu, also had connections in the Nationalist government. W. S. New was acquainted with many leading politicians through his family, as his mother was a sister of the matriarch of the Soong family. F. C. Yen was a good friend of H. H. Kung, minister of industry and the brother-in-law of T. V. Soong, the minister of finance. J. Heng Liu was a Harvard classmate of Soong's, and had known Mme. Chiang when she studied at Wellesley.

The board met in February 1929, and again a year later, to recommend initial policy directions for the Ministry of Health. These included such important matters as regulations governing pharmaceuticals, industrial hygiene, rules for the examination of unregistered physicians, administration of medical schools, and issues related to state medicine.[14] The Chinese government extended invitations to Dr. Ludwik Rajchman, director of the Health Organization of the League of Nations; Dr. Victor G. Heiser, director for the East of the International Health Division of the Rockefeller Foundation; and Sir Arthur Newsholme, formerly chief medical officer of the Local Government Board, England, to serve on the International Advisory Council. Though Newsholme declined because of advanced age, the others accepted. Their presence proved to be very beneficial since both the League of Nations and the Rockefeller Foundation were to play active roles in health planning and development in the Nationalist decade.

The five administrative departments in the Ministry of Health were General Administration, Medical Administration, Health and Sanitation, Epidemiology, and Vital Statistics. These departments were responsible for a myriad of functions ranging from supervision of the local health administration, medical practice, and health education to development and control of health services, sanitary inspection, epidemic prevention, and quarantine. Their work was predominantly in the field of public health services, and it reflected the major concerns of the new ministry in its early years. In fact, the health administration declared the four official "fundamental issues" to be the development of administrative principles, the training of health personnel, the establishment of an efficient quarantine service, and the control of epidemics.[15] It is significant that in the original proposal for the establishment of a health ministry, Liu had argued that, although preventive medicine would be the primary focus of the ministry in the beginning, it would become increasingly necessary for the government to provide for curative functions in its medical administration. In fact, he insisted that the need for such functions was greater in China than in most other countries since "through government it would be possible to give the population a minimum degree of the benefits of curative medical science at a relatively small cost, which will take decades to become available if left to the evolution of a private curative medical profession."[16] What Liu envisaged, therefore, was a ministry whose activities would encompass the traditional categories of public-health and medical-care services. Clearly, it would be the state's responsibility to meet the public-health and medical-care needs of the population.

On paper, there were a number of organizations constituted under the Ministry of Health, including the health bureaus of the provincial governments and special municipalities. In practice, at the beginning of the Nationalist era, the government had direct jurisdiction over only the provinces of Jiangsu, Zhejiang, and major portions of Anhui, Fujian, and Jiangxi.[17] In Zhejiang, public-health work began soon after the Nationalists came to power. A provincial health commissioner was appointed in the Department of Civil Affairs to direct health-care work. Health-education goals included the creation of a medical school, a modern hospital, and a training school for midwives. Various public-health projects such as school hygiene, control of malaria, and the improvement of environmental sanitation were initiated.[18] But, as in the cases of Jiangsu and Anhui—both under the Nationalists' direct jurisdiction—there was no independent provincial health bureau since departments of civil affairs in all three provinces were in charge of health matters. In areas controlled by Chiang Kai-shek's allies, health bureaus might be set up but direct interference by the Ministry of Health would be minimal. In most cases, the ministry had to yield control over local health agencies to provincial governments, which at times were reluctant to share their power over provincial matters. Thus, the role of the ministry was essentially one of defining the broad principles of health policy.[19]

The ministry also claimed direct authority over health matters in the seven municipalities of Nanjing, Peiping, Shanghai, Hankou, Tianjin, Qingdao, and Canton. Canton, Peiping, Shanghai, and Nanjing already had established municipal health departments—in 1920, 1925, 1926, and 1927, respectively. In the Special Municipality of Greater Shanghai (excluding the foreign concessions, which had their own services), the health organization had four divisions in charge of various health responsibilities, a health commissioner, a secretariat, a public-health laboratory, and two rural health centers.[20]

The Ministry of Health did draw up plans in December 1928 for the establishment of health organizations at the provincial and local levels: health bureaus of provincial and municipal governments and health divisions under departments of public safety at the *xian* level.[21] The inauguration of such administration was dependent upon the establishment of certain minimum standards and guidelines by the ministry as well as on the availability of funding and personnel. In the meantime, the ministry urged local governments to at least address the most urgent health priorities, among them the prevention of communicable diseases and vaccination campaigns.

There were other agencies under the direct jurisdiction of the Ministry of Health. The Central Hygienic Laboratory (*Zhongyang weisheng shiyan suo*), founded on 1 March 1929 in Shanghai to conduct chemical and pharmaceutical analysis, bacteriological and pathological examinations, and laboratory research, exercised control over drugs and patent medicines. The National Epidemic Prevention Bureau (*Zhongyang fang yi chu*), which had existed in Peking since 1919 under the Ministry of the Interior and was now placed under the jurisdiction of the new ministry, was responsible for research on and production of sera and vaccines. In January 1929, the National Midwifery Board was established jointly by the Ministry of Health and the Ministry of Education to promote modern midwifery training. The First National Midwifery School was founded in Peiping nine months later. To study industrial health problems, a joint Commission on Industrial Health of the Ministry of Health and the Ministry of Labor and Commerce was organized, and factory health services were planned in selected cities. Initially, the ministry also had ambitious plans for a National Health Officers Training School but it had to settle for short-term courses because of lack of funds.[22] Finally, in 1931, as a result of cooperation with the League of Nations Health Organization, the Central Field Health Station was established to undertake technical activities related to public health and hygiene such as surveys, research, special projects, and the training of technical personnel.

The National Health Administration

As a result of the world depression in 1931, the government found it necessary to retrench. It streamlined the central administration by combining ministries hitherto autonomous (such as the ministries of Health, Agriculture, and Labor) and with few or no provincial organs. On 3 April 1931, the Central Political Council decided to change the status of the health ministry from an independent body to a semiautonomous service within the Ministry of the Interior and change its name to the National Health Administration (*Weisheng shu*).[23] J. Heng Liu became director of the new administration but he now reported to the minister of the interior in the Executive Yuan. Liu was not convinced of his future independence of action, despite verbal assurances from Chiang Kai-shek himself, and he contemplated resigning from his post.[24] Since the League of Nations Health Organization had agreed to a program of technical cooperation with the Ministry of Health, the government also had to assure Dr. Ludwig Rajchman, the league's representative, that the vital work of the ministry would be maintained in the new administration.[25] But in the summer of 1933 rumors that Chen Guofu, a staunch supporter of traditional Chinese medicine, would soon be named the minister of the interior was enough to create panic among the medical modernizers.[26] Advocates of modern and traditional medicine feuded over the role of the two systems in China's medical development. Indeed, the need to placate important political allies in the party or the government may have led some Guomindang leaders to softpedal the push for rapid implementation of certain westernized healthcare programs. Further, T. V. Soong resigned as finance minister after a disagreement over fiscal policies with Chiang in the latter part of 1933, and there was speculation that Liu's political fortunes would decline since he was a close associate of Soong.[27] But Liu remained in his post and was confirmed as director of the Central Field Health Station in late 1933, with Dr. P. Z. King as vice-director.

The structure of health administration was simplified after the ministry was abolished. The original five administrative departments were consolidated into three, while their duties remained basically unchanged. Another bright aspect of the change was that more technical personnel were provided for.[28] Nonetheless, the Central Field Health Station was removed from the National Health Administration, becoming one of the technical services of the new National Economic Council. The functions of the National Health Administration were now basically administrative, relating to matters of legislation, supervision, and registration. The Central Field Health Station emerged as the agency in charge of technical matters and the coordinator of the local health services, the subsidiary organizations nominally under the jurisdiction of the National Health Administration, and special health services undertaken by other ministries. Together the two agencies constituted the National Health Service.[29]

During the Nationalist decade, the National Health Service was expanded to include a host of organizations, some of which had been controlled formerly by the Ministry of Health or other ministries. Directly under the National Health Administration were the National Quarantine Service, formerly under the Ministry of Finance, with its headquarters at Shanghai; the Central Hygienic Laboratory; the Northwest Epidemic Prevention Bureau, established in 1934 to study and manufacture biological products, primarily for use in controlling animal diseases; the Mongolia-Suiyuan Epidemic Prevention Bureau, also founded in 1934 to investigate epidemics in that region; the 340-bed Central Hospital in Nanjing; the First National Midwifery School and the Central Midwifery School, both of which offered regular and short-term courses; the Central School of Nursing; and several urban and rural demonstration stations. The National Epidemic Prevention Bureau, located at Nanjing with branches in Peiping and Lanzhou, was administered directly by the Central Field Health Station. At the same time, the National Health Administration and the Ministry of Education worked together to set policies for health-related education through several bodies, among them commissions on medical education, health education, and nurse education (see Appendix 1).

The Depression also affected municipal health organizations. In 1930, the Peiping Health Department was incorporated into the Police Department, while those at Tianjian and Nanjing were abolished outright (in 1931 and 1932, respectively). The latter two cities maintained only a health subbureau within the municipal government.[30] At the provincial level, the National Health Administration recommended in 1932 a model plan for the establishment of provincial health services consisting of an administrative office, hygienic laboratory, provincial hospital, nursing and midwifery schools, and an urban health center in the capital of the province. Much of the initiative for setting up such services rested with the provincial governments, although the National Health Administration usually provided technical and personnel assistance. By 1937, health organizations of this type had been introduced in Jiangxi, Hunan, Gansu, Qinghai, Ningxia, Shaanxi, Zhejiang, Yunnan, and Fujian, while efforts were underway to expand the model to Guangxi, Shanxi, and Sichuan.[31] In 1934, the National Health Administration adopted as standard a rural-health scheme that focused on the *xian* health center, with a clinic and hospital, and subdivisions administering health stations and substations.[32]

As these plans were implemented, hospitals at both the provincial and *xian* levels emerged as key institutions. In provinces and *xian* where health bureaus or centers had not yet been organized, hospitals provided both curative and preventive services while doubling as some sort of administrative center. In fact, many *xian* hospitals practically functioned as health centers.[33] The number of government hospitals remained small, however, and their slow development became one of the major obstacles to the introduction of state medicine. In 1930, more than half of the five hundred hospitals in China were missionary institutions or private concerns run by Chinese or foreign nationals.[34] Some early attempts at cooperation were made, however, by both the government and missionary hospitals. Missionary hospitals in Anhui decided in early 1935 to share personnel and resources with the provincial health authorities and the National Health Administration. Missionary hospitals in some rural areas also were recruited by the government to assist in promoting public health. As Christian missionary groups became increasingly involved in the rural reconstruction movement in the mid-1930s, these and other private hospitals generally were willing to cooperate with the health administration, serving as links in the state medical system. The larger ones functioned as provincial hospitals and the smaller as *xian* health centers.[35]

As we have seen, the Nationalist government was anxious to consolidate state control over health policy and development, and the establishment of central administrative and technical agencies, as well as a hierarchy of health organizations, reflected this fundamental concern. In choosing this centralized administrative model, health planners shared certain ideas about state medicine with their Eastern European counterparts. The involvement of the League of Nations in health planning in the 1930s strengthened this approach.

The Role of the League of Nations

The effort to establish a modern health administration was supported by the League of Nations, which, even before the founding of the Nationalist regime, had been invited by the Chinese government to plan a national health program. In 1926, Dr. Ludwig Rajchman, director of the Health Section of the League, visited China, although the chaotic political situation prevented the development of any concrete plans for cooperation. Contacts between the League and the Chinese government continued, with visits to China by Albert

Thomas, director of the International Labour Office, in 1927, and by Joseph Avenol, then deputy secretary-general of the League, just prior to the formal establishment of the Nationalist government in 1928. As noted above, the new Ministry of Health invited Dr. Rajchman to serve as one of the members of its International Advisory Council. Moreover, in September 1929, the Chinese Foreign Ministry officially requested the League to send a "sanitary mission" from its Health Organization to study China's port health and quarantine matters. With the League's approval, Dr. Rajchman visited China again in late 1929. The subsequent exchanges between the Ministry of Health and the League, together with Rajchman's report to the League, submitted in early 1930, formed the basis of the collaboration between the two sides.[36] Significantly, John Grant and J. Heng Liu viewed the League's involvement as crucial to ensuring stability and continuity in China's health reconstruction. As Grant pointed out, the presence of the League representative most likely would shield the personnel engaged in activities that the League considered important, despite any political changes that might occur at the top, because "any new government in China is going to be desirous of international goodwill inasmuch as the eventual success of any party will depend upon reconstruction measures." Even a new political regime, he felt, would be compelled to honor previous agreements made with the League.[37]

The League's involvement in China was confined to four areas. First, the League might send a small number of experts or representatives to China for a long period to assist with a specific technical service. Second, certain highly specialized experts might be sent to China on a temporary mission to advise the Chinese on important issues. Third, the League might facilitate the study abroad of Chinese specialists. And last, specific committees within the League might be assigned to study technical problems that the Chinese government deemed important.[38] Beginning in the summer of 1930, Dr. Borislav Borcic, former director of the State Institute of Hygiene at Zagreb, Yugoslavia, was stationed at Nanjing as a full-time representative of the League to provide technical advice. From 1933 to 1936, Dr. Andrija Stampar, former director of public health at the Ministry of Social Assistance and Public Health, Belgrade, served as the League's expert in China. Although the role of the League's Health Organization in the 1930s also included rural-health developments, the immediate concern here is with its contribution to the organization and administration of health services.

The Ministry of Health's initial proposal for collaboration with the League was submitted in December 1929. It emphasized the need for the development of administrative principles and facilities for training personnel before such long-term goals as effective child, school, and industrial health, epidemiology and communicable disease control, and general sanitation could be met. As a result, the ministry proposed to create a Central Field Health Station in Nanjing, which would serve as the technical headquarters for public-health work and the nucleus of an eventual national field health service. It would perform much the same functions as did the institutes and schools of hygiene in Europe. Initially, the station would limit its activities to designated areas. A network of medical and public-health institutions would be created to serve not only as models but as training centers for public-health personnel. A national hospital would be established to serve as a national institution for undergraduate instruction and postgraduate training. Other reforms in medical instruction would be introduced as well. The provincial hospitals, located in the provincial capitals, would be used as bases from which to extend public-health programs gradually to the *xian* and lower levels. Finally, the Quarantine Service would be reorganized with the help of the League's Health Organization.

After approving the proposals in March 1930, the League began working closely with the Chinese government to further define specific areas of cooperation.[39] In April 1931, the new National Health Administration announced a Three Year Plan to implement some of these ideas. The plan focused on the creation of the Central Field Health Station, the Central Hospital, and an experimental medical school; the gradual extension of the National Quarantine Service; and the coordination of public-health work. Seven months later, the National Economic Council formally included the plan in its general program of national reconstruction.[40]

The key component of the plan was the Central Field Health Station, which, together with the Central Hospital, was to become the nucleus of national medical and health services. League experts provided not only the organizational charts of the Health Station but its name as well—a title of which J. Heng Liu was not particularly fond.[41] From the beginning Dr. Rajchman insisted that the Chinese should assume most, if not all, of the burden of establishing the station, arguing that this would result in a stronger institution, despite the fact that the lack of a foreign contribution probably would delay "the accomplishment of the project."[42] In an interview with Roger S. Greene, he resisted the Rockefeller Foundation's suggestion that it be allowed to contribute to the expense of organizing the agency. He did not, however, reject the foundation's offer to send Chinese fellows abroad for public-health training. He did express doubts about the wisdom of sending all the fellows to Johns Hopkins and Harvard, arguing that the returning fellows would feel frustrated after having been exposed to a system that they could not hope to duplicate in China. Even Dr. Borcic, the League's expert in Nanjing since the summer of 1931, had once expressed dismay over the fact that "he could never build up in Nanking anything at all comparable to the PUMC."[43] Both the Rockefeller Foundation and the League did provide fellowships for Chinese personnel to further their training. By July 1935, twenty-eight members of the Health Station and affiliated organizations had been sent to study in Europe and Singapore, while thirty-two had gone to the United States.[44] The foundation also sent Brian R. Dyer, a sanitary engineer, to advise the station on sanitation and the training of personnel.[45]

It is apparent that Rajchman was very concerned over the influence wielded by the Rockefeller Foundation in China's development at that critical stage, and feared the possibility of friction between the League's representatives and experts from the foundation's International Health Division. He went so far as to intimate that the foundation and the League's Health Organization should accept a geographical division of their activities: the former concentrating its efforts in north China, focusing on the work of PUMC, and the latter operating in central and south China, focusing on government health initiatives.[46] Significantly, this "division" also reflected to a large extent the different approaches that health planners in the Nationalist decade tried to reconcile: the "Johns Hopkins model" adopted by the PUMC, which stressed high-powered research and clinical work; and state medicine, which aimed to extend benefits to the greatest numbers through preventive medicine and public-health work.

The Implementation of the Three Year Plan

The Central Field Health Station began operation in May 1931 in a temporary location in Nanjing. In 1933, it moved to a new building constructed with a subsidy from the National Economic Council.[47]

The scope of its work was vaguely defined as "the establishment of experimental and investigating institutions, the demonstration of practical field work, and the training of the technical staff."[48] In practice, the station played a pivotal role in the planning, the organization, and (to some extent) the financing of most of the major health programs implemented during the Nationalist decade. The broad extent of its work is reflected in the wide-ranging areas of concern encompassed by its nine departments: Bacteriology and Epidemic Disease Control, responsible for the study and control of infectious diseases; Chemistry and Pharmacology, responsible for research in pharmaceuticals and Chinese drugs; Parasitology, responsible for investigating and controlling parasitic diseases, especially malaria; Sanitary Engineering, responsible for the planning and improvement of environmental sanitation; Medical Relief and Social Medicine, responsible for the planning and application of social medical relief; Maternity and Child Health, responsible for the organization of maternal and childrens' health programs; Industrial Health, responsible for developing programs of medical relief for workers and the prevention of occupational diseases; Epidemiology and Vital Statistics, responsible for the gathering and analysis of birth, morbidity, mortality, and epidemiological data; and Health Education and School Health, responsible for the organization of propaganda, instruction, and school health work.[49]

In the realm of organization and administration of health services, the station was charged with establishing laboratories and branch stations in various parts of the country. By early 1934, it was maintaining specially equipped field stations in thirty-five localities in eight provinces.[50] In that same year, in cooperation with various provincial governments, it helped to establish health bureaus and agencies in Shaanxi, Gansu, Qinghai, Ningxia, and Jiangxi. In those provinces, the station also operated laboratories and training centers and carried out public-health work. It also provided financial, technical, and personnel assistance for rural health demonstrations.[51] Despite natural disasters (such as the Yangzi flood of 1931 and the cholera epidemic of 1932) and wars (including the Nationalist campaigns against the Communists and Japan's attack on Shanghai in 1932), which compelled the station to send personnel and materials to locations where help was most needed, the station continued to grow, assuming an increasingly important role in the development of public health and health manpower.

Another component in the Three Year Plan's attempt to establish central, guiding, technical institutions was the creation of the Central Hospital in Nanjing. Conceived as a center for modern medical research and instruction, the hospital launched operations in temporary quarters in January 1930. Despite problems caused by the absence of public services such as a reliable supply of water, gas, and electricity, and the disposal of waste water, as well as interruptions caused by the Japanese attack on Shanghai in 1932, new buildings were completed in June 1933. The new hospital had 340 beds and a large outpatient department. It was instrumental in training a number of doctors for public hospitals and clinics through a system of internship. The Central Midwifery School, founded in the fall of 1933, and a School of Nursing also were attached to the hospital, which was controlled and maintained directly by the government.[52]

The third component of the plan, the creation of an experimental medical school to train personnel for the planned state medical and public-health service, failed to materialize by the end of the three-year period owing to financial restrictions and difficulties in reorganizing the existing medical-education system.[53] There was some controversy also over the value of such an institution. It was not until 1937 that the school finally opened at Nanchang, in Jiangxi, and then the outbreak of the Sino-Japanese War forced it to move inland. These circumstances prevented the school from realizing its full potential as planned.[54]

In the coordination of public-health work, the emphasis remained on the health administration's efforts to encourage and coordinate local health activities and provide support for health campaigns and public-health education. These activities will be dealt with in more detail below.

Supervision of Medical Practice

One objective of the health administration was to assert national control over medical practice and standardize the requirements for the registration of physicians, dentists, pharmacists, nurses, and midwives. As we have seen, before 1928 these groups practiced without much interference from a central authority and without uniform standards. While dentists and nurses were not required to register with the government until October 1935 and January 1936, respectively, the government promulgated provisional regulations for the registration of physicians, pharmacists, and midwives in 1928–29, immediately after the founding of the Ministry of Health.[55] Pharmacists with diplomas from a government-approved Chinese or foreign pharmacy school, or persons with licenses from foreign countries, could register with the government. Persons who had successfully completed a two-year course on midwifery in government-approved Chinese or foreign schools, or who had practiced for three years prior to the promulgation of the regulations, could do so as well. Persons in both groups could obtain a license to practice if he or she passed a government-administered examination. Since the overwhelming majority of babies were still delivered by old-style midwives, in July 1928 the government also promulgated rules governing their work. They were now to be called *jieshengpo* (literally, 'delivery ladies') and were required to register with the government. Only women between the ages of thirty and sixty would be considered qualified, and these had to enroll in a two-month course on sepsis and the rudiments of modern midwifery. This latter measure was a tacit recognition on the part of the new Ministry of Health that it would be years before China could train enough modern midwives. In the meantime, old-style midwives with some modern training would be recruited. Unfortunately, few local authorities had the funds to offer training classes. For most of the country, the impact of the new regulations was minimal.

A more stringent approach was adopted in the Ministry of Health's attempt to register physicians. During this period, the number of modern doctors was still small. Most had received their training at institutions in Japan, England, Europe, or the United States, or at the few modern medical schools in China. Some, however, were graduates of schools not recognized by the government, or of hospital-training courses only. On the other hand, the large numbers of practitioners of native medicine were usually trained by means of an apprenticeship. It will be recalled that modern doctors had called for the abolition of native medicine as early as the 1910s. Not surprisingly, the domination of the new Ministry of Health by a group of physicians who generally dismissed traditional medicine as unscientific and were anxious to standardize licensing requirements led to a bitter dispute between the two sides. In January 1929, the ministry published provisional regulations for the registration of doctors without distinguishing between practitioners of modern and native medicine. The requirements clearly were based on standards and training that few traditional doctors possessed. They included possession of a diploma from a government-approved Chinese or foreign medical school, or a medical license from a foreign country, or successful completion of a government-administered examination based on modern medical knowledge.[56]

Liu and his colleagues seemed bent on outlawing native medicine altogether. The first conference of the National Board of Health (convened in February 1929) passed a resolution abolishing native medicine. Its practitioners henceforth would be required to obtain additional training in modern medicine before receiving a license to practice. And no new licenses would be granted after 31 December 1930.[57] The following month, a massive petition organized by practitioners and supporters of native medicine was submitted to the Guomindang. The petition, which demanded the repeal of the resolution, succeeded in forcing the government to table it. The Nationalist party actually split over this issue, with supporters of indigenous medicine found mostly in the higher echelons of the party and in the legislative branch of the government, while modern medicine received its support mainly from organizations in the executive branch, especially in the ministries of health and education.[58] The rift in the party injected a political dimension into the feud between the two groups and, as we have seen, reinforced the desire of supporters of scientific medicine to maintain a tight grip over the health administration.

Ignoring opposition, the ministries of health and education pushed ahead with their attempts to restrict the activities of native practitioners. They issued regulations changing the names of schools of native medicine to "training institutes" (*quanxisuo*), renamed hospitals as clinics, and barred native practitioners from using certain modern instruments and equipment.[59] In May, 1930 the Ministry of Health finally promulgated regulations for the licensing of modern physicians: graduates of government-recognized Chinese or foreign medical schools or persons with licenses to practice medicine in foreign countries could now take a government licensing examination. Successful candidates could register to practice with the government.[60] No similar regulations were promulgated for practitioners of native medicine.

The status of native practitioners remained unclear; they had been relegated to legal limbo. The Ministry of Health lacked the political clout to outlaw them outright, but it did not have to recognize them officially. In May 1930, supporters of native medicine organized an Institute of National Medicine (*Guoyiguan*) with the goal of securing for native medicine some legal status. It also tried to promote the scientific study of native medicine. Three years later, twenty-nine members of the Central Political Council supported a resolution entrusting the regulation and supervision of native practitioners to this institute. The National Health Administration and supporters of modern medicine denounced this move as usurpation by a non-government organization of the power of the legally constituted administration, which was, at that very moment, trying to create a unified national health system. The resolution was blocked finally by Wang Jingwei, president of the Executive Yuan and a supporter of modern medicine, who argued that China would "lose face" in the international community if it were to allow a nongovernment organization such great executive power over health matters.

Although defeated on the issue of supervision, the Institute of National Medicine succeeded in persuading the Fifth Guomindang Party Congress, in November 1935, to pressure the government to promulgate finally the "Regulations for Chinese Medicine." Under these rules, traditional doctors could obtain a license to practice if they met one of the following criteria: passing a government examination, graduating from a school of native medicine, receiving a permit from the government, or having practiced for more than five years. With this success in hand, supporters of native medicine pushed for the addition of a vice-director to the National Health Administration. This appointee would have knowledge of native medicine and would deal specifically with traditional medical matters. In the end, they had to be content with the creation of a Commission on Chinese Medicine under the National Health Administration in February 1937. On paper, the commission was responsible for matters relating to the registration and supervision of native practitioners, but in fact it remained advisory in nature and was largely ineffectual in influencing the policy of the health administration.[61]

Medical modernizers, however, viewed these developments with alarm. Although traditional doctors were now required to register with the government, the fact that anyone who could claim to have been practicing for five years could continue that practice nullified the attempt to upgrade and standardize licensing requirements. Nor was the National Health Administration able to enforce its registration regulations, for it lacked not only the political power but the manpower to verify the registration status of doctors. Supervision of practitioners of native medicine rested basically with local authorities. In reality, many thousands of traditional doctors remained unregistered and unregulated, operating outside the medical sphere controlled by modern doctors, by practicing among the millions of Chinese untouched by modern medicine. In the final analysis, in their zeal to establish scientific standards, modern medical leaders overlooked, or refused to accept, the potential usefulness of traditional practitioners as allies in the expansion of public-health activities to segments of the population that were not reached by the small number of modern doctors and public-health specialists. Certainly this failure adversely affected the development of health manpower in China.

Health Expenditures

In dealing with the issue of native medicine, lack of political influence was not the only problem facing Liu and his colleagues. The viability of the new health administration and the expansion of services depended upon adequate funding from the government. Unfortunately, military and political exigencies and the fiscal policy of the Nanjing regime conspired to limit government spending in the health sector. From 1928 to 1937, military appropriations constituted the largest single item, averaging 44 percent of total national expenditures. Even this figure may understate expenditures since the Guomindang provided substantial amounts of indirect assistance to military-related activities in particular regions. In fact, military spending steadily increased during this period, from $210 million in fiscal year 1929 to $312 million in 1931.[62] The next largest item was debt service, accounting for an average of 35 percent of total national expenditures during the same period. Thus, at least 79 percent of the national budget was devoted to two items, both of which were nonproductive and basically lost to the national reconstruction effort.[63]

The fiscal problem was compounded by the a lack of tight control over the level of spending despite the passage of numerous budgetary laws. Chiang Kai-shek pressured Soong for funds without regard for budgetary constraints. In fact, Soong resigned as finance minister in late 1933 partly because of his conflict with Chiang over excessive military spending.[64] Ultimately the Guomindang, not the government, controlled the purse, and expenditures that would strengthen the position of the party—whether military, political, or economic— had priority over other items.

It is difficult to construct a clear picture of health-related expenditures, partly because so many agencies were involved and partly because the published figures did not always match the amounts spent. Moreover, some funds went directly from the Ministry of Finance to the Ministry of Health, never appearing in the budget at all. In general, all health spending constituted a minuscule percentage of total national expenditure, and health agencies had to compete for funds with other agencies of the civil government. Appropriated funds would be channelled through the National Health Service for allocation to its agencies and projects. In 1929, the Ministry of Health's first fully operational year, $698,836 was budgeted for the health service. This accounted for approximately .11 percent of the total national budget.[65] With the announcement of the Three Year Health Plan in 1931, the government declared its intention to allocate $3 million annually for health work. But the budgeted amount, which was less than the pronounced target, represented only .22 percent of total expenditures.[66] By 1936, although the health budget was almost ten times larger than that of 1931, it still represented only .7 percent of the total budget, or roughly 2.4 cents per Chinese citizen.[67]

The pattern of health spending provides some insight into the priorities of the health planners. For instance, were expenditures concentrated on the technical aspects of public health? What were the respective allocations for urban and rural areas? An examination of the health budget for 1931–33 provides some answers to these questions. For each of these three years, if we combine the annual allocations for the medical and technical portions of the health budget, including funds for the Central Field Health Station, Central Hygienic Laboratory, National Epidemic Prevention Bureau, North Manchurian Plague Prevention Service, the Central Hospital and the Chinese Drug Research Institute, they account for 58 percent, 53 percent, and 53 percent of the respective total budgets, yielding an average of 55 percent for the three-year period. The rest of the funds were allocated to the National Health Administration, the national midwifery schools, the nursing school, the quarantine service, and urban and rural health demonstrations. Thus, more than half of the health budget was devoted to the scientific and research aspects of public health, confirming the strong influence of the American model.[68] Although by 1936 some health leaders were calling for a shift away from this approach, the technical agencies' share of the budget remained at 53 percent in 1937.[69]

Apart from some small subsidies given to certain provincial projects, the central health administration had no control over expenditures at the provincial and *xian* levels. It had power only over the municipalities directly administered by the central government. Health spending in Nanjing and Peiping almost doubled between 1931 and 1936, while in Shanghai it had increased only slightly. Per capita health expenditures for these three cities in 1936 were: Nanjing, $1.06; Peiping, $.37; and Shanghai, excluding the foreign concessions, $.21 (the average for all major cities was $.45). As a whole, the average amount of health spending among the major municipalities in that year accounted for 6.5 percent of total health expenditures. This compares most favorably with the average of .74 percent for the provinces and .99 percent for the *xian*.[70] There is an obvious bias in favor of the mostly curative health services provided in urban areas.

Provincial health budgets were determined by the provincial governments. Sources for health funds were not often reliable, although provinces such as Jiangxi and Fujian assigned portions of their regular revenue for health purposes.[71] As for the *xian*, in 1936 only 473 out of a total of 1,098 *xian* in sixteen provinces reported some spending on health activities, and this amounted to only about 1 percent of the total outlay for all the provinces that year. Moreover, health spending varied greatly from province to province. Jiangxi, with an average of $9,055 per *xian*, ranked first; while Hubei, with an average of $172 per *xian,* was last.[72] It is important to note that the Nationalist government placed a much greater emphasis on the construction of railways and roads, which had obvious strategic importance. For instance, in 1934 the National Economic Council allocated $10 million—about a third of the council's budget for that year—to road construction.[73]

To raise additional funds for the many projects of the health administration, J. Heng Liu appealed for support from different sources. One was the Sino-Belgian Boxer Indemnity Fund Commission, which granted the National Health Administration a subsidy of $20,000 for the construction of an obstetrics hospital in Nanjing in 1935.[74] It is not surprising that Liu sometimes used his personal connections to raise funds for certain projects. The fact that Liu was close to Soong and Mme. Chiang proved advantageous not only in political matters but also in the extraction of funds from the treasury. John Grant testified that Liu had to resort to this short-cut many times, bypassing regular channels, in order to get "an immediate handout for something which 'had to be done immediately.'" These funds would be sent directly to Liu from the Ministry of Finance, and they were not recorded in the budget. This was necessary because, as Grant put it, the regular budget provided the health administration with only enough to sustain a "skeleton organization." When Soong resigned as finance minister in late 1933, Grant worried that Liu's source of extra financial support would dry up.[75] Later, Liu got into trouble over his methods of finding additional money for the expansion of the health administration's work. In mid-1936, he was investigated for fraudulent reporting of health revenue. Apparently Liu had not remitted to the government all the earnings of the Central Hospital and some units of the administration, applying the funds to construction of a new building for the serological division and to the expansion of other projects. To do that, he allegedly kept a double set of books. Although Liu's integrity was never questioned, he came in for much criticism as a result of the investigation.[76]

The limited amount of funds available, and the unreliability of their sources, had an adverse effect on health planning and programs. Many projects had to be left to local initiatives, which often were lacking. This was especially the case in the field of rural health care, and the substantial urban-rural differentials in health expenditures exacerbated the geographic maldistribution of services. Without any social insurance schemes, many people were unable to pay for the primary health care that the government had hoped to provide through the introduction of state medicine. On the other hand, the government could only provide support for health care in a few areas. Because of limited resources, the health administration decided to concentrate on a few health demonstrations, both urban and rural, in order to develop techniques that could be applied elsewhere. It also hoped to develop, with the cooperation of provincial and local governments, selective projects that would further the basic objectives of state medicine.

The model of Chinese state medicine advocated by health leaders at the time stressed the establishment of central guiding institutions, both administrative and technical, and the development of a hierarchy of health organizations to provide curative and preventive care to the largest possible numbers of people. It must be remembered that the Chinese government had no control over private health institutions such as those financed and run by foreign missionary boards or nationals. And, throughout this period, the country was far from united under one central government. Nonetheless, by 1937

the Nationalist government had established central health institutions comparable to those existing in some European countries, and
these were functioning with reasonable efficiency despite financial
and political constraints. The attempt to extend health care to the
masses, however, was repeatedly frustrated by political unrest, limited funding, insufficient personnel, lack of local initiatives, and the
failure to recruit traditional doctors into public-health work. It was
in the countryside that health planners saw the most urgent need for
health protection and conservation efforts, and it was there that
they met the greatest challenge.

4

The Evolution and Organization of Rural Health

In the context of early-twentieth-century China, where more than 80 percent of the roughly 450 million people lived in the countryside, the promotion of public health necessarily meant the development of large-scale, rural, health programs that could address directly the massive problems of unsanitary living conditions and the virtual absence of modern health care. In its plans for the development of a modern health-care system in China, the health administration of the Nationalist government did not ignore the rural areas. In fact, as we have seen, the attempt to introduce state medicine was a response in part to the acute health needs of the rural population. Health planners certainly recognized that appalling conditions existed in the villages and small towns, and they constantly stressed the need to develop preventive and public-health programs with a rural bias. In practice, the government tried to establish a hierarchy of rural health-care organizations and introduce programs of curative and preventive medicine. It also consolidated and coordinated efforts initiated by individual reformers or groups. Although progress toward the organization of rural health services was halting and slow, the decade preceding the outbreak of the Sino-Japanese War proved to be an important period in which models of rural health were tested and developed. The system that eventually emerged, though extremely limited in scope, had consequences extending beyond 1949.

67

The Special Needs and Problems of Rural Health

In order to understand the difficulties and problems associated with the development of a rural health service, it is necessary to examine the socioeconomic conditions under which peasants lived and worked in the 1920s and 1930s. We have noted briefly the factors contributing to rural distress: chronic political disorder, social ills, economic collapse, massive poverty, famine, and natural disasters. These conditions themselves contributed to, and were exacerbated by, such public-health problems as poor environmental hygiene, the prevalence of infectious disease, high mortality rates, and widespread malnutrition. Despite the nominal unity imposed by the Nationalist regime after 1928, socioeconomic conditions in most of the Chinese countryside did not improve significantly. Rather, for a variety of reasons, they had worsened in many respects. The prolonged military struggle between the Nationalists and the Communists in the late twenties and early thirties not only devastated farmland but it created instability in the countryside.Significantly, the success of Communist land reform in certain areas forced the Nanjing regime to develop competing programs addressing the deteriorating rural economy. China's increasing involvement in the world economy and the growing interdependence among financial, commercial, and agricultural interests in the 1920s and 1930s led to the gradual collapse of the traditional rural economy. One indicator of this trend was the decline, and even the disappearance of, many basic rural industries. By 1930, competition from both foreign and native machine-spun yarn had virtually wiped out the hand spinning of cotton, formerly one of the most important sources of supplemental income for the rural population. Rural industries such as tea processing, silk reeling, paper making, flour milling, and oil pressing declined dramatically in the late 1920s and early 1930s.[1] There was also a steady flight of capital from the hinterland to the coastal cities, especially Shanghai, which offered relief from civil war and social unrest and provided safer investment opportunities. In 1932, the Bank of China reported that about 64 percent of domestic remittances handled by the bank went from the interior to coastal ports. That percentage increased to 72 just one year later.[2] This outflow of capital seriously limited the availability of rural credit and helped to inflate the already usurious rates of interest demanded by the money-lenders.

Other factors worked to reduce the incomes of farming communities in the 1930s. The worldwide depression caused the price of agricultural products to decline after 1931, and farmers whose subsistence had been precarious in the best of times now faced the threat of starvation. The economic crisis led to an increase in tenancy and in some areas hastened the proletarianization of the peasants. Ironically, land values depreciated due to the chaotic conditions in the countryside, and the tax rate was soon unduly high compared to the value of the land. From 1930 to 1931, it can be estimated that the tax burden actually rose an average of 25 percent even if real tax increases are not taken into account.[3] In many rural districts, in fact, the land tax increased rapidly, sometimes by as much as 90 percent, in the late 1920s and early 1930s, and some military authorities in the Yangzi provinces were collecting land taxes as much as twenty to forty years in advance.[4] Compounding these problems was a series of natural calamities that affected the northwest and the Yangzi and Huanghe provinces from 1928 to 1934: the great famine of 1928 created close to 20 million refugees in the northwest, the Yangzi River flood of 1930–33 destroyed crops worth an estimated $90 million, and the Huanghe flood of 1933–34 affected more than 6 million acres of farmland.[5]

Since the health problems in the countryside were already colossal, one may argue that such developments had little or no significant impact on the health of the peasants. The infant mortality rate had always been higher in rural areas than in the cities (in the mid-1930s, it was 164 per 1,000 live births versus an urban rate of 122).[6] Epidemics raged unabated in many parts of the country. There were serious outbreaks of plague in Shanxi, Shaanxi, Xinjiang, South Manchuria, and Fujian between 1931 and 1935, and a widespread cholera epidemic in Shanxi, Shaanxi, Suiyuan, and Henan in 1934.[7] The level of understanding of modern sanitary and health measures among the rural population remained low and there was an obvious shortage of trained health-care personnel. What did take place, however, was further erosion of the ability of the peasants to pay for medical care, and a lessening of the capacity of local authorities, even if they were willing, to finance new organizations or institutions associated with the introduction of modern health services.

Studies undertaken in the 1930s concluded that, on average, a farmer spent thirty cents annually for all his medical services, an amount equal to about .75 percent of his yearly income.[8] Since modern medicine was expensive and still unknown or distrusted in many parts of the country, it was highly unlikely that a farmer would spend half of that thirty cents on modern health care even if he could.

With a diminished income, it was likely that he would postpone seeking medical intervention until the last possible moment. Most rural people did not have a clear notion of the meaning of public health and they generally identified it with medical relief. So in general they were more willing to pay for drugs than to spend a few cents on a smallpox vaccination, and some officials felt obliged to build their rural health framework around clinical service.[9]

Such an approach, however, was prohibitively costly for a farming community. In the 1930s, the minimum annual salary of a modern private physician was $600. Assuming that each person in a rural area contributed about twelve cents from his "normal" yearly health expenditure, at least five thousand people would be required to maintain a modern physician. And this did not include the cost of an office, equipment, or drugs, all of which required an additional annual outlay of about $500. Thus, another five thousand people would have to be recruited in order to support a modern private physician in the countryside.[10] The poverty of the rural population virtually precluded such an arrangement. Not surprisingly, overwhelming numbers of rural patients turned to practitioners of native medicine for medical relief. At the same time, it is doubtful that local authorities, already hard pressed for funds to implement other reconstruction projects, were willing to expend a sizable portion of their budgets on modern health projects.

The introduction of rural health services therefore demanded a different strategy. As already noted, J. Heng Liu and other health planners identified preventive medicine and active state intervention at the local level as the two approaches most appropriate for the development of organized rural health. The social side of medicine was to be emphasized. With the state's backing, programs of protection and prevention would be developed to eliminate social ills with a medical component: malnutrition, poor housing, and the many social diseases.[11] Certainly, health planners would have liked to introduce modern medicine into the countryside, applying scientific knowledge to better people's lives. But as C. C. Chen, who had gained valuable experience in his work at the Mass Education Movement at Dingxian, pointed out, scientific medicine would be meaningless "in the absence of concurrent improvements in other phases of social life," and that "only in localities where the local government, the economic organization and other phases of social life are undergoing reforms, are there signs of the medical service taking root."[12] In short, it was clear that the introduction of health services in the country-side would have to be carried out within the general context of rural reconstruction.

Rural Reconstruction

Despite verbal commitments from Nationalist leaders to the cause of rural rehabilitation, the first few years of the Nanjing regime witnessed limited efforts in that direction. These included attempts to quell banditry and rural unrest, in order to restore peace and order in the countryside, and the creation of institutions to improve agricultural production. In August 1929, the government promulgated an Agricultural Extension Law to initiate a nationwide extension program. With the cooperation of local authorities, a number of experimental stations were organized in various parts of the country.[13] In 1930, the government also promulgated a land law capping rent at 37.5 percent of the value of the main crop, although in practice the provision remained largely on paper. To encourage economic development, the government promoted development of the cooperative movement—one of the items in the "seven campaigns"—to aid farmers in matters of rural credit, business and marketing, rural industries, improvement of farming techniques, and mutual security and support.[14]

The Nationalist government's technical cooperation with the League of Nations also included an agricultural component, albeit a rather small one in comparison with the emphasis on road construction, industries, and hydraulic projects. In October 1932, two experts from the League, Prof. Carlo Dragoni of the International Institute of Agriculture and the University of Rome, and Dr. Guido Perris of the same institute, arrived in China to survey agricultural conditions. Later that year, another League expert was studying methods to improve the sericulture industry in rural districts.[15] One of Dragoni's recommendations was adopted immediately: the creation of a Rural Reconstruction Committee serving under the National Economic Council to coordinate reconstruction efforts. The committee held its first meeting on 20 March 1933 and made plans for the expansion of extension work, economic surveys, and the cooperative movement.[16] But during these years Chiang Kai-shek was preoccupied with his consolidation of power and his campaigns against the Communists, and it was not until after 1932 that the Guomindang began to consider seriously the implementation of comprehensive programs of rural reconstruction. Confronted with the success of Communist recon-struction efforts and its own setbacks in trying to deal with Japanese aggression, Chiang's government resolved to initiate a series of co-ordinated rehabilitation programs—especially in Jiangxi after the Nationalists made significant inroads into eliminating the Commu-nist stranglehold in that province.

Health Centers and Demonstrations

J. Heng Liu and his colleagues in the Ministry of Health began for-mulating plans for a rural health service soon after the founding of the ministry. Between 1929 and 1932, although concerned mainly with creating and consolidating central administrative organs and guiding technical agencies, they were also experimenting with strategies for implementing the second aspect of state medicine: the provision of medical relief to the largest possible number of people. Faced with limited resources and few personnel, Liu decided to con-centrate on the strategy of using health centers (*weisheng yuan*) as demonstration areas for testing ideas and techniques. According to him, China would have to develop methods that were "adapted to conditions prevailing." A small number of "typical regions" would be selected "in which to work out the details of effective and eco-nomic methods."[17] In other words, by concentrating on practical research in restricted areas, a feasible health program could be devel-oped and extended to other regions by means of demonstration and application. To Liu and like-minded medical modernizers infused with optimism over the potential benefits of applying scientific methods to problems of social reform, the centers would serve as social laboratories in which applied medicine would be combined with social sciences to effect change.[18] As Andrija Stampar put it, the physician, making use of social science, now "applies his learning to the people as a whole, thus extending his knowledge and becoming a physician of the whole community."[19]

In adopting the idea of health centers as a major part of the rural program, Chinese leaders acknowledged their debt to models that had been developed in the United States and Europe.[20] In the United States, the idea of relating health services to a definite population or district began to emerge before the First World War and drew much attention in the twenties and thirties. Health demonstration centers were established by child-welfare societies, antituberculosis agencies, and private social agencies and foundations such as the Metropolitan Life Insurance Company, the Milbank Memorial Fund, and the American Red Cross. What is ironic is that the American health-center movement was primarily concerned not with medical care but only with "coordinating health department programs and local voluntary agencies within a particular neighborhood."[21] What came closest to the Chinese reformers' concept of the health center was a 1920 proposal by Hermann M. Biggs, health commissioner of New York state, calling for a network of health centers to be established in New York's rural districts to compensate for the lack of medical personnel in those areas. His institutions would consist of a hospital, an outpatient clinic, a laboratory, and a center for public-health work. Despite support for Biggs's proposal from public-health and social-welfare groups, tremendous opposition from the medical profession to what it called public-health intervention in medical care spelled its doom.[22] To the Chinese, however, Biggs's model embodied the features that they wanted to implement in their own countryside. Their community health centers would combine curative and preventive medicine to serve defined populations. The emphasis would be on primary care, with much attention paid to health-related environmental concerns.[23]

Another source of inspiration for Chinese medical leaders was the work of the Rockefeller Sanitary Commission (1909–14), and later the International Health Board, in the eradication of hookworm in the southern United States. The commission chose selected demonstration counties as sites in which to educate local people about the benefits of public health and sanitation. At the same time it attempted to generate support for the organization among local health departments and lobbied for the enactment of public-health legislation.[24] Later this experience in the rural south was transferred to Eastern Europe through the International Health Board, which provided funding for many rural sanitation programs as well as the reconstruction of state health services after the First World War.[25] Unlike the United States, the governments of several European countries, including Yugoslavia, Hungary, and Czechoslovakia, created health centers that became part of national health services. The Yugoslavian health structure, for example, combined a central Institute of Hygiene with a number of provincial institutes and district and rural health centers.

These examples helped to shape the Chinese perception of the functions of health centers. First, health centers would "demonstrate" modern public-health techniques and train students. Second, they would act as part of the government's health administration by providing curative and preventive services to the rural populations that needed them most. In Chinese health centers established in the late 1920s and 1930s, both functions were present, although generally the initial intention was to use them strictly as demonstration centers.

The first attempt to apply the concept of community health care to China, however, was not initiated by the Chinese themselves. As we have seen, it was John B. Grant, professor of hygiene and public health at PUMC, and concurrently the Rockefeller Foundation's International Health Board's representative in China, who spearheaded the founding of the Peking First Health Station in 1925. Labelled a "medical Bolshevik" by some, Grant had been interested in using community health centers to promote both preventive and curative services ever since his work in 1917 in the Rockefeller Foundation's county health program in Pitt County, North Carolina.[26] The Peking First Health Station gave Grant the opportunity to realize his goal. It was launched with financial contributions from and cooperation between PUMC, the Rockefeller Foundation International Health Board, the National Epidemic Prevention Bureau, and the Peking Police. The station combined the features of a demonstration center for community health care with curative and preventive services. It also served as a training site for PUMC students. This was the first modern health center in China and it served as the model for many others, both urban and rural.

Since the Peking First Health Station exerted such far-reaching influence, it is important to examine in some detail its organization and operation. The station served a city ward with a population of 95,956 (in 1929). Its three divisions encompassed the functions of sanitation, including sanitary inspections of food and drinking water; vital statistics and communicable disease control, including the registration of births and deaths and the administration of preventive measures; and medical services, which maintained a health center with preventive and curative clinics and public-health nursing services. It also directed a school health service for 1,800 students and an industrial medical service for 1,200 workers. Grant believed that the example of curative clinics producing readily appreciable results would be necessary to win over those who were still skeptical about modern medicine. The medical staff of the station consisted of six physicians, seventeen nurses, one pharmacist, one dental hygienist, and three sanitary inspectors. Students from PUMC were required to fulfil a three-week clerkship there during their fourth year.[27] One indicator of the station's success was steady growth in the volume of its work. From 1929 to 1931, the annual number of curative treatments increased from 47,316 to 80,471 while such preventive services as smallpox, cholera, and typhoid vaccinations rose from 7,163 to 10,660. During the same period, home visits by public-health nurses increased from 25,126 to 34,565. The training of public-health personnel also gained ground. Twenty-eight medical undergraduates completed clerkships in the station in 1931, compared to eighteen in 1929, and the number of nursing undergraduate clerkships rose from nine to ten in the same period.[28] Significantly, the station served as a training ground for many future health leaders and officials in both the private and public sectors. One of them, Dr. P. Z. King, the station's chief of medical services, served as health commissioner at Hankou in 1927. Later he joined J. Heng Liu in the new Ministry of Health.

Private and Local Health Demonstrations

The Peking First Health Station provided Chinese reformers with a model of how community health demonstrations could be developed in a controlled practice area. In the 1920s, individual reformers already had embarked on rural reconstruction projects that embodied some public-health activities. Organized rural health work finally began in 1929, though it was not initiated by the new Nationalist government. In that year, four health centers began operation: one at Xiaozhuang, near Nanjing, as part of the Rural Normal School Movement; one at Dingxian as part of the Mass Education Movement; and two at Gaoqiao and Wusong, both near Shanghai, with support from the municipal government of Greater Shanghai. Dr. Li Tingan, a 1926 PUMC graduate, was instrumental in helping to establish the Shanghai stations with help from Grant.[29]

These centers represented the two varieties of rural health demonstration as they existed in the Nationalist period. The first was established through private initiatives with some support from local governments. The second was a city or *xian* initiative with support from other agencies. In the case of the Gaoqiao and Wusong centers, the Shanghai government provided the administrative machinery while the National

Shanghai Medical College and the National Tongji University provided the medical expertise. The rationale behind both types of demonstration was similar. They were to experiment with the introduction of modern health care in a small, defined area with the hope of applying the results to other, larger areas. Each center was staffed by three doctors, several nurses and midwives, and one sanitary inspector. It is interesting, in view of the friction that existed between practitioners of modern and native medicine, that fifteen doctors of native medicine served on the Gaoqiao medical staff, although all had been judged acceptable by the Ministry of Health. The activities of the stations included curative clinics, communicable disease control, public-health publicity, maternity and child health, school health, environmental hygiene, sanitary inspection, and the collection of health statistics. There were even some efforts to train public-health personnel. All of these activities, however, were still rather limited.[30]

The Xiaozhuang Rural Normal School Movement was initiated in 1927 by Tao Xingzhi, a noted educator, in the village of Xiaozhuang outside Nanjing. His objective was to reconstruct rural life through the promotion of rural education, especially elementary education. He believed that education should be part of people's daily lives and that schools should lead the countryside in social change. To accomplish this, he organized a network of normal schools, with affiliated elementary schools, to train teachers. The curriculum also included manual work in fields or gardens. The students were encouraged to embody the movement's motto, "Live With the Farmers!"[31]

Health work in Xiaozhuang began in 1929 when C. C. Chen, who had graduated from PUMC that year, was invited to organize a rural demonstration program. When Tao discovered that Xiaozhuang did not have enough funds, J. Heng Liu agreed to pay Chen through the Ministry of Health.[32] Chen had been influenced by Grant's ideas of community health care and he strove to establish an organization that emphasized experimentation, demonstration, and popular participation. He opened two clinics, and during his tenure a hospital was built. Most importantly, he injected modern medical information into the curricula of the normal schools, training teachers in the rudiments of first aid, vaccination, and environmental hygiene. His idea of using rural schoolteachers to spread public-health information proved to be one of the most important innovations in the rural health movement. Chen later admitted that his sojourn at Xiaozhuang taught him much about the ways to develop rural health programs, and this experience proved invaluable later when he became the head of the health department of the Mass Education Movement at Dingxian.

The Xiaozhuang project was closed down by Chiang Kai-shek in April 1930, apparently in response to student demands that the facility be socialized, and to Tao's criticism of Chiang, an indiscretion that led to Tao's arrest.[33] Chen left for postgraduate study at Harvard and in Germany with the support of a Rockefeller Foundation fellowship.

The health program of the Mass Education Movement at Dingxian, a *xian* with a population of about 390,000, was far more elaborate. Begun in 1923 as a National Association, James Yen's Mass Education Movement initially concentrated on promoting literacy through specially prepared texts (the "One Thousand Character Text") and teacher training. Three years later, the movement went on to Dingxian where in 1929 it launched a *xian*-wide rural reconstruction project. Social surveys were carried out to lay the foundation for programs concerned with literacy, agricultural development, citizenship training, and public health in what Yen called the "living laboratory."[34]

The movement's health program in Dingxian had financial support from the Milbank Memorial Fund. J. Heng Liu also instructed the Department of Civil Affairs of Hebei to co-operate.[35] A health department was established in 1929 to develop a system "practicable under existing conditions, to make elementary medical relief and health protection available for the masses."[36] It was headed initially by a graduate of PUMC who tried to apply his experience at the Peking First Health Station to the countryside.[37] Two years later, C. C. Chen took over as head of the department after his return from Europe. The relationship between PUMC and Dingxian remained close. In 1932, PUMC and the Mass Education Movement signed an agreement of cooperation. PUMC began using on-site health-training facilities at Dingxian while its hospital served as a base for the movement's medical-relief work. PUMC provided experts in public health to assist in the movement's work as well as facilities and fellowships for qualified members of the movement's health department who wished to undertake special studies at PUMC.[38]

C. C. Chen's stewardship vastly strengthened the administration of the health department. His work at Xiaozhuang had taught him that public-health practices must be integrated into the people's lives and that successful programs required their active participation. He concentrated on developing programs that were economically feasible and based upon utilization of local resources, sound organization, effective local leadership, and the concurrent improvement of socio-economic conditions. The provision of health care was designed to work effectively within the three rural administrative units—the *xian*, the *qu* (subdistrict), and the *xiang* (rural district)—so as to facilitate the patient's access to health care even at the lowest level. At the *xiang* level, health substations were staffed by nurses or village health workers, local people who had received some basic training in preventive treatment and simple medical procedures, usually for ten days. These workers were responsible for first aid, vaccinations, the reporting of births and deaths, health publicity, and the improvement of sanitary conditions, especially the construction of drinking-water wells. On the second level, the subdistrict health station was usually located in a market town. It was staffed by a doctor, a nurse, and a dresser. Their duties included the operation of daily clinics, the dispensing of preventive vaccinations, supervision of health workers and village midwives, and promotion of health education. On the highest level was the *xian* health center, located in the *xian* capital. Acting as the administrative headquarters, it maintained a thirty-bed hospital and a laboratory and was responsible for sanitation and communicable-disease control, health education, school health, and the training of physicians, nurses, and midwives. The objective of the health program was to gradually increase the number of health stations at the *xiang* and *qu* levels so that medical relief and preventive treatment could be made readily available to the rural population.[39]

To keep costs low, C. C. Chen and his colleagues drew as much as possible upon the local resources of Dingxian. Instead of relying on outside experts, who were expensive to maintain, village health workers were extensively utilized. Teachers were trained to meet minor medical needs and provide guidance and supervision in school health programs. Village health workers charged only 1.1 cents per treatment, which included materials and labor, and patients requiring hospitalization paid only about 40 percent of the average daily cost, about $1.79.[40] Prevention was emphasized. Extensive public-health education was undertaken through the organization of demonstrations and exhibits. Textbooks in the People's Schools run by the movement contained much health information. To reinforce these measures, drinking-water wells, public bath houses, and pit latrines were built so that healthful practices could be integrated into the people's daily lives.

As Chen has pointed out, the Dingxian program challenged the existing model of private physicians and hospital-centered care. It addressed the problems of an impoverished rural population virtually devoid of modern resources. It provided basic care within the economic limitations of the community while linking that community to centers of scientific medicine in the cities.[41] The Dingxian experiment thus illustrated the crucial nature of economic feasibility in the development of health programs and the clear link between health improvements and socioeconomic reform. The use of local resources, especially the training of village health workers as paramedics, and to a lesser extent the incorporation of schoolteachers, helped to augment rural health manpower and develop local leadership. It must be remembered that public health was only one aspect of the general program of rural reconstruction at Dingxian. As James Yen put it,

> we are trying to develop not just rural education alone, or rural health, or economic improvement, or citizenship, each individually and by itself, but to coordinate and correlate all these varous aspects of community improvement and social up-building for the remaking of the Chinese *hsien* [*xian*] and the Chinese citizen.[42]

Another rural reconstruction initiative with a health component was Liang Shuming's project, initiated in Henan and later moved to Shandong. In May 1929, Liang, a former professor at Peking University, joined with other reformers to establish the Henan Village Government Academy to promote research in village government, agricultural reform, moral uplift, and health education, as well as to train personnel in rural reconstruction. These efforts were terminated by Chiang Kai-shek in the fall of 1930 after he defeated the warlord Feng Yuxiang and occupied Kaifeng, the capital of Henan. Fortunately, Liang was able to launch a more ambitious project at Zouping, in northern Shandong, upon the invitation of Han Fuqu, the new governor of that province. Centering upon the Shandong Rural Reconstruction Institute, the Zouping experiment aimed to develop new forms of social and economic organization through the revival and reform of traditional culture. It hoped to increase rural production through the cooperative movement, develop agricultural technology, and mobilize the people for purposes of character building and moral improvement. At the same time, it adopted preventive medicine and public-health education as the means of improving health conditions. A clinic was opened, with support from Shandong

Christian (Cheeloo) University's School of Medicine, and a small
hospital was established in 1935. The institute planned to organize a
health substation in every *xiang*. Similar to the Dingxian effort,
laymen who had received some training in modern preventive techniques and simple medical procedures were employed to provide primary care. Training classes in midwifery were organized for local
women and the hospital's maternal and child-care program contributed to a dramatic decline in the infant mortality rate.[43]

Nationalist Rural Health Policies and Programs

Medical leaders in the Nationalist government such as J. Heng Liu, P.
Z. King, and Robert Lim recognized the usefulness but also the limitations of such private, local initiatives. They agreed that state medicine
and government-sponsored national programs were necessary. The
Dingxian program, in particular, offered a concrete example of a
rural demonstration center in action, and it encouraged them to establish similar projects in which new techniques would be developed
and extended to other *xian*. But Liu and his colleagues' interest in
these centers went beyond mere demonstration. Organizationally,
the three-tiered structure of Dingxian's health program proved to be
an important model for the planned rural health service and the
health centers that were to be part of the national administration.
Beginning in 1929, the Ministry of Health would adopt a dual approach in building a rural health system: selecting and establishing
demonstration centers directly under the government's sponsorship,
and drawing up long-term plans for a national rural health service.

The Central Field Health Station played a major role in the ministry's plans for the rural health service. In its proposal for technical
cooperation with the League of Nations, drafted in 1929, the ministry had emphasized the station as the nucleus of an eventual health
service. In April 1931, the National Health Administration announced
a Three Year Plan. Creation of the Central Field Health Station was
one of its key components. As early as May, when the station commenced operation, it became deeply involved in the training of health
personnel and the development of rural health centers, hospitals,
and laboratories in various parts of the country, providing crucial
technical, and at times financial, support. The technical staff of the
regional health centers and demonstration centers was linked with
the station. Thus, data collected from the center were transmitted to

the station for use in evaluating existing and future national or regional health policies, and the expertise of the station staff was put at the disposal of the regional centers.

Even before the Three Year Plan was formally launched, the government had established (in January 1931) a demonstration center at Tangshan, a small town in Jiangning *xian*, Jiangsu Province, about twenty miles east of Nanjing. The Tangshan Rural Health Station was the first demonstration center initiated directly and supported entirely by the central government. In the first year, its budget was about 1 percent of the total *xian* budget. Five years later, it had risen to about 5 percent (or 9.3 cents per capita per annum, a fairly substantial amount compared to other health programs at that time).[44] The station was designed to develop health programs at the most basic levels, to make these programs applicable to other areas, and to train public-health personnel. Its work was at first confined to about ten villages, with the town of Tangshan as its center, but it was extended to twenty villages with 6,199 people in July 1933.[45]

In Tangshan, the National Health Administration established a health station that maintained a clinic staffed by a doctor, two nurses, one midwife, one sanitary inspector, and a part-time health officer. The work of the station encompassed both public health and medical services. With the aid and cooperation of various local departments, and organizations such as the Public Safety Bureau and Peasant Education Association, the station tried to improve sanitary conditions in the villages through the passage of sanitary regulations and the digging of new wells with funds and materials provided by the central government. It organized special classes to train policemen as sanitary inspectors who could exercise their law-enforcement powers in the interest of public health. The modern-trained midwife provided pre- and postnatal care, delivering babies and conducting classes for traditional midwives. The progress of work in maternal and infant care was slow at first, but it grew steadily. During one twenty-six-month period, the midwife supervised sixty-two deliveries, which was only about 30 percent of total births in the area. This was a significant step, however, since even traditional midwives were scarce in Tangshan and deliveries had been left to the general female population. School health programs, which included periodic examinations and treatment for common problems, were also initiated in the eight local schools, serving a total of about 450 students. Teachers were trained to conduct such health work as vaccinations and first aid.

Vaccination campaigns against common diseases like smallpox and health-education campaigns were considered important means of arousing the health consciousness of the population. The station also maintained a clinic to provide medical relief from many ailments, the most common of which were trachoma, skin problems, malaria, and gastro-intestinal disease. Except for a registration fee of a few cents, the medical service was free. The clinic was so well attended that the station soon opened ten branches in the primary schools. What is encouraging about attendance at the clinic is that first visits increased steadily from 3,392 in 1931, to 4,891 in 1932, and 6,480 in 1933. There was also a high rate of return visits. To provide service to outlying sites, a mobile medical team was formed.

In many ways the Tangshan Rural Health Station resembled the *qu* station of Dingxian. It also emulated Dingxian's use of paramedics and schoolteachers in health work. In 1933, the entire Jiangning *xian*, with 1,600 villages and a population of 450,000, was designated as one of the ten "*xian* reconstruction experiment areas" (*xian zheng jianshe shiyan qu*) under the Nationalist government's National Regulation for Experimental *Xian*. The three-tiered division of health services pioneered at Dingxian was to be introduced and the original Tangshan demonstration center was incorporated into the *xian* health structure. Students of public health in Nanjing institutions were sent to the *xian* for practical training.[46] Significantly, the staff of the Central Field Health Station, which was closely involved with developments at Tangshan, realized that it would be virtually impossible to build the rural health system from the top down, that is, by extending public-health activities gradually to the *xian* level from the provincial hospital, as the Ministry of Health had originally envisioned in its proposal to the League of Nations in 1929. Instead, the Dingxian model of a *xian*-based health center with a hospital as the focal point of *xian*-wide programs of both curative and preventive service proved to be far more practical and feasible. The *xian*, after all, was the economic as well as the political center of rural China. Following the existing administrative divisions, and linked through the use of mobile medical teams, the health network was to provide the population with modern health care.

From 1932 to 1934, the National Health Administration took additional steps to formulate the organizational structure of the national rural health service. While the demonstration centers in Tangshan and Dingxian were useful, in that they experimented with practical techniques for the application of modern medicine in rural China, they required significant outside support—both financial and in manpower. Initially, at least, it would be difficult for small towns or villages to duplicate those experiments. The second strategy adopted by the National Health Administration was the introduction of general medical and preventive services for the *xian* as a whole through the *xian* hospital. The hospital would be supported by the *xian* government and would act as the center for health activities in the *xian* until a full-fledged health center could be established. In the meantime, the base hospital would try to extend medical and preventive services to the lower levels.

In the fall of 1932, a Rural Health Service was organized under the Department of Medical Relief and Social Medicine of the Central Field Health Station in order to expand the demonstration program begun at Tangshan in selected sites and to promote the establishment of *xian* hospitals or health centers to provide curative and preventive services.[47] During the Second National Conference of Civil Affairs, held in December, the government reaffirmed, at least on paper, the need to establish public-health organs, especially *xian* health centers or hospitals.[48] The Central Field Health Station also helped to establish hospitals in a number of *xian*, concentrating at the beginning on the province of Jiangsu, the Nationalist power base. To demonstrate the feasibility of such programs, in October 1932 the Central Field Health Station organized model hospitals in Tai *xian* and Yancheng *xian*, both in Jiangsu. The hospitals provided curative and public-health services, including vaccination campaigns, maternal and child care, and health propaganda. After the Nationalists overran the Communist stronghold in Jiangxi, the National Health Administration worked with the provincial government to establish hospitals in many *xian*. In fact, by 1935, Jiangxi had the largest number of government-approved *xian* hospitals.[49]

To a lesser extent, health programs were launched in a few *xian* in the provinces of Anhui, Shandong, and Hunan in 1934, and, with the expansion of Nationalist power in the southwest, in Yunnan in 1935. In February of that year, a Northwest Investigation Team was dispatched to investigate rural health conditions in Shaanxi, Gansu, Qinghai, and Ningxia. In several *xian* in Shaanxi, health centers were established with assistance from the Central Field Health Station. Dr. Stampar, the League representative, was directly involved in the establishment of health services in the Northwest provinces and in Yunnan.[50]

A most important step in the development of a rural health service was taken in April 1934 at the First National Health Conference, convened by the government and attended by health officials and medical leaders to discuss national policies. The Central Field Health Station's plan for *xian* health organizations was formally approved and the conference urged local governments to implement the new rural health structure.[51] The government's plan provided for the establishment of a health center in each *xian* to be located at the capital. Each center was to be equipped with a forty-bed hospital and would be responsible for curative and preventive work throughout the entire *xian*. It would combine administrative and technical tasks within five sections: clinic and hospital, diagnostic laboratory, drug supply, health education, and administration. At the next level, *qu* health stations would be established in the larger market towns, serving groups of fifty thousand people. The health officer in charge, assisted by a nurse, would be responsible for conducting daily clinics and implementing preventive programs such as vaccinations, sanitary inspections, and school health. *Xiang* health substations, located as often as possible in a school in the central village, would each serve between five and ten thousand people. The nurse, with public-health and midwifery training, assisted by village health workers, would conduct a daily clinic for simple medical procedures, carry out pre- and postnatal care and visits, and perform general preventive work. These health organizations would be staffed by personnel similar to those employed in Dingxian. The lowest level of care would coincide with the *baojia* system, which the Nationalist government revived in 1932. This system organized families in groups of ten for mutual surveillance and security purposes (mainly against the Communists), and the fourth level of the health system would be on the *bao* level, consisting of one hundred households (ten households constitute one *jia* and ten *jia* form a *bao*) and staffed by a village health worker (see appendix 2).[52]

To underscore the importance of the *xian* as the foundation of rural reconstruction, attempts were made to coordinate health services with other reconstruction programs. The government proposed in the Second National Conference of Civil Affairs, held in 1932, the creation of a number of "*Xian* Reconstruction Experiment Areas." Within each designated *xian*, all ameliorative programs, including education, cooperatives, local industries, and health services, would be correlated, and the experience gained would be applied to other *xian* reconstruction efforts. By the end of the following year, ten *xian* in the provinces of Jiangsu, Zhejiang, Shandong, Shanxi, Henan, and Hebei had been chosen. Those with *xian* health centers already in place included Jiangning in Jiangsu (the Tangshan Health Center), and Dingxian in Hebei. In Shandong, hospitals were built in the designated *xian* of Heze and Zouping, the last one already serving as the headquarters of Liang Shuming' rural reconstruction organization.[53]

The expansion of rural health services depended upon, among other factors, the availability of funding and manpower. A major problem was the cost of the facilities, and the National Health Administration or the National Economic Council usually provided small subsidies, especially in politically sensitive areas such as Jiangxi. The construction of a hospital with thirty beds cost about $10,500, while the maintenance of such a facility required an average monthly outlay of $1,500.[54] Without guaranteed financial support from the *xian* government, such projects could not be undertaken. It may be recalled that most provincial and *xian* governments did not have fixed budgets for health work. The National Health Administration urged local bodies to levy taxes specifically for rural health activities but these would have to be added to the already exorbitant tax burden that the peasants had to bear. Jiangxi and Hunan tried to set aside portions of their budgets for use as capital and operating funds for health work.[55] But without a steady source of local support, the National Health Administration and the National Economic Council effectively became the arbiter of where health programs could be introduced. As for manpower, the innovative use of laymen such as village health workers and schoolteachers, the development of schools as centers for the dissemination of public-health knowledge, and the use of mobile medical teams not only reduced the cost but also enhanced the health consciousness of the people. But it took time to change the beliefs and perceptions of the rural population about modern health care. And, despite support from the central government, funding remained restricted and unreliable and there continued to be a lack of modern health manpower.[56]

With all these problems, it is not surprising that most local governments were slow to implement the plans recommended by the National Health Administration. By 1936, out of a total of 1,098 *xian* in 16 provinces, only 181 *xian* health centers in 12 provinces had been established. In addition, there were 86 health stations and substations and 91 rural clinics. Compared to the findings of Li Tingan's survey of 1934, which showed only 17 *xian* health centers, these figures were a tremendous improvement.[57] Yet the extent of preventive and curative work, as well as the training of public-health personnel, varied widely, and it is difficult to assess their effectiveness. As Stampar noted in his study of rural health programs in China, some *xian* health centers invested too much time and attention in the *xian's* principal city and not enough in the villages, overemphasized curative work at the expense of public-health measures, or adopted a fee-for-service policy when care should have been free.[58] Still, most health leaders considered the scheme to be the best means of introducing modern health care into the countryside. In March 1937, the Nationalist government ordered provincial governments to organize *xian* health centers based on this plan as quickly as possible.[59] Just prior to the outbreak of war with Japan, the number of *xian* health centers increased to a total of 217 in 13 provinces.[60] But the number was infinitesimal when the number of *xian* and the size of the population were taken into account, and the majority of the people in the countryside remained outside this health-care network.

The Jiangxi Reconstruction Program and Rural Health

For J. Heng Liu and his colleagues in the National Health Administration, the Dingxian model of a *xian*-based system with its hierarchy of health organizations formed the basis of state medicine. As was discussed above, formulation of the plan was also influenced by models from other parts of the world, and by the League of Nations experts—Borcic and Stampar, both from Eastern Europe—who were in China at the time. But the three-tiered structure was clearly Chinese and it followed the existing administrative divisions. Indeed, C. C. Chen has argued that he and others had developed the idea of a *xian* hierarchy prior to the League's active involvement.[61] There certainly were differences between the Chinese plan and some of the Eastern European models. The *xian* health centers were not welfare facilities, as were the *zadrugas* of Yugoslavia, nor were the village health workers second-grade physicians like the *feldshers* of the Soviet Union. As Mary Bullock has pointed out, the Chinese *xian* structures "were circumscribed by the economic and social limitations of the Chinese village, and differentiated so as to diffuse medical care throughout the region."[62]

The most direct involvement of the League in rural reconstruction in China was in the ambitious project launched in Jiangxi in 1934. Instead of a modest attempt to create a "*xian* reconstruction experiment area," this would be a coordinated, comprehensive, province-wide effort. In November 1933, the National Economic Council sent three League experts, Max Brauer, E. Briant-Clausen, and Dr. Stampar, to investigate rural conditions in Jiangxi. The Nationalist government had launched its fifth encirclement and suppression campaign against the Communists' central soviet base area two months earlier. The League experts recommended development of a multifaceted project aimed at restructuring the system of rural tenancy and creating, at the provincial level, a Welfare Center, a Commission on Education, a Commission on Cooperatives, an Agricultural Institute, and a Health Department. While the government rejected the recommendation for reform of the tenancy system, it pushed ahead with the other programs, the most important of which was the Provincial Welfare Center, which would direct all social services in the province. Under this agency would be a number of rural welfare centers at the *xian* level, each including departments for education, agriculture, cooperatives, home industries, and health. The activities of these departments would be coordinated and supported by the respective provincial commissions, and together they would improve the living conditions of the people by providing technical information and support in all areas of social amelioration. Politically it was hoped that this program would win the support of the rural population, which had recently been under Communist control.[63] Unlike the projects at Dingxian and Zouping, which relied mostly on local initiatives, the Guomindang's program at Jiangxi attempted to impose social and administrative change from above.

Initial funding for these projects came entirely from the National Economic Council. Grants were made to the provincial commissions on cooperatives and education, and to the Agricultural Institute. Among the health agencies, the Provincial Health Department received $360,000. The rural welfare centers' set-up costs and expenses, estimated to be $350,000, were fully met for the first year, though funding was decreased by a quarter in each succeeding year as local governments assumed a greater share of the budget.[64]

With these generous contributions from the central government, the provincial health institutions were quickly set up between 1934 and 1936. The provincial Health Department was organized in 1934 to direct the program. A new hospital at Nanchang, the provincial capital, was opened in temporary quarters in 1934. It moved to its new three-hundred-bed facility, built at a cost of $300,000, in March 1936. The medical staff consisted of five chief doctors, thirteen assistant doctors, eleven interns, four pharmacists, two technicians, and forty nurses—a well-staffed institution compared to other provincial hospitals at that time. It housed the Provincial Nanchang Nursing School, which offered a three-year course. A midwifery school was opened in Nanchang with seventy-six students in 1936. The school maintained forty beds for deliveries and averaged about sixty patients per month. A unique development, made possible by the infusion of funds, was the creation of a separate Center of School Health, supported by the Commission on Education and the Health Department, to organize school health programs in the province. Ordinarily such activities were relegated to individual schools or to the *xian* health centers (if one existed) in other provinces. Other provincial agencies included an opium hospital and a diagnostic laboratory, both located in Nanchang.[65]

Ten rural welfare centers were formed between August 1934 and January 1936, although the locations and dates of their establishment depended to a large extent upon the course of the political and military struggles between the Nationalists and the Communists in the province. All activities of the welfare centers (education, agriculture, home industry, cooperatives, and health) were to be coordinated. According to Zhang Fuliang, director of Jiangxi Rural Reconstruction, each center was "intended to mean a point of service and influence which will radiate into surrounding districts with its purpose and example."[66] Essentially, this was the same concept that underlay the *xian* health centers, the difference being that the welfare centers—which bore the imprint of Stampar's Yugoslavian experience—were more comprehensive in their approach and subject to greater provincial supervision. They also enjoyed more financial support from the provincial government. Half of the yearly budget of $10,000 for each welfare center was allocated to meet the salaries of technical workers and was paid by the provincial government. The rest, including operating expenses and the salary of the executive secretary, was borne by the National Economic Council for the first year, with gradual reductions in succeeding years.

The Health Department of each welfare center was staffed by a doctor, an assistant, and a midwife, the first two being sent directly from the Provincial Health Department. Each center had four to fifteen beds for emergency cases and operated a daily clinic. It disseminated knowledge about modern medicine and public health. Health and sanitation were promoted through smallpox vaccination campaigns, school health programs, and people's organizations, as well as through the construction of model wells and latrines. Regulations prohibiting unsanitary practices were introduced. By March of 1936, there had been more than 42,000 clinic treatments in the centers, 33,000 smallpox vaccinations, and 329 deliveries. Improvements had been made in 204 wells and 163 latrines. These activities, it was claimed, would promote "healthful living in a healthful environment."[67]

However, the Jiangxi rural reconstruction project was not confined to these attempts to make concrete improvements in the environment. To combat Communist ideology, Chiang Kai-shek also placed great emphasis on the rural masses' spiritual regeneration. As we have seen, his New Life Movement, launched in Nanchang in February 1934, in conjunction with the welfare programs, was viewed as the ideological underpinning of the national effort at rebuilding, not just for rural reconstruction and certainly not just for Jiangxi. There was symbolic significance in the decision to introduce the movement in Jinagxi where the Communists had gained a strong foothold before being ousted by Chiang. The New Life Movement hoped to inspire the masses to revolutionize their lives through, among other things, improvement in their personal hygiene. A government publication promoting the movement in the countryside asserted that the poor health of the rural population was one of the basic causes of the "irrationality" of Chinese rural life. To rectify this problem, health education and propaganda, clean-up campaigns, the abolition of practitioners of traditional medicine, and free health care for all would be implemented.[68] However, better hygiene and improved sanitary conditions were only one part of a total reconstruction scheme based upon spiritual regeneration. The people were urged to cultivate traditional Confucian virtues, which would imbue them with a fresh spirit, the spirit of the New Life.

While the attempt to improve personal and environmental hygiene was beneficial to a certain extent, moral platitudes proved to be less relevant in meeting the immediate needs of the impoverished rural masses. By the end of 1934, the New Life Movement, launched with much fanfare at the beginning of the year, had lost its momentum. The task of health improvement in rural Jiangxi was assumed in the main by the health departments of the welfare centers. But, despite the tremendous amount of time and money invested in these efforts, their impact on the province as a whole was rather small. It has been estimated that the ten welfare centers reached at most 400,000 people, a small fraction of the province's population. In fact, to reach the rest of the population, an additional 292 centers would have been needed.[69] Interestingly, the development of *xian* health centers, independent of the welfare-center movement, continued without the publicity accorded the latter. By 1936, the provincial government of Jiangxi claimed that within each of its 83 *xian* there was either a health center, a health station, or a substation.[70] Although the number may have been exaggerated, if true it represents a remarkable accomplishment considering the fact that the lion's share of reconstruction funds was channelled into the welfare centers.

The Christian Church and Rural Health

The Jiangxi reconstruction project was notable also for the direct involvement of Christian groups who were interested in social reform as part of their mission in China. The anti-Christian movement of 1922–27 had forced many missionaries to reevaluate their role in a rapidly changing society in which social issues were coming to the fore.[71] For the first time, mission societies began to seriously contemplate the contributions they could make to China's reconstruction, especially after the founding of the Nationalist regime. Christian colleges and universities such as Shandong Christian (Cheeloo), West China Union, and the University of Nanjing developed their own rural reconstruction programs, focusing on agricultural research and education and on village-aid projects.[72] In 1927, Shandong Christian University founded a Rural Institute at Longshan, a market town near Jinan, consisting of a school, a recreation center, and a dispensary.[73] The National Christian Council, an organization composed of most of the leading Christian groups in China, urged its members in 1930 to launch a "Rural Community Parishes" movement. At appropriate sites, Christian groups would organize rural units in which a six fold program encompassing evangelism, education, health, livelihood, recreation, and women and the home would be introduced to create the base for a Christian social program for China. To coordinate these and other activities, two years later representatives of churches and institutions working in the field established the North China Christian Rural Service Union.[74]

The launching of the Jiangxi rural reconstruction program saw the beginning of close cooperation between Christian groups and the Nanjing regime. Zhang Fuliang, the rural life secretary of the National Christian Council, was loaned to the National Economic Council in April 1934 to direct the program in Jiangxi. A year later he resigned from his position in the National Christian Council. In late 1933, Mme. Chiang Kai-shek invited Christian groups to establish a rural center at Lichuan, a *xian* in southeastern Jiangxi Province, as part of the rural reconstruction program about to be launched there. The National Christian Council accepted the invitation. A Jiangxi Christian Rural Service Union was formed to establish a model rural center under church auspices. The Rev. George W. Shepherd, a Congregational missionary from New Zealand, was put in charge of the center, which opened in the summer of 1934.

The work of the center included not only agricultural extension, village industries, village organization, and religious training but also the promotion of public health, providing curative and preventive services under the direction of a doctor and a nurse. The Christian doctor and staff, however, encountered apathy and suspicion among the populace, all the more so since Lichuan was in a backward and isolated part of the province. Suspicion was directed not only at modern medical practices but, more significantly, at the emphasis placed on Christian teaching. Although there was little overt expression of anti-Christian sentiment, there was an undercurrent of hostility against the church in many parts of the country. The problem in Jiangxi was compounded by the difficulty of finding a Chinese doctor willing to relocate to such a depressed part of the province. One candidate interviewed by Shepherd commented that "during his entire course in a Christian medical school nobody ever brought up the subject of what a Christian doctor might do for the great masses of people in need of better ways of living." Shepherd also complained that students in nearby medical schools were less than enthusiastic in cooperating with the center.[75] The Lichuan center also suffered when Shepherd, its enthusiastic leader, left to assume the post of adviser to the New Life Movement in mid-1936.

The relationship between the church and the Nanjing government in the New Life Movement and Lichuan project revealed the ambivalence of Christian attitudes toward Chiang and his regime. Christians themselves, Chiang and his wife were anxious to recruit Christian groups for the national reconstruction effort. Mme. Chiang, in particular, hoped that rural reconstruction would have a revitalizing effect on both the church and China. On a more practical level, the well-educated graduates of Christian colleges would be extremely important in China's development, then and in the future. The cooperation of mission bodies also would prove useful in Chiang's attempt to gain western support. On the other hand, Christian groups were attempting to make their message relevant to the transformation of China, and, although some were chary of Chiang's authoritarian regime, they were even more worried about the spread of Communism. Rural reconstruction projects appeared to be the most appropriate forum in which both entities could cooperate to bring about social change. This partnership extended beyond the Lichuan project into the work of the North China Council for Rural Reconstruction (in 1936) and the New Life Movement as a whole. When the movement was launched, and the church was asked to cooperate, many Christian leaders hesitated, unsure of its political motives. Many also found the methods of regimentation a potential danger. After repeated appeals from Mme. Chiang, and with Shepherd retained as an adviser to the movement, the National Christian Council finally recommended that its groups and individual members participate. Many Christian leaders now maintained that the objectives of the movement and the aims of the church were not so different after all.[76]

The government also tried to seek the mission institutions' cooperation in its plans for state medicine. Dr. Edward Hume, former dean of Xiangya Medical College at Changsha, was invited back to China in 1936. He was entrusted with the task of persuading foreign, especially American, institutions to coordinate their work with the National Health Administration at the local and central levels. As representative of both the Chinese health administration and the Missionary Division of the Chinese Medical Association, Hume traveled in the provinces, discussing the ways in which cooperation could be accomplished. The consensus was that the various institutions should establish close ties with towns and villages around a strong central hospital.[77] Some mission hospitals already were cooperating with the health administration, serving as provincial or *xian* health centers. J. Heng Liu argued that mission medical institutions could be incorporated into the government's expanding state system. He cited, in particular, an example of collaboration in a village in Jiangning *xian*. There a community health committee, formed with mission cooperation, had established a health center. By 1937, it had been brought into the *xian* health service as a substation.[78] Christian medical schools, too, made an effort to cooperate in the health administration's efforts to reorganize China's medical-education system and train adequate personnel to meet the needs of state medicine.

The Rockefeller Foundation and Rural Health

Despite attempts by the National Health Administration and the National Economic Council to consolidate private and government efforts to promote rural health care, the work was far from coordinated. As early as the fall of 1931, James Yen had urged the newly established National Economic Council to coordinate the various rural reconstruction activities. He called for a comprehensive survey of existing programs so as to identify the work being done and the results obtained. Based on these data, a blueprint for a national program could be drawn up. The National Economic Council would act as the coordinating agency, assigning specific projects, reducing duplication of effort, and conducting annual reviews to determine appropriate levels of government financial support. A national policy would be formulated to extend the techniques developed to other regions. Rural reconstruction tasks that the council considered basic but neglected would be assigned to some existing institution or a new agency.[79] Yen's grand scheme was not acted upon by the government, which did not have the political control or the resources to bring about such change. Although the government did attempt to formulate long-term plans for a national health service, before 1937 little coordination was effected.

Impetus for such coordination did come from the Rockefeller Foundation in 1935. The foundation, which had been providing support for PUMC and other medical-education institutions, began to reevaluate its approach in China in the early 1930s in view of the economic downturn, the need for retrenchment, and the sociopolitical conditions there. Selskar M. Gunn, vce president of the foundation in Europe and a public-health expert, visited China in 1931 and 1932. In January 1934, he submitted a proposal recommending radical reorientation of the foundation's approach to China. He urged the development of practical programs firmly rooted in China's institutions and designed to promote rural reconstruction. He described the previous activities of the foundation as outdated, and singled out PUMC as an institution thoroughly unprepared to meet the challenge of a new social order. He urged the foundation to change its emphasis from pure research to social medicine with its strong public-health component. What he had in mind was an all-inclusive concept of rural reconstruction combining the application of medical science with knowledge derived from the social sciences, an approach that had informed the early experiments of John Grant, James Yen, C. C. Chen, and J. Heng Liu. The difference between their efforts and Gunn's was that, while Gunn was also interested in the practical application of medical and social-scientific knowledge, he was able to marshall a much broader range of resources to test his concept in the field.[80]

Gunn's ideas were endorsed by the foundation, which launched a new program—the China Program—later that year with a three-year grant of one million dollars to promote rural reconstruction. The largest grant went to Dingxian to establish a training center in education, health, local government, and economics so that its personnel could become knowledgeable about Chinese conditions. Nankai's Institute of Economics received a second grant for research in rural reconstruction and administration. Finally, Yanjing University was to direct some of its science programs toward the study of rural problems.[81] Apparently, John Grant influenced the formulation of this program. In fact, Grant was the only westerner appointed to the North China Council for Rural Reconstruction, founded in April 1936 as part of the China Program to coordinate specific tasks assigned to each of the program's six members.[82]

The council's main area of responsibility was to train university students in different aspects of rural reform. These included agriculture at the University of Nanjing, sanitary engineering at Qinghua University, economics at Nankai University, education and social administration at Yanjing University, social medicine at PUMC, and public health, agriculture, economics, and public affairs at Dingxian. In 1936–37, the fieldwork of the council was divided between Dingxian and Jining, in Shandong, the former focusing on education and social medicine and the latter on economics, agriculture, engineering, and civil and social administration. In these two centers, the university departments lost "their individual identity and function[ed] solely through the Council as their coordinating agency." Since the council was given the power to appoint its personnel to official government posts, the universities were able to control the operation of government organizations through the appointment of staff members to important administrative positions. The council considered such initial control essential to providing the social scientists with "controlled 'laboratory' facilities" for their work.[83] It is revealing that, of the 289 fellowships that the Rockefeller Foundation granted to the China Program in 1936, 106 were in public health and 32 in nursing.[84] This promising beginning was soon cut short, however, by the outbreak of the Sino-Japanese War in 1937, despite attempts by leaders of the council to revive its work in Guizhou. Indeed, the war and its accompanying destruction, political upheavals, and social and economic dislocations forced the suspension or cessation of many of the projects described above. When the Nationalist government moved inland, it renewed its efforts to develop rural programs appropriate for the interior. But for all intents and purposes, a chapter had been closed on the Nationalist attempt to provide health services to the rural population.

Limitations of the Health Programs

In evaluating the Nanjing regime's success or failure in its rural health programs, one can easily identify many of its limitations. Despite all the efforts, scientific medicine still reached only a very small percentage of the rural population. In 1937, Wu Lien-teh estimated that even in the most developed rural districts more than 65 percent of the population continued to rely on practitioners of native medicine, while about 26 percent died without receiving any treatment at all.[85] The number of health centers, stations, and substations was far too small and their sphere of activity too restricted to have a significant impact on the population as a whole. Stampar, as we have seen, pointed to the overemphasis placed on the work in the *xian* city in many of the health centers. He was particularly critical of the welfare centers in Jiangxi, arguing that with the same personnel and expenditure the centers could have trebled their coverage beyond the ten-mile radius that they seemed capable of influencing.

The extent of each center's work was to some extent restricted by funds and manpower. We have noted the minuscule, and often unreliable, amounts of money made available for health work. When there was a generous infusion of funds from the central or provincial governments, as was the case in Jiangxi, the tendency was for the centers to become too dependent on outside support, lessening their attempts to develop programs in accordance with local economic realities. Even at Dingxian, where C. C. Chen and James Yen were most conscious of the need to develop local resources, the health center's proximity to and collaboration with PUMC proved to be highly beneficial. In his reminiscences, John Grant in fact criticized the Nanjing government for adopting the Dingxian model as the basis for state medicine without careful refinement. As he saw it, other health centers would not have at their disposal the financial and manpower resources that PUMC was able to provide at Dingxian.[86]

For the rural health movement as a whole, the increasing demands of a modernizing state simply outstripped the ability of the economy to provide adequate resources, especially since the military and its related sectors had priority over reconstruction efforts. There was also a dearth of manpower to staff even this limited number of rural health programs. Most young Chinese doctors were unwilling to abandon the cities to serve in the countryside. Many newspaper articles charged that modern physicians had forgotten their "social responsibilities to serve the Chinese people."[87] In 1935, nearly half of these physicians were concentrated in the coastal provinces of Jiangsu and Guangdong, and most of these were practicing in the large cities. For most, independent private practice was the professional norm, and there certainly were strong economic incentives to maintain the status quo. The PUMC model of medical education, so widely admired and copied, encouraged the training of specialists dependent upon sophisticated biomedical equipment and research, all of which were lacking in the countryside. There seemed to be a need for some reorientation in medical education.

There was also, of course, a large group of practitioners of traditional medicine whom the government could have utilized in the promotion of rural health care, especially since they had the confidence of most of the rural population. Unfortunately, in almost all the health demonstrations and projects, traditional doctors were ignored or rejected. The emphasis was always on promoting scientific medicine, which, it was claimed, would eventually replace the "superstitious practices" of the countryside.[88] As we have seen, the Ministry of Health had actually tried to outlaw native medicine, provoking a bitter and prolonged feud between supporters of traditional and modern practice. Modern physicians generally rejected any attempts to include traditional medicine in the curricula of medical schools and dismissed proposals to establish short-term courses to train traditional doctors in the rudiments of modern medicine.[89] The Ministry of Health and its modern-medicine supporters were unwilling to recruit and train traditional practitioners to promote public health. The only notable exception was the attempt to train some old-style midwives in the basics of modern obstetrics and sepsis. Some supporters of traditional medicine organized their own public-health classes but most adopted a negative attitude toward government-sponsored activities in the countryside.[90] Thus, the opportunity to use this very important group was not actively exploited. Even in Dingxian, a survey in 1933 showed that, among the population of about 390,000, 67 percent relied on traditional doctors for medical relief, while 4.3 percent relied on modern medicine. The balance, 28.7 percent, had no access to any kind of health personnel.[91] These figures underline the fact that traditional medicine was too much a part of the people's social and cultural lives to be uprooted by the rather limited intrusion of its modern counterpart. Deeply rooted cultural and religious attitudes toward health and disease and competition from traditional practitioners all played a part in retarding the spread of modern medicine. A fundamental change in the people's attitude toward modern health practices and their relationship to traditional medicine would be an important factor in the successful implementation of modern health-care programs.

The rural population, in fact, at times received contradictory messages from the authorities. Chiang Kai-shek was urging them to return to traditional values in the New Life Movement while health workers were promoting scientific medicine in a way that tended to undermine elements of traditional culture. At a time when modernizers were condemning the superstition of the masses, some health workers were proclaiming the benefits of scientific medicine at local festivals honoring Guanyin, the Goddess of Mercy.[92] The reality is that religion and traditional culture continued to be the vital factor governing the lives of rural people, and to most the health centers remained tangential to their daily existence.

Given time and a stable political environment, the health programs might have taken hold. Unfortunately, the survival of separatism in the provinces during the Nationalist decade precluded the option of a concerted national effort. On the other hand, one can fault the Guomindang for failing to make an unqualified commitment to rebuilding the countryside. The Guomindang was too concerned with its political longevity to introduce reforms that might undermine its base of support. It considered health programs at the local levels to be part of the party's political attempt to extend its control and win the support of the masses. To Chiang Kai-shek, military control was essential in dealing with the village problem. He confided to George Shepherd that "as soon as the armies enter a district," they must organize "Christian farmers and workers" to establish "law and order."[93] The reconstruction program in Jiangxi, for example, was clearly related to the reassertion of control over an area formerly occupied by the Communists. What impressed Robert Haas, a League expert who visited China between January and May of 1935, including a stop in Jiangxi, was not the health activities but the provincial authorities' "organisation of the population," through the development of the *baojia* system of mutual security and control, to which the government had attached "most value."[94] Administration of the Jiangning experimental *xian* in Jiangsu and the Lanxi experimental *xian* in Zhejiang were turned over to the C. C. Clique, a conservative faction within the Guomindang. Instead of trying to mobilize people in support of a broad range of reconstruction programs, local bureaucrats imposed their will at the sub-*xian* levels. With the emphasis on security and control, reconstruction efforts were focused almost exclusively on road construction and the improvement of agricultural technology.[95] Yet, in the final analysis, as Prasenjit Duara's study has shown, the Nationalists were unable to build political organizations linked to state structures from the grass-roots level up.[96] Part of this failure stemmed from the party's unwillingness to tackle the crucial, and most explosive, issue of the countryside—land tenure. Most observers at the time agreed that the small size of landholdings and the tenancy system were the main causes of social unrest since they depressed the standard of living and contributed to general poverty. Zhang Fuliang, director of the Jiangxi reconstruction program, defended the slowness of land reform by insisting that such change required careful surveys and records, which took much time to complete.[97] But equally important was the government's concern not to alienate its allies in the countryside.

With no fundamental alteration in the working and living conditions of the peasants, health workers found it difficult to effect lasting change through the rather limited health services they provided. In fact, to be truly effective, the provision of health services would have to have been accompanied by a scheme of general rural reform. It should have been an integral part of a rural-reconstruction scheme that aimed at the improvement of general socioeconomic conditions. Based on his observations in China, Dr. Stampar concluded that "successful health work is not possible in areas where the standard of living falls below the level of tolerable existence."[98] The Dingxian experiment had demonstrated that the successful implementation of rural health programs involved the introduction of social reforms aimed at altering the behavioral pattern, the socioeconomic system, and the living environment of the peasantry. While most Chinese reformers working in rural health programs seem to have been aware of the close relationship between these various components, the development of comprehensive programs designed to uplift the peasantry as a whole was beyond their capability. Such programs would require active government intervention. The Nationalist government, as we have seen, was unwilling to make a major commitment to a system of rural health care implemented with concomitant socioeconomic reforms. The outbreak of the Sino-Japanese War in 1937 finally destroyed any hope of establishing a viable national health-care system in the Chinese countryside under Nationalist leadership. We should not, however, dismiss the Nationalist effort as a complete failure. The isolated health projects stimulated some interest in rural health reforms and they enhanced, albeit in a limited way, modern public-health knowledge among some of the population. Most importantly, the planners tested various methods of establishing rural health services, and the lessons learned proved extremely valuable to medical reformers developing a system of state medicine for a new China after 1949. The village health workers find their parallel in the barefoot doctors of the 1960s, and the hierarchy of the rural health structure was later adopted, with slight modifications, by the Communist government. Programs developed after 1949, in fact, would be directed by some of the pioneers of state medicine in the 1920s and 1930s.

5

The Development of
Organized Public Health

If one defines public health as "the application on the community level of existing medical knowledge,"[1] then it can be argued that all societies have some form of health protection. But in 1926, when a syllabus developed by PUMC's Department of Hygiene and Preventive Medicine asserted that "China has not really begun public health," the author had in mind a specific form of the movement, one that traced its origins to recent developments in the West and to modern scientific medicine.[2] This assertion is revealing because what took place in the development of Chinese medicine and health care in the Nationalist decade was shaped to a large extent by the introduction and subsequent dominance of scientific medicine. The boundaries of public-health work in China after the founding of the Nanjing regime were delimited by health leaders who were believers in scientific medicine anxious to transfer western health practices into China. It is not surprising that this syllabus faithfully reproduced Charles-Edward Amory Winslow's definition of public health. It was

> the science and art of preventing disease, prolonging life and promoting physical health and efficiency through organized community efforts for the sanitation of the environment, the control of community infections, the organization of medical and nursing services for the early diagnosis and preventive treat-

100

ment of disease and the development of the social machinery which will ensure to every individual in the community a standard of living adequate for the maintenance of health.[3]

In the context of China in the mid-1920s, leaders aspiring to fulfil such broad claims for public health's jurisdiction may seem overly ambitious, but it is to the credit of health planners like J. Heng Liu, Robert Lim, P. Z. King, C. C. Chen, John Grant, and others that by 1937 China had introduced and developed, on a limited scale, many if not all of the activities listed in Winslow's definition. We have seen how medical authorities tried to create an administrative structure for health care. In this chapter, our concern is with the development of specific public-health activities undertaken to prevent diseases of the individual and in the community.

For Chinese health leaders in the Nationalist decade, the introduction of a modern public-health system offered both an opportunity and a challenge. By the turn of the century, public health in the West had advanced beyond the sanitation movement associated mainly with environmental cleansing in the combat against epidemics. Breakthroughs in bacteriology and developments in scientific medicine in general led to the emergence of new public-health programs supported by the germ theory of disease and a statistical approach to disease problems. The subsequent shift from environmental to individual concerns, focused on personal hygiene and medical examinations, was reflected in the widespread use of diagnostic techniques, promotion of changes in maternal and child care, and the introduction of school health programs. While this transformation allowed the medical profession a prominent role in public-health activities, it did not completely resolve the conflict over the proper boundary between public-health agencies and the medical establishment.[4] Medical leaders in Republican China did not face this conflict, however, since they were the architects and practitioners of modern public health and they fervently embraced its model. China's immediate needs were much more basic than those of the West—the improvement of sanitary conditions and the control of a multitude of communicable diseases—which required the doctors to assume a more active role in social change. Undeterred by the enormity of the problem, Chinese medical leaders embarked upon a course that tried to combine the social and technical components of public health.

Actions taken by the Nationalist health administration reflected these dual concerns. On the one hand, it passed legislation designed to change the pattern of people's lives. This ranged from regulations concerning the proper disposal of refuse and handling of foods to the registration of births and deaths and mandatory notification of the occurrence of certain diseases. At the same time, the health authorities attempted to implement elaborate machinery promoting health protection: maternal and child care, school hygiene and medical examination of children, industrial health, sophisticated biomedical laboratories for the study of epidemics, and the manufacture of vaccines and sera. In fact, the first Sanitary Code issued by the Ministry of Health in December 1928 encompassed all these areas of concern.[5] This comprehensive approach was revolutionary at a time when most people had little or no knowledge of modern hygiene and when many still thought that public health entailed only occasional street cleaning and the removal of night soil. Popular public-health education would have to be a large and important part of the work of the health agencies.

The Collection of Vital Statistics

Since the Nationalist regime had claimed the responsibility for public health, it assumed for itself regulatory powers over what was considered unhygienic social behavior. It also asserted its right to introduce measures that would, it claimed, enhance the welfare of the public. That the definition of health that now governed acceptable social behavior was based on the prevalent precepts of scientific medicine not only confirmed the power of its advocates in the health administration, but it reflected their confidence in the efficacy of behavior modification. Social reform, they believed, could be effected through the promulgation of rules and regulations explicating the benefits of modern science.[6]

A prominent theme in the optimistic plan for improvements in public health was the application not only of medical expertise but of the knowledge derived from social surveys and the statistical approach to disease problems. The collection of vital statistics—births, deaths, causes of deaths, and epidemiological data—became fundamental to the calculation of morbidity and mortality rates, the study of disease prevalence, and the construction of health profiles of the population, all essential steps in laying a sound foundation for public-health work. In the short run, such information, according to Dr. T.

F. Huang, would reveal the appalling nature of China's health conditions and "invariably stimulate action of a public health nature."[7]

Before 1928, there were no uniform government attempts to gather and maintain such data. Information was meager. After all, most births were handled by old-style midwives and deaths by local undertakers who had no understanding of the need, and in most cases no legal obligation, to report births and deaths. China had no modern health service demanding accurate vital information. A few statistics were collected by missionary clinics and hospitals, foreign consulates in major treaty ports, the customs services, and the North Manchurian Plague Prevention Service. In 1925, the National Epidemic Prevention Bureau made the first systematic attempt to collect data on the incidence of important communicable diseases in China, publishing the results in the first *Monthly Returns of the Prevalence of Communicable Diseases in China*. Although its findings were not extensive, due to the lack of reporting agencies in other parts of the country, they were accepted by the League of Nations Health Organization. The publication was later continued by the Ministry of Health.[8]

A few cities, such as Peking, Shanghai, and Canton, did try to register births, marriages, and deaths, but enforcement of pertinent regulations was lax and often nonexistent. In Canton, where a municipal health administration had been organized in 1920, physicians were supposed to sign death certificates, although this was not enforced. Although the Department of Public Safety was responsible for the registration of births, marriages, and deaths, the statistics collected often were inaccurate. For example, the figure for total deaths reported in 1921 would have given Canton the remarkable crude death rate of only 3.7 per 1,000.[9] When the Peking First Health Station was established in Peking, a Division of Vital Statistics was created for the "compilation of birth, mortality and morbidity statistics and the reporting, diagnosis and prevention of communicable diseases."[10] But the absence of a standardized, modern, medical terminology in the Chinese language created numerous problems in the reports (pneumonia, for example, was the "witchy wind"). John Grant and his staff had to develop a standard terminology for the translation of Chinese folk terms into a modern medical vocabulary.[11]

In 1925, the National Epidemic Prevention Bureau sent letters to foreign and Chinese modern doctors urging them to report, using a standard form, routine information on the occurrence of the ten communicable diseases designated as major by the League of Nations

Health Organization: plague, cholera, smallpox, epidemic meningitis, diphtheria, dysentery, typhoid, influenza, relapsing fever, and typhus. The response was so encouraging that the author of the resulting report had high hopes that the data collected would generate interest among the public and the government regarding the need for more epidemiological and statistical work in China.[12] Indeed, the regulations for the prevention of communicable disease promulgated by the new Ministry of Health in 1928 stipulated that doctors should report to local health authorities within twelve hours the diagnosis of nine prevalent diseases in China: abdominal typhus, typhus exanthematous, dysentery, smallpox, plague, cholera, diphtheria, epidemic meningitis, and scarlet fever.[13] The ministry operated a Department of Vital Statistics, which was responsible for collecting health and other statistics. The ministry also urged local authorities to report accurate data on births, deaths, and the incidence of disease, and to assemble health statistics from schools, industrial institutions, and other organizations.[14] In fact, the few provincial, municipal, and rural health administrations that were established during this period always contained departments of vital statistics, though the level of activity varied greatly. A survey of vital-statistics work in nineteen major cities from 1924 to 1931 reveals that death registration was carried out in only seven of the cities examined and birth registration in three. And only three cities mandated the reporting of notifiable infectious diseases.[15] In the countryside, only a few health centers, including those at Dingxian, Tangshan, Wusong, and Gaoqiao, reported any consistent compilation of vital statistics in 1933.[16]

To standardize the process of data collection, the National Health Administration in 1931 adopted the practice of sending to hospitals monthly communicable-disease report cards. These were to be filled out and returned to Nanjing. The Central Field Health Station compiled the information and distributed the results to government health agencies, hospitals, and universities. In October 1932, a Department of Epidemiology and Vital Statistics organized within the Central Field Health Station expanded and improved the system of notification of reportable diseases. Information was solicited from local government agencies as well as hospitals. By 1935, the station was receiving monthly data from more than six hundred respondents nationwide. Other projects of the department included the compilation of statistics on cholera epidemics and on physical defects among school children.[17] In 1934, it selected Nanjing and a nearby *xian* as sites for an urban and rural experiment in census taking, the collection of vital statistics, and the training of investigators. A uniform system was developed, and in 1936 it was extended to other cities and *xian*.[18] By that time, the Central Field Health Station had expanded the number of reportable diseases to nineteen with the addition of such maladies as kala-azar, leprosy, schistosomiasis, hookworm, filariasis, and malaria.[19]

Sanitation and Communicable-Disease Control

Despite the limited and sometimes sporadic nature of data collection, statistics confirmed the wide variety of communicable diseases prevalent in China. In addition to the nine diseases whose registration was mandatory, statistics revealed a high incidence of beriberi, malaria, tuberculosis, leprosy, enteritis, schistosomiasis, and kala-azar.[20] This is hardly surprising in view of the generally unsanitary conditions prevailing throughout China, and health leaders certainly recognized the relationship between poor environmental hygiene and disease. Construction of the necessary sanitation infrastructure proved difficult, however, given political instability, inadequate funds and manpower, and the general lack of modern health knowledge among officials and the people. Except in times of epidemic, when emergency measures were taken, or in a few cities where some components of a modern sanitation system had been implemented, most sanitary work before 1928 was confined to street cleaning and the disposal of refuse and sewage.

In 1928, the newly established Ministry of Health laid down elaborate plans for sanitation and infectious-disease control. The enforcement of regulations, however, was the responsibility of municipal health departments or rural health organizations, if and where they existed.[21] Even after promulgation by the Ministry of Health of regulations for street cleaning and refuse removal in 1928, such activities remained largely an urban phenomenon. Only in such large cities as Nanjing, Shanghai (especially in the International Settlement), Peiping, Tianjian, Qingdao, and Canton was the work carried out systematically with the support of special allocations. In 1934, Canton spent the most—about half of its total health budget—on such activities.[22]

The active intervention of the Central Field Health Station accelerated the development or reorganization of street sanitation work in some cities and in rural areas served by health centers. For example, the station assisted the municipal government of Greater Shanghai in reorganizing its sanitary work in 1935. In rural health centers it helped to introduce simple measures regulating sewage disposal, periodic chemical and bacteriological examinations of wells, and the improvement and disinfection of latrines. As much as possible, bored-hole latrines were installed and provided with ventilators. Such improvements were important in impressing upon the people the benefits of modern sanitation and in changing their health habits.[23]

Another potential health hazard was contaminated water. A piped water supply was rare, especially in the countryside, and most water came from wells, ponds, or rivers. Only a few cities were served by water-supply companies. Since it is likely that most of these sources were contaminated, the incidence of sickness would have been much higher if it were not for the fact that the Chinese seldom drank unboiled water. The Ministry of Health's regulations governing well-water supplies (announced in June 1928) remained largely on paper.[24] After 1928, a number of cities began organizing water-supply companies, private or public. Nanchang in Jiangxi, for instance, did not complete the construction of infrastructure for a water supply until 1934. Before completion, water was drawn from the river and from unprotected wells, a service that brought the city a huge financial burden every year.[25] By 1935, at least eighteen cities, including Nanchang, Canton, Xiamen, Nanjing, Shanghai, Chongqing, Tianjian, and Peiping, were being served by their own water-supply companies.[26] As in the case of street sanitation, the Central Field Health Station provided technical expertise in analysis and purification of water in some cities, and it trained waterworks operators in its own plant.[27] In many rural health centers it assisted in the design and digging of wells protected from sources of contamination, and in Tangshan and several centers in Jiangxi it constructed small-scale experimental water-supply plants in 1934.[28]

Many of these environmental improvements involved sanitary engineering, which was essential in the creation of a milieu favorable to health. Government-sponsored efforts did not begin until April 1931 when Brian R. Dyer, a sanitary engineer, was loaned by the International Health Division of the Rockefeller Foundation to the Central Field Health Station. He organized a Department of Sanitary Engineering to plan improvements and train personnel.[29] By 1936, the department had graduated fourteen sanitary engineers from its one-year course. For the first six months this course included specialized training in the operation of water and sewerage plants, surveying and design, well and latrine construction, delousing, and bacteriology. The last six months were devoted to field practice.[30] The first graduates were involved in sanitation work in flood-relief camps and epidemic areas, in reorganization of municipal sanitation and sewerage systems, and in field investigation of rural sanitation. They also assisted in the construction of hospitals and public buildings and in organizing delousing units for military camps. The demand for their expertise was so great that beginning in 1932 the department, in conjunction with the Department of Health Education of the Central Field Health Station, offered special courses to train sanitary inspectors, twenty of whom were graduated by the end of 1933.[31]

Improvements in environmental sanitation, proper disposal of sewage, and the provision of uncontaminated water certainly helped control the spread of communicable disease. But developments in bacteriology, immunology, and scientific medicine in general also made it possible for physicians to add to their arsenal such weapons as vaccines. To Chinese health leaders, such biomedical advances epitomized the power of scientific medicine in controlling communicable disease. Dr. Li Tingan, for example, argued that the first measure adopted to control tuberculosis should be medical, including registration of cases and the establishment of clinics for early diagnosis and treatment, laboratories for diagnostic and curative services, and sanatoria for treatment and isolation of open cases. The second step would be education of patients and the public with respect to personal and public hygiene, and the last would be improvement of the living standard of the people.[32] Certainly, environmental improvements were important. But, given the difficulties of actually implementing many health measures in a backward and politically divided country, and in trying to raise the standard of living of the majority of the population to a level that would make those same measures viable, the ability to effect broad health improvements through the research, manufacture, and use of sera and vaccines proved to be extremely attractive. Indeed, as indicated above, more than half of the health budget of the National Health Administration during this period was devoted to the technical and biomedical aspects of medicine.

In 1928, one of the first health regulations promulgated by the Ministry of Health dictated mandatory smallpox vaccination. It designated 1 March 1929 as National Smallpox Vaccination Day,[33] and urged local jurisdictions to launch mass inoculation campaigns against smallpox, cholera, typhoid, and diphtheria. To encourage such activities, the National Health Administration distributed small-pox vaccine free of charge to various local health authorities, and the National Epidemic Prevention Bureau provided free prophylactic vaccinations against smallpox, cholera, and diphtheria in Peiping.[34] These campaigns proved to be one of the few, and sometimes the only, public-health activity undertaken in many communities. As was the case with other health programs, only in major cities and rural health demonstration areas were such campaigns carried out fairly regularly. For instance, every summer the municipal government of Nanjing, in conjunction with the city party branch, the police, and the National Health Administration, conducted regular inocu-lation campaigns, while Shanghai scheduled spring smallpox vacci-nations for its citizens regularly.[35] Dingxian had regular vaccination programs every spring and autumn.[36]

One indicator of the relative success of these campaigns was an increase in the number of people vaccinated. In Shanghai, the num-ber of persons receiving smallpox vaccinations and anticholera inocu-lations rose (respectively) from 67,131 and 48,906 in 1927–28 to 246,063 and 577,200 in 1933–34.[37] A survey of preventive work in six *xian* health centers and in hospitals in Zhejiang and Jiangsu showed that in 1934, 33,791 persons received smallpox vaccinations, and 18,446 received anticholera inoculations, compared to the 1932–33 figures of 23,869 and 16,915.[38] Whether this was a result of easy accessibility, better organization, or greater health consciousness among the populace, a comparison of the Shanghai and xian fig-ures highlights the glaring difference between urban and rural China in the people's response to one of the most essential public-health activities. Statistics from other areas also suggest that, in general, while the public was willing to be vaccinated against smallpox, most people were reluctant to be vaccinated against other diseases, espe-cially diphtheria. This was probably due to the fact that the diph-theria toxoid inoculation was new in China in the mid-1930s, and the public had not been persuaded of its effectiveness through special publicity and health education.[39] But two developments were en-couraging. The first was the fact that people agreed to be vaccinated at times when there was no epidemic raging, indicating some degree of acceptance of preventive medicine. Second, increasing numbers of children were being immunized against some of the most common infectious diseases.

Several government agencies were involved in the manufacture and production of sera, vaccines, and drugs used in the prevention and control of disease. They were the North Manchurian Plague Prevention Service, the Central Hygienic Laboratory, the National Epidemic Prevention Bureau, the Northwest Epidemic Prevention Bureau, and the Central Field Health Station. Since its founding in 1912, the North Manchurian Plague Prevention Service, under the directorship of Wu Lien-teh, had been in the forefront of the fight against plague in the northeast, conducting research and manufacturing sera and biological products for prevention and control. Despite the political turmoil in that area, the service continued operating until the Manchurian Incident of 18 September 1931 when the Japanese invasion effectively ended its work. By that time, Wu had been appointed director of both the Central Cholera Bureau and the National Quarantine Service, and the staff of the Plague Prevention Service followed Wu to Shanghai.[40]

The work of the Central Hygienic Laboratory in Shanghai was confined largely to chemical and pharmaceutical analysis, bacteriological and pathological examinations, and laboratory research. Although its main function was to regulate drugs and patent medicines, its research also contributed to the control, and in some cases the eradication, of communicable diseases. The National Epidemic Prevention Bureau was the primary agent in these efforts, however. It produced large quantities of sera and vaccine using standards approved by the League of Nations. In response to a growing demand for its products, the bureau established a branch facility and laboratory in Lanzhou in 1934, and moved its headquarters from Peiping to a new facility in Nanjing in 1935 (its former Peiping laboratory then served as a branch facility). By 1935, it was manufacturing more than forty kinds of sera, vaccine, and antitoxin drugs for use against such diseases as diphtheria, tetanus, cholera, pertussis, dysentery, smallpox, and plague. The Northwest Epidemic Prevention Bureau, on the other hand, was established in 1934 mainly for the purpose of manufacturing vaccine and biological products for the control of animal diseases such as anthrax and rinderpest and of diagnostic antigens such as mallein and tuberculin.[41] As a result of these efforts, the government claimed in 1935 that China was not only able to produce enough vaccine and sera to meet most of its needs but it was exporting some of them to Taiwan, Korea, and Hong Kong.[42]

The scope of the work carried out by the Central Field Health Station related to communicable disease control was much broader, involving not only laboratory research but field investigations and, as indicated above, the initiation of sanitary projects. Laboratory work in the station placed great emphasis on the bacteriological study of disease, and its Bacteriological Laboratory devoted much time and effort to research, tracing the sources of infection and isolating bacteriological strains. In 1931–32, for example, it provided technical support for a concerted anticholera campaign in Shanghai and Nanjing, assisted by the chief statistician of the League of Nations Health Organization. On the other hand, the station's Chemical Laboratory, organized in May 1931, focused on chemical and pharmacological analysis. Its major activities included the analysis of water sources to determine their chemical and bacteriological content, and analysis of patent medicines.[43] The two laboratories also provided bacteriological, serological, and pathological examinations, free of charge, to hospitals, physicians, and other medical institutions in Nanjing and its vicinity. In 1934, they performed more than twenty-four thousand examinations.[44] To facilitate on-site work, the station also helped to set up laboratories in various parts of the country in order to carry out bacteriological and parasitological studies at the local level.

The Department of Bacteriology and Epidemic Disease Control and the Department of Parasitology of the Central Field Health Station conducted extensive field investigations and collected a wide range of data for their studies. Major diseases investigated included kala-azar, plague, malaria, and schistosomiasis. Kala-azar, a parasitic disease that causes anaemia, distended bellies, and enlarged spleens or livers, was endemic in Shandong and Hubei, in most of Shanxi, and in parts of Henan, Shaanxi, Jiangsu, and Anhui. PUMC faculty and students long had been active in the study of this disease but it was not until 1940 that the dog was identified positively as the reservoir host and the sandfly as the vector host.[45] The first major field study of the disease undertaken by the Central Field Health Station was launched in June 1934 with the establishment of a Kala-azar Research Station located in Qingjiangpu in northern Jiangsu, to investigate methods of control and prevention. As part of the study, 982 residents of ten villages were given medical examinations between August and December. Of these, 242, or 24.6 percent, were found to be infected with the disease. In one village, more than 83 percent of the residents suffered from it.[46]

Another disease affecting huge areas and a large percentage of the population was schistosomiasis, caused by the blood fluke *Schistosoma japonicum*, which, after entering the human body, ulcerates the intestinal walls, causing enlargement of the spleen, anaemia, ascites, and eventually death if the patient is left untreated. In China, schistosomiasis was found in all the Yangzi River provinces, where it was affecting at least 10 million people in the early 1930s. Systematic field investigation of the disease began in 1932 when the Central Field Health Station selected a *xian* in Zhejiang in which to begin the collection of data and the study of preventive measures. Owing to Communist activities in that area, the team moved to another locality in April 1934 and continued the work of environmental studies, parasitological examinations, biological research, and clinical treatment of patients. Much research was also done on oncomelania snails—the intermediate host of the disease—determined to be the best place to attack the *Schistosoma japonicum* during its life cycle. By the end of the year, the health team had investigated conditions in eighty-nine villages and had provided medical treatment for more than three thousand persons.[47]

Two other common diseases, plague and malaria, received much attention from the National Health Administration and the Central Field Health Station. It may be recalled that the devastating plague in Manchuria in 1911–12 had led to the founding of the North Manchurian Plague Prevention Service, which devoted itself to the prevention and control of this deadly disease. But outbreaks of plague continued in various parts of China: in Manchuria in 1920–21; in parts of Shanxi, Shaanxi, and Suiyuan in 1928–30; and again in Shanxi and Shaanxi in late 1931. The Central Field Health Station dispatched a team to the latter two provinces to initiate control measures and to study the feasibility of establishing permanent prevention stations to monitor regional conditions.[48] In Fujian, plague also broke out in 1934, and continued into 1935, culminating in a severe outbreak in the southern part of the province. Responding to an appeal for help from the provincial government, the National Health Administration and the Central Field Health Station dispatched a team to the town Longyan in south Fujian. The team began organizing antiplague activities and undertook a systematic epidemiological study. With the support of the National Health Administration, the provincial government established a Fujian Provincial Plague Prevention Bureau headed by a representative from the National Health Administration. An Experimental Plague Prevention

Station also was established in Longyan to assemble incidence and prevalence data and to develop methods to control the disease.[49]

The attempt to control malaria also involved a large number of epidemiological studies and field investigations. In November 1931, specialists from the Central Field Health Station accompanied Professor M. Ciuca, an expert of the Malaria Commission of the League of Nations, on a fact-finding trip along the Yangzi Valley to determine the endemicity of malaria. Not surprisingly, malaria was found to be present at all the major stops, from Nanjing to Wuchang, although endemicity was highest in the rural areas. The following year, the Department of Parasitology organized an entomological laboratory to conduct research on mosquito bionomics and their relationship to malaria. It began conducting field surveys in several experimental districts in Nanjing and at the Tangshan rural health center. One important feature of these investigations was the examination and treatment of school children.[50] The department provided materials and technical support to investigation teams sent in 1934–35 to newly recovered areas in Jiangxi and Fujian where malaria was widespread.[51]

In addition to kala-azar, plague, schistosomiasis, and malaria, the Central Field Health Station conducted research on diseases such as tuberculosis, leprosy, and dysentery. Undoubtedly, the station's findings were invaluable in obtaining the necessary epidemiological and medical data about these and other diseases, but to a certain extent the technical work was undertaken at the expense of many preventive measures that, ironically, were determined to be too expensive for most rural areas. For instance, after an extensive investigation of malaria in a small district northeast of Nanjing in late 1934, the parasitology department of the station concluded that the best means of controlling malaria effectively would be to destroy the mosquito population, a course of action that was deemed financially prohibitive. Even the cost of such simple preventive measures as using mosquito nets and window screens was beyond the reach of the impoverished population. The report therefore concluded that the only way to deal with malaria was to register the population, so that it could be examined and tested every spring and fall, and set up curative clinics to treat those succumbing to the disease.[52] The problem with such an approach is that the majority of the rural districts really were too poor to undertake the effort needed to suppress malaria below an acceptable level or to adopt effective preventive measures.

With the limited funds going mainly to curative services, most of the rural population did not benefit from the scientific work of the Central Field Health Station.

The studies of the station did show clearly that the people of the countryside were most severely affected by these communicable diseases. In 1935, about 60 percent of them were suffering from hookworm, 35 percent from kala-azar, 47 percent from leprosy, and 62 percent from schistosomiasis.[53] But the work of the National Health Administration and the Central Field Health Station did not extend far beyond the technical research and curative stage. Despite recognition of the need to involve the population through popular health education, the government lacked either the will or the machinery to penetrate the basic levels of society and mobilize the people in the effort to eradicate disease. This situation contrasted sharply with Communist efforts in the post-1949 period when mass mobilization became a key element in China's health campaigns.

One particular reconstruction project—highway construction—received abundant funding from the National Economic Council. To protect construction crews against communicable disease, the National Economic Council created a Highway Health Service under the Central Field Health Station to coordinate a network of highway clinics, temporary hospitals, and health protection units. With the cooperation of provincial authorities, this network began operating in May 1933 in conjunction with the initial road projects in Jiangsu, Zhejiang, and Anhui. The service was extended into neighboring Hubei, Henan, Hunan, Jiangxi, and Fujian as road construction began in those provinces. Later another network was developed in the northwestern provinces.[54] Since the major road system ran through the valley of the Yangzi and its tributaries, a primary breeding ground for malaria-carrying mosquitoes, much attention was paid to the creation of mobile teams to combat the disease. The programs of the health service also included curative work, health education, and public-health activities such as smallpox vaccination, anticholera inoculation, sanitary inspection, and supervision of conditions at work sites and in the dwellings of workers, construction of public latrines, and disinfection of wells.[55] Such work was not permanent, however, as the health units soon moved on to new construction projects, and in most cases the benefits did not last. There was an attempt to develop a railway health service with the reorganization of the two main lines—the Nanjing-Shanghai and Shanghai-

Hangzhou-Ningbo—in early 1933. The planned service would not only have cared for railroad employees and passengers, but it would have undertaken sanitary and communicable-disease control work along the rail lines. Unfortunately the proposal never received much support from the National Health Administration.[56]

Industrial Hygiene

The welfare of road construction crews received extra attention from the government because of the strategic importance of the highways and the involvement of the League of Nations. But at about the time when the highway health service took shape, the health administration also began formulating protection policies for factory workers. These, after all, were essential in the economic reconstruction of the country. Industrialization had brought with it the many problems of occupational disease, unsanitary working and living conditions, and child labor. In the 1920s, Christian groups such as the YMCA had spearheaded reforms in a few factories but as late as the early 1930s medical facilities for workers were inadequate in many of the factories, both foreign and Chinese owned. In a survey of twenty-four factories conducted in 1934, about one-third had one or less than one infirmary bed per thousand workers.[57]

The first major attempt to establish an industrial health program was initiated in 1926 by the Peking First Health Station, later renamed the Peiping Special Health Area, in a local rug factory employing about a thousand employees, all of whom lived in dormitories. The station agreed to provide free medical services while the factory assumed the cost of treatment and hospitalization as well as maintaining several health workers (including a full-time nurse) on the premises. The duties of the medical staff, both curative and preventive, included physical examinations, treatment of illness and accidental injuries, inoculations, improvement of working conditions, remodelling of latrines and some living quarters, first-aid classes, and general health education. Although the results were encouraging, the impact of such experiments was limited given the absence of labor-health legislation.[58]

In 1929, the new Ministry of Health joined with the Ministry of Labor and Commerce to create a Commission on Industrial Health, which established a demonstration area in the industrial center at Wuxi, a complex consisting of 200 factories employing 120,000 workers. The ministry set up an industrial health station to provide curative and preventive services in four free clinics. Another demonstration project was begun in the Gaoqiu Health Center where a paint factory with about 350 employees cooperated with the medical staff of the center to conduct curative clinics and other health activities.[59] But it was not until 1933 that the government provided badly needed enforcement in the form of a Central Factory Inspection Bureau organized under the Ministry of Industries. The bureau included a Division of Industrial Health created with the support of the National Health Administration. It initiated such projects as health surveys of various industries, publication of literature on industrial health and occupational diseases, and joint development of local committees on industrial health with provincial and municipal authorities. Work on industrial health and hygiene was undertaken in cities such as Shanghai, Qingdao, Tianjin, and Hankou.[60] By 1935, based on reports from various parts of the country, the health administration claimed that 69 percent of the nation's factories were equipped with some form of medical facility, 17 percent had none, and 13 percent had made arrangements with nearby hospitals for the treatment of their workers.[61] But the expansion of industrial medical services was slow and most programs were confined to simple curative services, supervision of sanitary conditions, and health education. Without health insurance or some form of compensation for accidents, workers with serious illnesses or injuries often were left to fend for themselves.

The National Quarantine Service

The detection and control of communicable diseases and the improvement of health conditions took on added significance at the international level under the Nationalists as the government strove to regain sovereign rights lost in the treaties of the nineteenth century. As the legitimate government of a unified China (however nominal that unity might be), the Nanjing regime, under the direction of T. V. Soong, finally won tariff autonomy from the treaty powers in 1929. Immediately it began reorganizing the customs administration. The new regime also reasserted jurisdiction over the administration of salt revenues, which up to that time had been controlled by a foreign staff under a Chief Inspectorate of Salt Revenues.[62] Against a background of heightened nationalism, the issue of developing a

Chinese-controlled quarantine service assumed both symbolic and real significance. It was symbolic because it would signal the foreign powers' acceptance of the legitimacy of China's health improvements based on scientific medicine. It was real because establishment of a Chinese-controlled service was a victory in China's fight for sovereignty. In addition, it would mean the reversion to the Chinese government of lost revenues in quarantine services.

It was no accident, therefore, that China's initial petition to the League of Nations for technical cooperation in 1929 was a request initiated by the Foreign Ministry, not the Ministry of Health. The League was asked to "dispatch a sanitary mission from the Health Organization of the League to make a survey on port health and maritime quarantine."[63] Chinese leaders shrewdly recognized that the launching of a national quarantine service would bring to the fore conflicting interests among different nations. The collaboration of the Health Organization of the League would be "a source of strength," which would "ensure a friendly spirit of reciprocity and helpful mutual confidence."[64] At the same time, the Chinese were anxious to make use of the knowledge and experience of League experts in order to create a service of such a high international standard that foreign powers could not reject it out of hand. The concern for national sovereignty that played such a crucial role in the organization of a modern quarantine service similarly affected other health developments during the Nationalist decade.

Dr. Rajchman and Dr. Frank Boudreau, both of the League, visited China in late 1929. The following year, Dr. C. L. Park, an expert in epidemiology and chief of the Quarantine Division of the Australian Health Service, on loan to the League, was sent to China to survey port conditions and to discuss the proposal for a modern quarantine service with T. V. Soong, J. Heng Liu, and officers of the Customs Administration. The League subsequently approved Park's report, which included a plan for the reorganization of the service. The plan called for the establishment of a National Quarantine Service with headquarters in Shanghai, the promulgation of modern quarantine regulations, and the gradual extension of the service to the other Chinese ports where some form of quarantine administration already existed: Andong, Yingkou, Qinhuangdao, Tianjin, Tanggu, Qingdao, Xiamen, Shantou, and Canton.[65] In theory, port health work at that time was carried out by Chinese Maritime Customs, under the Ministry of Finance, with the exception of Qingdao and Canton where the municipal governments had taken over. But, since quarantine activities had been conducted in the past by authorities of the foreign concessions in the treaty ports, the chief port officers were usually foreign medical officers, sometimes in private practice, and the administration of the ports was largely controlled by the consuls of the treaty powers. The inauguration of the National Quarantine Service in July 1930, under Wu Lien-teh, was the Chinese government's assertion of control over an integral part of its health infrastructure. As a first step, the Quarantine Service promulgated new regulations, based on the International Sanitary Convention of 1926, in both Chinese and English.

The takeover by the National Quarantine Service of the port of Shanghai provides a good example of the process by which China regained sovereign rights. Before that time, the Shanghai Sanitary Service had been responsible for quarantine activities. It was administered by the Shanghai Commissioner of Customs on behalf of the government and the Consular Body at Shanghai. The latter had veto power over any quarantine measures imposed in the port, and the port health officer, a retired British doctor, considered himself an employee of the Consular Body. Fumigation and disinfection were handled by a private foreign firm. The Chinese found this unacceptable. Under Wu Lien-teh, a new staff was assembled, and fumigation and disinfection were taken over by a fleet of barges and launches owned by the Quarantine Service. The backing of the League of Nations and the service's willingness to provide monetary compensation to the former fumigation firm ensured a smooth transition. A new headquarters was built, containing laboratories, wards, and other features of a modern quarantine station. In addition, five Chinese officers were sent to Europe and the United States to study quarantine and public-health practices.

With the operation in Shanghai in place, the National Quarantine Service formally took over the Xiamen station in January 1931, the Hankou station in November, the Tianjian, Tanggu, and Qinhuangdao stations in April 1932, and the stations in Shantou and Canton four years later. The service also maintained hospitals in Shanghai, Xiamen, Tanggu, and Qinhuangdao.[66] The stations in Andong and Yingkou were lost to China after Japan's invasion of Manchuria in September 1931. During the Shanghai War, which broke out in January 1932, Japanese bombardment severely damaged some of the city's quarantine facilities, although the service continued to function throughout the conflict.[67] By 1937, besides the Shanghai headquarters, the service had five branch offices at Xiamen, Shantou,

Canton, Hankou, and Jintangqin, the last being a consolidation of the three stations in Tianjin, Tanggu, and Qinhuangdao.[68] However, after Japan's full-scale invasion in the summer of 1937, and its subsequent occupation of most of the eastern seaboard, the service was moved to Hankou, and later to Chongqing. From the date of its inception, the Quarantine Service maintained close ties with the League of Nations' Eastern Health Bureau in Singapore, the Health Organization in Geneva, and the International Public Health Office in Paris.

The major functions of the Quarantine Service were to detect infectious agents, infected persons, or implicated hosts and vectors and to prevent their introduction into China or their export to another country. Its activities included medical inspection of incoming vessels, isolation and treatment of infected persons, examination and vaccination of emigrants, inspection of outgoing vessels, and fumigation and disinfection. The work of the service was so successful that after only two years the League of Nations Health Organization reported that with the exception of Canton, which at that time still administered its own quarantine station, the National Quarantine Service was "now in a position to ensure the effective health supervision of all the Chinese rivers and maritime ports of concern to international traffic." The service had "inspired with confidence the officers of vessels of the many countries entering Chinese waters."[69]

While this recognition certainly was important to the Nationalist leaders, Chinese jurisdiction over port traffic was far from complete. In most countries, outgoing vessels would be inspected and obtain a bill of health from the quarantine service. But, since many countries enjoyed extraterritoriality in China—a legacy of the treaties of the nineteenth century—ships flying the flags of those countries bypassed the Quarantine Service, instead obtaining bills of health from their respective consular authorities. Obviously these bodies did not possess the necessary equipment to carry out a proper inspection.[70] The Chinese were unable to correct this situation as long as extraterritoriality continued to exist. Nonetheless, the Quarantine Service greatly improved conditions for Chinese emigrants leaving for the Philippines, the East Indies, or the Straits Settlements. Before the inauguration of the service, these emigrants were examined and vaccinated by the medical and port officers of the countries to which they travelled. Their treatment was often capricious and demeaning. Sometimes emigrants were required to line up on deck and strip to the waist, even in inclement weather. The National Quarantine Service took over these medical duties, vaccinating and inspecting all departing passengers and issuing health certifications. At the port of Xiamen, from which the majority of Chinese emigrants embarked, new facilities were built in 1931. In 1933, a special section of the quarantine hospital was set aside to house rejected emigrants who were no longer literally thrown into the streets.[71] The acceptance by foreign countries of Chinese health certifications shortly following the establishment of the Quarantine Service was a recognition of its high standards and efficiency. It also testified to the determination of Chinese leaders to impress upon the foreign powers their right to regain control over other areas of Chinese sovereignty.

The National Quarantine Service also engaged in public-health and medical activities in collaboration with municipal and district authorities. The service was in an excellent position to collect epidemiological data since the various stations regularly reported disease information to the Shanghai headquarters. To ensure that the ports would be able to operate without interruptions caused by epidemic outbreaks, the quarantine offices implemented strict precautions and conducted public-health campaigns to control infectious disease. In collaboration with the National Health Administration, the Quarantine Service became the headquarters of a new Central Cholera Bureau, created in 1930 to coordinate efforts along the coast. In 1932, the service conducted a systematic study of plague in eastern ports, assembling valuable information on the rat and rat-flea populations.[72] Such efforts proved quite successful, at least in the eastern ports, and after 1935 cities such as Shanghai, Tianjin, and Tanggu remained relatively free of communicable disease. Although there was an outbreak of plague in Fujian in 1935, the Quarantine Service localized the disease in the town of Longyan so that Xiamen was not affected.[73] The work of the service initially was confined to the coastal ports, but one of its objectives was to incorporate health work in all the main sea and river towns of the country. That goal was never realized, of course, as the Sino-Japanese War forced the service to move its operation inland.

Maternal Welfare and Child Health

Attempts to protect the Chinese population from communicable disease caused by factors inside China or by international traffic were only part of the ambitious public-health program initiated by the health administration under J. Heng Liu. As we have seen, Chinese health leaders were telescoping several stages of public-health development, as it was experienced in the West, into a relatively short period of time. In addition to making improvements in environmental sanitation, an emphasis prominent in the American public-health movement in the mid and late nineteenth century, they were trying to apply the new findings in bacteriology and scientific medicine that had shaped American efforts at the turn of the century. At the same time, the focus on the individual spawned a new concern to introduce preventive examinations and health education. Programs promoting pre- and postnatal care, preventive examinations of infants and children, and school health were eagerly embraced by medical leaders as integral to China's health program in the course of national reconstruction. After all, as one leader put it, the task of reconstruction "must fall on the shoulders of the children of China today and of future generations."[74]

Organized programs to promote the health of mothers and children were urgently needed in view of the high maternal and infant mortality rates. The concept of modern care was new, however, and had little or no relevance to the vast majority of the people who tended to view childbirth—whatever the outcome—as a natural phenomenon. Also, as C. C. Chen pointed out, modern midwifery, defined in its broadest sense as the practice of assisting women in childbirth as well as providing pre- and postnatal care for both mother and infant, and the concept of child welfare had "no economic foothold in the tradition of the people."[75] Midwifery was never considered a profession; old women usually became midwives because of the number of children they had borne. Thus, the transition to modern maternity and child care would mean overcoming old customs and philosophy, the acceptance of modern medical practices, a gradual change in the conception of adequate care of pregnant women during the complete cycle of pregnancy, and the provision of care—preventive and clinical—for all infant births.[76] It was a formidable task.

In 1928, the Ministry of Health adopted a twofold approach in dealing with this problem. It planned to train personnel for maternal and child health care (including modern midwives and retrained old-style midwives, as well as public-health nurses) and develop a nationwide service to provide preventive and clinical care for pregnant women, infants, and young children. Early in 1929, the ministry announced a Five Year Program aimed at implementing both of these plans. A National Midwifery Board was set up under the joint auspices of the ministries of health and education to develop plans and programs, especially with regard to midwifery education.[77] In October, with support from the Rockefeller Foundation, the First National Midwifery School was opened in Peiping with Dr. Marion Yang (Yang Chongrui) as director. Affiliated with the school was a forty-five-bed maternity hospital.

Marion Yang, a graduate of the Union Medical College for Women, had done postgraduate work at the Johns Hopkins School of Hygiene and Public Health. She was the moving spirit behind many of the efforts to improve maternal and child health during this period. She had taught at PUMC and worked in the Peiping Special Health Area where she developed a child-health program. Her program encompassed prenatal care, including antenatal clinics and home visits by public-health nurses; obstetrical care, including twenty-four-hour delivery assistance and home visits; infant welfare, including infant clinics and well-baby care; preschool health, including periodic physical examinations and children's clinics; and midwifery training.[78] She was eminently qualified to fulfil the mission of the First National Midwifery School, which was to train modern midwives, to develop a child-health program, and to collect vital statistics in cooperation with the local government.

Several developments during the next few years bolstered improvements in maternal and child health in the capital city of Nanjing. Cooperation between the Central Hospital and the Nanjing Municipal Health Station in 1932 led to maternal and child-welfare initiatives in the city as well as in the hospital. A year later, a second national midwifery institution, the Central Midwifery School, opened in the city. Concurrent with her position in the First National Midwifery School, Yang was appointed chief of the newly organized Department of Maternity and Child Health in the Central Field Health Station, which now oversaw the pilot programs in Peiping and Nanjing.[79]

In Peiping in 1930, under the direction of Yang, a Child Health Institute was quickly set up to develop a model maternity and child-health program and to act as a training center for students of the First National Midwifery School. In 1934, the program was officially entrusted with the responsibilities of "mothercraft"—the training of mothers in home economics, hygiene, and the care of newborns and infants; the provision of health consultation for mothers and children under five years of age; the study of medical problems and their prevention, including promotion of the mother's health by "regulating the number of children"; provision of health education for mothers; the collection of birth and death statistics; and the registration and supervision of midwives.[80] The most controversial feature of the program was its promotion of birth control. Yang strongly believed that the pressure of excess population upon the limited resources of China would "thwart effectively every effort at broad social and economic reconstruction."[81] To promote family planning, Yang, James Yen, Ida Pruitt of the Social Service Department of PUMC, and several professors from Yanjing University's Department of Sociology and Social Work organized the Peiping Committee on Maternal Health in February 1930. Its members included John Grant, Li Tingan, and other Peiping health leaders. The committee opened clinics for birth control and sterilization but the response was disappointing. During the three-year period from March 1930 to February 1933, only ninety-nine cases were treated, and most of the patients came from middle- and upper-class backgrounds.[82] Health leaders usually included birth-control publicity in rural health campaigns, although success eluded them. Birth control ran against the deeply rooted Chinese tradition of ancestral worship and the need to perpetuate the family line through male heirs. Ironically, it was the high infant mortality rate, caused mainly by tetanus neonatorum, that had always functioned to limit the size of Chinese families.[83]

The Peiping Child Health Institute opened seven branch stations during its first five years of existence. From July 1933 to June 1934, the main station and two of its branches recorded 817 free deliveries, 3,384 prenatal examinations, and 406 postnatal examinations.[84] Although figures from the other stations and from private practitioners are not available, it can be assumed that the total number of deliveries by modern midwives and doctors, as well as the number of women receiving care before and after their pregnancies, was extremely small in a city with a population of about 1.5 million. This is understandable in view of the newness of the concept of maternal health and the fact that prenatal care (which was preventive in nature) required the expectant mother to present herself for it—a course of action that was highly unlikely when most people had no clear understanding of the value of preventive health care and when such care was seldom readily available.

To overcome the reluctance of expectant, apparently healthy

mothers to seek prenatal care the municipal health administration of Nanjing under Wang Zuxiang initiated in 1932 a unique program to seek out pregnant women and assist them in obtaining care and free delivery. Police responsible for registering households were asked to supply the health department with information on expectant mothers recorded on a standard form. The department would then contact the women about obtaining prenatal care from the municipal urban health demonstration at Sipailou in the city, with follow-up home visits to be supplied if necessary. The number of prenatal examinations rose from 7,061 in 1933 to 9,078 during the first ten months of 1934. At the time of delivery, the health department provided car fare for those unable to pay to ensure that deliveries would be performed in the municipal health station. Students and graduates from the Central School of Nursing and the Central Midwifery School helped in the deliveries. From 1932 to 1937, the program handled an average of five hundred deliveries per month.[85] The Central Midwifery School, since it was affiliated with the Central Hospital, benefited from this innovative program. The school also introduced maternal and child-care services in five municipal substations in conjunction with the Nanjing Municipal Health Station, and it carried out tasks similar to those of the Child Health Institute in Peiping. By 1936, its programs were reaching about one quarter of the city's population.[86]

In Shanghai, the other major urban center in Jiangsu Province, maternal and child health-care programs were carried on in the municipal health stations where free deliveries were also available.[87] A glimpse of the impact of these health programs on different social classes is provided by data on the backgrounds of women who sought care at the Provincial Midwifery School and Hospital in Nanchang. During 1931–34, an average of one thousand women per year were attended to by the school and hospital staff. Of these, 20 percent came from well-to-do families, 60 percent from the middle classes, and 20 percent from the poorer classes. The percentages suggest that the message of the benefits of modern health care had found a more receptive audience among the middle and upper classes. Most likely these were also the women with the best access to facilities in the city.[88]

In the provincial and *xian* maternal and child-welfare programs, conditions varied greatly. Jiangsu Province maintained the largest number of service centers, all of them in theory under the direction of the Provincial Midwifery School in Zhenjiang. By 1937, there were twenty maternal homes in as many *xian*, and in the health demonstration center at Jiangning *xian* a model maternal and child-health service had been established.[89] Next came Jiangxi, with ten maternity programs located in the welfare centers established between 1934 and 1936, each with its own modern midwives. In these centers, expectant mothers were enrolled in classes on the care and feeding of babies. Postnatal care was provided and nurseries were organized during the planting and harvest seasons. By the spring of 1936, however, these centers had performed only 329 deliveries, a small number for ten centers during a two-year period, especially compared to the monthly average of 500 deliveries recorded by modern midwives in Nanjing.[90] Except for demonstration centers established in some of the provinces, provincial or *xian* maternal and child-health programs were not organized until the mid-1930s.[91]

In general, maternal programs were hard to develop. This was the case even in Dingxian where the health program had been introduced as early as 1929. At first, in Dingxian, the health department tried to install a modern midwife and a fairly experienced obstetrician. But the villagers were suspicious of a twenty-five-year-old midwife. Nor did the number of abnormal births justify the maintenance of a full-time physician. In fact, it was estimated that each delivery cost at least five dollars, a fee far too high for the local people. Attempts to retrain traditional midwives also proved frustrating. As C. C. Chen put it, "it was practically impossible to correct the habits of a lifetime, or even to enforce cleanliness." Often, even when younger women desired the assistance of a modern midwife, their mothers-in-law would not allow it. In 1936, Chen reported that the number of deliveries and prenatal and postnatal visits did not show any dramatic increase over previous years. He was moved to comment that "the improvement of midwifery practice seems to be a question of two to three generations, even provided continuous education is carried on."[92]

School Health

The national health administration's concern for child health extended into the schools. It was seen as the government's responsibility to provide students with a reasonably sanitary environment and to protect their health. This would ensure that a new generation of physically strong, Chinese youth would be trained to carry on the nation's reconstruction.[93] Although Chinese leaders emulated the American model of school health, they combined it with environmental and individual concerns in the programs of the 1920s and 1930s. Thus, the focus was not merely on the control of communicable disease and the maintenance of sanitary conditions. It also included a strong medical component of disease prevention, the detection of physical and mental defects, and establishment of procedures for the correction of such impairments. Unlike the situation in the United States, where the boundaries of public health conflicted with physicians' interests, in China the physicians controlled the entire process. Although the school programs were administered by both the Ministry of Education and the health administration, and attempts were made to train teachers to perform simple examinations, the power and jurisdiction of the modern doctors were never challenged.

In the early years of the Republic, some schools had hired visiting physicians to treat sick children, but the practice was neither organized nor widespread. The first organized attempt to provide school care was made at the Peking First Health Station in 1925. There a model program was introduced in eight schools (there were fifty schools in the station's service area with a total student population of 4,454). The program had three components. The first was medical service, which included physical examinations performed by two general practitioners, two specialists, one dentist, and two nurses; the correction of defects in the school clinics or nearby hospitals; the establishment of school clinics to provide immediate care for minor ailments; provision of preventive inoculations, especially against smallpox, typhoid, scarlet fever, and diphtheria; and the introduction of nursing service, responsible for the supervision of treatment and follow-up care. The second component of the program was provision and maintenance of general sanitation in the schools. Its areas of concern included ventilation, lighting, sanitary toilet facilities, and safe playgrounds. The last component was health education, which aimed to instill good habits in the students and incorporated health information in the curricula.

From 1925 to 1928, the station carried out 3,575 physical examinations and 1,417 smallpox vaccinations. The chief physical impairments identified were trachoma and dental defects: 21.8 and 34.5 percent of the students suffered from these problems, respectively.[94] In fact, trachoma and dental defects were the most common of the various problems identified in the student population from 1929 to 1938. For that period, the percentages were 37.6 for dental defects and 48.5 for trachoma.[95] Although some early health programs had been introduced by Christian missionaries in their schools, it was the program in the Peking First Health Station that became the model for all subsequent attempts in other parts of the country.[96]

After the Ministry of Health was founded, it negotiated with the Ministry of Education to form a Joint Committee on School Health, which was established in February 1929. Two months later, when the committee held its first conference, it not only established school-health procedures but it recommended that *Essentials of School Hygiene*, a handbook prepared by the Peking First Health Station, be used in the development of programs throughout the country.[97] Later that year, the Ministry of Health also promulgated regulations governing the medical examination of school children.[98] The Guomindang, too, made an important addition, insisting upon vigorous physical education in all schools at the secondary and higher levels. Emphasizing the need to strengthen the student's body and character, the Guomindang made mandatory military training and physical education part of its *San min zhuyi* (Three People's Principles) educational program designed to instill in students the virtues of discipline and self-sacrifice. Thus, physical education became an essential instrument of national strengthening and reconstruction.[99]

To further standardize the planning for school health programs throughout the country, in 1931 the Central Field Health Station created under its Department of Health Education a Central School Health Service. The service undertook fieldwork in a few school districts in Nanjing in 1931, and it initiated a program of school health in Peiping the following year. Further cooperation between the National Health Administration and the Ministry of Education resulted in the establishment of a National Planning Commission on School Health Education in 1934. Among other things, the commission attempted to develop guidelines for budgets and facilities. It even recommended the proper height for chairs.[100] Local authorities were urged to establish commissions on health education to implement these ideas, and by 1935 Peiping, Nanjing, Shanghai, Tianjin, Changsha, Hangzhou, and Canton had organized school health services. Peiping's service operated in 69 municipal schools with a total student population of 21,000, while in Nanjing the service dealt with 120 schools and 37,000 students.[101] School-health work was also carried out, to varying degrees, in the major rural health centers, especially those in Xiaozhuang, Tangshan, Dingxian, and Gaoqiao, and in some welfare centers in Jiangxi.

To ensure the availability of funds, the Ministry of Health urged schools to levy a fixed "health rate" of forty cents per year per student.[102] In April 1936, the National Health Administration convened a national conference on school health, which standardized the program for urban and rural schools and devised measures for the prevention and treatment of smallpox, skin diseases, and trachoma among students. By 1937, the government was claiming that about 200,000 students had received care through some sort of health service.[103] One innovation was the organization of students into school-health teams. Under the direction of a school-health leader, each grade had a team leader who supervised a number of subteam leaders, each in charge of divisions of ten to fifteen students. Team and subteam leaders received basic training in first-aid. They were responsible for ensuring the cleanliness of, and the practice of good health habits by, their group members by means of morning cleanliness drills and regular inspections. They also mobilized students in preventive work such as cleaning the school grounds and organizing inoculation campaigns.[104] This structure not only conformed with the Guomindang's stress on discipline and organization but it proved effective in reducing the number of professionals needed to carry out all aspects of school health work.

One aspect of the school health program, the inclusion of health information in the curriculum, met with many difficulties. First, because there was a dearth of instructional materials on hygiene, most schools had to develop their own. The situation was especially acute because the teaching of hygiene in primary schools and physiology in middle schools became compulsory after 1928. According to these new regulations, one hour per week in primary schools would be allotted to instruction in personal hygiene and public health. In the junior middle schools, instruction in subjects such as anatomy, disease prevention, and community health would be given one hour every week for three years. In senior middle schools, students were to receive instruction in social medicine and "sex hygiene."[105] But standardization of textbooks on these subjects for use in primary and middle schools did not take place until the conference on school health was held in April 1936. And, although the National Health Administration had a year earlier instructed local jurisdictions to allocate funds for school health work and the preparation of hygiene textbooks, the money in most cases was not forthcoming.[106] Finally, there was the problem of training enough instructors to teach health. Although short-term courses for teachers were introduced in normal schools and in the Central Field Health Station, difficulties were encountered in impressing upon educators the importance of health in their mission and the need to implement the guidelines approved by the National Health Administration.

Popular Health Education

As the discussion above has shown, success of the various programs, to a significant degree, hinged upon the extent to which people accepted or rejected the demands made on them to change their lives to conform to a new perception of hygiene. A doctor could successfully plan the clinical aspects of a campaign to stamp out cholera in a village but the disease would never be completely controlled unless the villagers understood and accepted the necessary preventive activities. Often such a change might be effected through popular health education and propaganda. Public-health education is not merely the removal of ignorance; it is a process whereby an individual changes an attitude and behavior through the acquisition of new knowledge. The knowledge not only persuades him to adopt preventive measures himself, but it also makes him so keenly aware of the health of others that he may support, and even initiate, preventive action by the community. This process eventually results in a change of habit or custom of the group.[107] To health leaders in early Republican China, popular public-health education was absolutely crucial in combating deeply rooted cultural, social, and philosophical barriers to the spread of scientific medicine.

It may be recalled that some uncoordinated attempts at popular health education were undertaken before 1928 by the North Manchurian Plague Prevention Service, the National Epidemic Prevention Bureau, the Peking First Health Station, and missionary organizations. In particular, the Council on Health Education, which was organized in 1916 with the support of several missionary groups, the National Medical Association and the Joint Council on Public Health, emerged as the most active nongovernmental bodies promoting modern health knowledge. But the council's work disintegrated after 1927 when its director, Dr. W. W. Peter, left for the United States.

For the Nationalist regime, which stressed the role of health improvement in national reconstruction, popular public-health education assumed a political dimension. This led to its attempt to motivate Chinese citizens to adopt health measures for the good of the nation. As we have seen, government propaganda constantly emphasized the link between health and China's economic rejuvenation, rural reconstruction, spiritual renewal, and social regeneration. The extent to which such nationalistic exhortations succeeded is difficult to gauge but it is clear that the Nationalist government saw the shaping of people's attitudes as a vital part of its overall program (witness the New Life Movement). Yet the problem remained that propaganda would be reduced to mere platitudes if it were not accompanied by socioeconomic transformation. Only this would provide the people with the opportunity to practice new behavioral patterns.

The government's popular health-education program combined the conventional approach of propaganda and campaigns aimed mainly at the individual with the use of model programs such as urban and rural demonstrations and school health programs to demonstrate the feasibility of community action. The center for many of these activities was the Department of Health Education in the Central Field Health Station. Organized in April 1931 under Dr. C. K. Chu (Zhu Zhanggeng), a PUMC graduate, and W. W. Peter, who was invited back to China for this purpose, the department prepared educational materials—health posters, pamphlets, books, lantern slides, and wax models—which were distributed free in all parts of the country. In 1936, it produced more than 1,600 books, 84,000 pamphlets, and tens of thousands of posters. One obvious drawback to printed propaganda was that most rural people were illiterate. So the station also prepared short films on the prevention of smallpox, diphtheria, and malaria. It also used weekly radio broadcasts on health topics and exhibitions in different localities to reach a wide audience. The exhibitions featured health lectures and lantern shows.[108]

At the local level, popular health education usually included such activities as conducting campaigns against a specific disease; mobilization of the population in a city or village to improve sanitary conditions through street cleaning or the killing of flies or mosquitoes; presentation of health exhibitions and talks; distribution of literature; and the organization of health contests. The Ministry of Health, in fact, designated the first of May and the fifteenth of December as the dates for national health campaigns to publicize environmental improvements and preventive measures against communicable disease.[109] Not surprisingly, such activities seldom extended beyond major cities or the provincial and rural health centers. And even in these sites the extent of popular health education proved to be rather limited. A survey of conditions prior to 1931 in nineteen cities with populations of 100,000 or more revealed that only seven conducted some kind of popular health education program in the form of exhibits, talks, or the distribution of health information.[110] The situation improved somewhat in the next few years. The number of health talks in Shanghai, for example, increased from 61 in 1930–31 to 232 in 1934–35, while home visits increased from 5,259 to 10,158 during the same period.[111] Another study of rural health conducted in seventeen health centers in 1934 concluded that the generation of publicity was one of the least frequent activities in the centers. The only exception was Dingxian, where, thanks to village health workers and the alumni of People Schools, the health education program reached the public through such means as the distribution of literature written in simple characters, personal visits, exhibits, classes, popular lectures, and, most important, the adoption of concrete measures such as the provision of free baths and the remodelling of latrines.[112]

Health publicity, especially in the countryside, also was hampered by the failure to incorporate practitioners of indigenous medicine. Though these practitioners were in an excellent position to act as agents of health education and to influence the behavior of the people, the bitter feud between modern doctors and native practitioners had kept them excluded from public-health activities. But, since traditional health practices constituted a significant part of the sociocultural fabric of Chinese society, any attempt to change attitudes and beliefs about health would surely require the close cooperation of the practitioners who had been responsible for local health before the intrusion of scientific medicine. Unfortunately this did not happen; the integration of traditional and modern medicine had to wait.

Some leaders also organized health associations to spread information among the people. Li Tingan and Wu Lien-teh, for instance, founded the National Anti-tuberculosis Association of China in Shanghai in 1933. But such activities were confined almost exclusively to urban centers.[113] These centers did witness some progress during this period. Health consciousness among the urban population does seem to have been heightened, and the term *weisheng* (hygiene) became very popular. In the 1930s, newspapers in cities such as Tianjin and Shanghai published weekly medical supplements, which discussed subjects ranging from the latest western medical discoveries to how to treat the common cold. The pages were filled with advertisements for all kinds of patent medicines. But, if nothing else, these publications helped to popularize some of the concepts and practices of scientific medicine.

Although the outbreak of the Sino-Japanese War in 1937 disrupted or terminated many of the programs discussed in this chapter, the ambitious and comprehensive program of organized public health launched by the Nationalists after 1928 served as the foundation for future efforts during and after the war. One of the most serious challenges that would have to be met in order to ensure the development and workability of these programs—indeed, of the entire health-care structure—was the training of health personnel in sufficient numbers to deal with the manifold problems of the country.

6

The Training and Supply of Health Manpower

Health manpower was a critical component in the state-medicine
service that Chinese leaders attempted to introduce during the
Nationalist decade. The success of the state health plans depended
to a significant extent upon both the quantity and the quality of
health-care personnel. These included public-health administrators,
doctors, dentists, pharmacists, nurses, midwives, and sanitarians, as
well as the practitioners of traditional medicine, if and when they
were incorporated into the organized service. In view of China's large
population and the enormity of its health problems, its manpower
needs were massive and varied. Among the host of policy issues dealt
with by the Ministry of Health in 1928 were deciding how scarce
resources should be allocated, the reorganization and establishment
of training institutions, the number and types of personnel to be
trained, and the role of private medical institutions in that training.
In order to understand the policies adopted by the ministry, and to
measure the extent to which they were successful, it is necessary to
examine the health manpower-needs of China in the 1930s and 1940s.

China's Health-Manpower Needs

In 1929, it has been estimated, there were 4,000 to 5,000 doctors
trained in modern medicine in China, although only 918 had registered with the new Ministry of Health that year. With a population
of about 450 million, the ratio of doctors to population was 1 to
somewhere between 90,000 and 112,500. This may be compared to

the figures of 1 to 800 in the United States in 1930, or 1 to 1,490 in England and Wales in 1927.[1] Certainly, it would be difficult, if not impossible, for China to train enough doctors to match the American ratio within a short period of time. Chinese planners therefore considered an improvement of the ratio to 1 to 8,000 as the goal for the next ten-year period. This would require the training of at least 5,000 doctors per year. Visiting China in 1930 as a representative of the League of Nations, Dr. Knud Faber of the University of Copenhagen identified thirteen medical schools, both government and private, with acceptable standards. These schools graduated 180 doctors. If one adds the 190 graduates of three private medical schools whose standards Faber found unacceptable, the total number of doctors produced in 1930 was still only about one-fourteenth of what was deemed desirable.[2] Even if all these graduates entered the state health service—a course of action that was most unlikely—the number of doctors still would be insufficient to meet the demands of the new health departments and organizations. Aggravating this problem was the type of training doctors received in the top medical schools. The college that best defines Chinese medical education at that time is PUMC. Almost all the best schools adopted the PUMC model, which in turn was based upon the curriculum of the Johns Hopkins School of Medicine in the United States. As one contemporary put it,

> PUMC was known for her emphasis on basic medical sciences, her stringent resident program, her strict academic standards . . . her full-time preclinical and clinical staffs, and her facilities for research work for all senior faculty members. These PUMC traditions guided those PUMC men who headed other medical colleges.[3]

PUMC's influence was strong in the 1930s and 1940s. Its graduates became officials in the health bureaucracy or formed the core of teaching staffs in other medical colleges. Consequently, the emphasis in most medical schools was on producing a few teachers and researchers whose training was highly specialized. It is clear that the demands of state medicine would require a redefinition of the kinds and relative numbers of schools needed and of the types of personnel to be trained in them. The role of practitioners of indigenous medicine, whose numbers were estimated to be about 1.2 million in 1930, had to be evaluated also in light of the massive needs of the population and the time required to train qualified modern doctors.[4]

The supply of other types of health personnel was also far from adequate. In view of the shortage of modern doctors, auxiliary personnel such as nurses and midwives assumed great importance. It may be recalled that in the mid-1920s there were an estimated 2,000 trained nurses in China. In 1928, except for a few medical schools in which nursing courses were offered, nurses were trained by individual hospitals or private schools without uniform requirements or admission standards. The task of the Ministry of Health and the Ministry of Education, therefore, was to reorganize nursing education and to establish qualified schools to train different types, including public-health nurses. Modern midwives also were badly needed since the lack of an understanding of sepsis and cleanliness on the part of old-style midwives was responsible to a significant extent for the high infant mortality rate. In 1928, there were an estimated 240,000 practicing midwives. But only 385 modern midwives were registered with the government in 1929.[5] New categories of health manpower, such as sanitary inspectors, sanitary engineers, and school-health personnel, also had to be developed. Since it took time to train qualified personnel of all types, the question was how to utilize existing personnel, especially old-style midwives and practitioners of native medicine. But China's health-manpower needs also were affected by the geographical distribution of existing and future personnel. And in 1928 the countryside was grossly understaffed in modern health personnel. In sum, in 1928, the new health administration of the Nationalist government faced the formidable task of providing adequate personnel to support the ambitious public-health programs that it was about to launch. It also had to ensure that personnel would be equitably distributed in the areas in which they were most needed.

Formulating Polices on Medical Education

Since there had been no special or coordinated efforts to develop medical education in China before 1928, the Ministry of Health and the Ministry of Education attempted to cooperate in formulating policies on the reorganization of medical education, despite the fact that unsettling political conditions in the ministries during the first two years of the new regime impinged upon the development of firm and consistent policies. Nonetheless, two initiatives were launched. First, a Commission on Medical Education was established by the Ministry of Education in early 1929, with participation by the Ministry of Health, to discuss policies, curricula, and other issues in the development of medical institutions. The commission's ideas would be submitted to the Ministry of Education for review and possible action. Unfortunately, except for special occasions when it was allowed to deliberate on specific policy matters, the commission had neither a steady source of funding nor a permanent staff to carry out its work. It did begin work on the standardization of medical curricula, and it issued recommendations for medical technical schools in August 1931 and for medical colleges in the early summer of 1935. But it was not until after July 1935 that the commission was reorganized, and became fully operational, with financial support from the Rockefeller Foundation. Its report on health-manpower training issued that summer was an important document outlining a new approach to the training and development of health manpower relevant to China's needs.[6]

The second initiative was taken in late 1928 when a special study committee was entrusted with the task of formulating a ten-year plan for medical education in China, focusing on the types of personnel to be trained and the standards and curricula of medical schools. The committee tried to address the quality-versus-quantity issue by recommending that two types of schools be set up. The first type would be medical colleges responsible for educating first-rate physicians through a highly selective process of recruitment and specialized training. The second would be "medical technical schools" (*yixue zhuanke xuexiao*) designed to produce a large number of doctors in a shorter period of time. Medical colleges would accept only students with two years of college or university premedical training and the course of study would last for five years (the final year being an internship in a teaching hospital). Thus, in all, the length of study would be seven years. On the other hand, graduates from senior middle schools could apply to the medical technical schools, which would have a four-year curriculum and a fifth year of internship in a hospital.[7]

The Ministry of Education did not accept these recommendations immediately. Instead it referred them to the Commission on Medical Education for further study. In the meantime, in August 1929, it promulgated new regulations governing the organization of all universities under the Nationalist government. Strangely, these regulations contained provisions that complicated the reorganization of medical education.[8] Article 22 of the regulations stated that universities (institutions with a minimum of three colleges, including at least one of science, agriculture, engineering, business, or medicine) or independent colleges (institutions with fewer than three colleges) could set up special courses such as teacher training, journalism, fine arts, library science, public health, and medicine. These courses, according to Article 25, must last for two to three years. The special medical course, however, was to be three years plus a fourth year of internship. Students graduating from these special courses would receive diplomas from the universities or independent colleges. In other words, a university or independent college could develop, in theory, a four-year special medical program to train "doctors" independent of the requirements of its regular medical school. The confusion that these provisions would entail—in curricula and facilities as well as for faculty and students—were never addressed by the Ministry of Education.

These provisions, in fact, contradicted the recommendations of the study committee, which maintained that there should be separate medical technical schools whose course of study would be five years (four years of study plus one year of internship). To add to the confusion, the Commission on Medical Education, which met in special session in February 1930, announced its approval of the study committee's recommendations. It also prescribed the required courses for the medical technical schools in August 1931, although apparently no school adhered to the proposal. The commission failed to come up with any recommendations for the curriculum in medical colleges.[9] This rather bewildering state of affairs resulted from unsettled conditions existing in the ministries of education and health. The former underwent a reorganization in the summer of 1929. Chiang Monlin (Jiang Menglin), the new minister of Education, abandoned a plan to divide the country into university districts (*daxue qu*) introduced earlier by Cai Yuanpei.[10] At that time J. Heng Liu had just taken over as acting minister of health. Despite the ministries' professed attempts to cooperate, coordination was poor and political uncertainties related to personnel changes hampered medical-education planning in the early Nationalist period.

By the end of 1929, however, J. Heng Liu and Chiang Monlin cooperated in seeking the League of Nations Health Organization's support in the reorganization of medical education, an objective that was included in Liu's request for technical assistance from the League. It may be recalled that one of the motives in seeking the League's cooperation was to lend China the League's international prestige and influence. Subsequently, Dr. Knud Faber of the University of Copenhagen visited China from September to December of 1930, as the League's representative, to study the state of medical education and make recommendations for its future development. Faber's report tried to address many of the issues confronting the health planners. Agreeing with the medical leaders, Faber insisted that China must produce doctors trained in modern medicine. He rejected the idea of introducing short-term courses to train doctors of native medicine in basic scientific practice, arguing that such a course of action "would do more harm than good" because it would be construed as "an official authorisation of native doctors."[11] To him, the solution to China's health-manpower problem lay in the development of a new tier of institutions to train doctors at the intermediate level.

This was essentially the proposal for medical technical schools put forward by the Ministry of Education's study committee. Faber endorsed the division of medical schools into higher and lower types to meet the demands of "quality" and "quantity" in the health service. He proposed the creation of a fairly large number of independent medical-technical schools, preferably one in each province. Each of these should, in the beginning, train at least sixty "practical physicians" yearly, with the number increasing eventually to about one hundred. The medium of instruction should be Chinese and the length of study four years, with the emphasis on clinical teaching in a provincial hospital. A fifth year of internship in the hospital would be optional. Graduates of these schools might be required to accept government health-service positions in small towns or rural areas.[12]

As for the higher medical colleges, basically Faber subscribed to the study committee's definition of their mission: to produce highly trained physicians "fitted to become leaders and teachers in the hospitals and schools of China."[13] He also endorsed the stringent entrance requirements and the length of the course of study proposed by the study committee, while emphasizing the need to train more specialists in different subjects. Yet he did not recommend the establishment of new national medical colleges, arguing that the existing institutions could be reorganized, expanded, and upgraded, so that the size of each graduating class could be increased from thirty to fifty students. For the training of auxiliary medical personnel, Faber urged the expansion of nursing education, with an emphasis on the recruitment of graduates of junior middle schools rather than primary-school graduates. He rejected the one-year college course in premedical sciences required for nursing students in PUMC as unnecessary and costly. Instead he proposed the creation of high schools or normal schools to train head nurses and supervisors. For the training of midwives, he also advocated a two-track system: a higher level of midwives with a two-year course, and a lower level with a six-month course. Graduates of the latter would be earmarked for rural service.[14]

In essence, Faber advocated the continuation of the Johns Hopkins model (training first-class teachers and researchers for a few elite colleges), while relying on medical technical schools to produce intermediate doctors and expansion of auxiliary personnel to meet the demands of state medicine. He did not support the idea of creating more gradations of medical personnel (between the intermediate doctors and auxiliary health workers) for the rural health service even if demands should outstrip supply. He rationalized this by explaining that "to send badly trained doctors of modern medicine out to compete with the native doctors might easily bring modern medicine into disrepute."[15] Since such personnel would require strict supervision by trained doctors, any attempt to create more categories of health manpower, in Faber's view, should await the expansion of the pool of intermediate doctors.

Faber's recommendations for a two-tiered medical-school system at the top and the expansion of auxiliaries at the bottom essentially coincided with the intentions of Chinese health planners. But the professed opinion of the new National Health Administration in early 1931 was that the two-tiered medical-school idea was essentially a temporary measure adopted to meet the immediate needs of China. The long-term objective was to create a new kind of "experimental" medical school, one better adapted to China's medical needs and health conditions. The Three Year Plan announced by the National Health Administration in April 1931 specifically included the creation of such an experimental school as one of its tasks. In the meantime, in June the government promulgated regulations for the establishment of medical technical schools in all the provincial capitals and in special municipalities. Each school would have a hospital equipped with two hundred or more beds for teaching purposes. The course of study would be four years with a fifth year of internship.[16] Three months later, the government announced that senior-middle-school graduates could apply for admission to medical colleges and medical technical schools. The length of study for medical colleges would be five years (one year premedical and four medical) plus a sixth year of internship.[17] This change from the recommended seven-year curriculum for medical colleges meant reduction of premedical science training to only one year, but the move actually rendered the two-tiered division rather meaningless since the only difference now was the one-year premedical course. Many observers wondered whether a single year's difference was enough to justify the division of the medical profession into two groups.[18] Nonetheless, the National Health Administration and the Ministry of Education expected the existing schools to adopt the new policy while pushing for establishment of the new medical technical schools.

To provide further guidance for the medical colleges and schools, the Commission on Medical Education finally announced the revised curricula for both types on 6 July 1935. For medical colleges, the first year of the six-year curriculum would be devoted to general subjects (including principles of the Guomindang and physical education) and basic science. The second and third years would cover preclinical subjects (including anatomy, histology, physiology, bacteriology, pathology, and parasitology), and the fourth and fifth years would address clinical subjects (including physical and clinical diagnosis, surgery, pediatrics, obstetrics and gynecology, and public health). The final year would be internship, including one month of public-health training in a health station. For medical technical schools, the curriculum would consist of four years of study, the first two concentrating on basic sciences and preclinical subjects, and the last on clinical subjects. Although officially an internship was not listed as mandatory in the curriculum, students were strongly encouraged to continue into the fifth year as an intern, including one month of public-health work in a health station.

The proposed curricula for both types of school also listed the number of hours to be devoted to each subject and specified that laboratory and practical work must occupy more than half of the hours allotted. To allow for some flexibility, about 20 percent of the total time was left open for electives. In fact, the two curricula were basically identical, the only exceptions being the number of hours devoted to the basic sciences, preclinical subjects, and the internship year, which most of the students in medical technical schools took anyway.[19]

The Reorganization of Medical Schools

In order to see how existing medical schools fit into the new system mandated by the government, it is necessary to examine those institutions and their developments. Medical schools had been established rather haphazardly in China. The systems and curricula of various countries were transplanted according to the training or national origin of the founders (a German-trained doctor was likely to adopt the German model, an American-trained doctor the American model, and so forth). Indeed, the medical community was divided into Anglo-American, German, French, and Japanese factions. In Japanese-controlled Manchuria, the medical school was operated along Japanese lines, while policies in mission schools usually reflected the desires of the mission boards of various countries. There also was diversity in the medium of instruction, the most common being Chinese, German-Chinese, English-Chinese, French, German, English, and Japanese.

In the 1930s, excluding the army's medical school, medical schools were grouped into three categories: national, provincial, and private. Depending upon the length of the course of study, they were also divided into medical colleges and medical technical schools. The central government directly controlled five medical colleges (plus the army medical school) but it had little jurisdiction, financial or otherwise, over the seven provincial medical colleges and medical technical schools, which generally tried to follow the guidelines laid down by the National Health Administration and the Ministry of Education. Although they might be registered with the government, the fifteen private medical colleges (excluding the Japanese Manchurian Medical College) enjoyed almost complete autonomy, especially if they were foreign-controlled. Thus, below the national level, the central health administration could do little to effect change without the cooperation of provincial or private authorities, especially with regard to establishing provincial medical colleges and medical technical schools.

Except for four single-sex institutions (two for men, St. John's and Army Medical College; and two for women, Hackett Medical College, which became coeducational in 1933, and Women's Christian Medical College), the medical schools were coeducational. The percentage of female students in the country was 16.9 in 1932–33 and 17.6 in 1933–34, and the general trend was for a gradual increase in female students. The percentage of women in individual schools, however, ranged from a low of 3 to a high of 29.[20] Class size in these schools also varied but the majority of classes were small, averaging less than 30 students. Assuming that a school would have five or six classes, each with 30 students, one would expect each school to have at least 150 to 180 students enrolled. This was not the case, however. In 1932–33, for example, less than 40 percent of the schools could claim that many students. And, except for a couple of private schools that graduated 100 or more doctors in that year, the number of graduates for the rest of the schools ranged from a low of 5 (Women's Christian Medical College in Shanghai) to a high of 39 (College of Medicine of National Peiping University).[21] Despite the Nationalist government's emphasis on the practical sciences (science, agriculture, engineering, and medicine), enrollment in medical schools remained small—in fact, it was the lowest among these four divisions. So was the number of medical graduates throughout most of the 1930s. The total number of graduates from all medical colleges and medical technical schools from 1931 to the end of 1935 was 1,664, compared to 5,067 for engineering, 2,022 for agriculture, and 3,435 for the sciences.[22] The length of the curriculum and the cost of medical studies were factors that discouraged higher enrollment.

Besides the Army Medical College, located in Nanjing, the five medical colleges directly controlled by the national government were the College of Medicine, National Peiping University; College of Medicine, National Tongji University in Shanghai; National Shanghai Medical College; College of Medicine, National Central University in Nanjing; and College of Medicine, National Zhongshan University in Canton. The National Peiping University Medical College, a name adopted in 1928, was founded in 1912 as the National Peking Medical Zhuanmen School. It was based on the German model, with a five-year curriculum, and the medium of instruction was Chinese. When Faber visited the school in 1930, he was appalled by the deteriorating conditions and lack of government support. It was affiliated with a hospital that had only about 20 beds available for teaching, although there were plans to build a teaching hospital with an enlarged capacity.[23] Faber recommended a complete reorganization of the institution so that it might qualify for the status of a medical college. In 1932, the curriculum was extended to the standard six years and the school acquired its own teaching hospital with 150 beds.[24] The change in status was accompanied by an increase in the teaching staff from thirty-four in 1932–33 to seventy in 1933–34. In fact, Peiping ranked second among the five national medical schools in total annual expenditures for 1933–34.[25] To strengthen the training program in public health, it affiliated itself with the Second Health Station in Peiping, which provided a site for the students to gain experience in practical public-health work.[26]

There were two national medical colleges in Shanghai. The National Tongji University Medical School originated in 1908 when a German doctor founded the Tongji German Medical School. This institution was turned over to the Chinese in 1917, and it became a national university in 1927. Its origin was reflected in its use of German as the medium of instruction and in its five-year curriculum, divided into two years of preclinical and three years of clinical study. The course of study was changed to six years in 1932 to conform to the new regulations. The preclinical course was reduced to one year and the sixth year was an internship served in the school's hospital and in Wusong Health Station (for public-health training).[27] In terms of numbers of teaching staff and total annual expenditures in 1933–34, it was ranked lowest among the five national colleges but its graduating class of thirty-three in 1932–33 was about the same size as that of National Peiping University Medical College. Faber's 1930 report faulted the school for poor clinical training, a weakness that apparently went uncorrected even in the late 1930s and 1940s.[28]

The other national institution in Shanghai, the National Shanghai Medical College, was superior to Tongji in many ways. Before 1932, however, it suffered a split personality as it was originally the school of medicine of the National Central University in Nanjing, which had undergone numerous name and administrative changes in the transition to Nationalist rule.[29] After completing two years of premedical studies in Nanjing, students undertook four years of medical training, two preclinical in Wusong near Shanghai, and two clinical in the Red Cross Hospital in Shanghai. The separation of theoretical from clinical work and the inconvenience caused by the disjoined facilities proved to be a major drawback.[30] In 1932, the medical school in Shanghai was removed from National Central University. Officially it now became the Shanghai Medical College, with a six-year course of study taught in Chinese and English. The Japanese bombardment of the city in 1932 destroyed the Wusong facilities but the new medical college continued operations in the Red Cross Hospital with the addition of two temporary buildings.

Help came from an unexpected source in 1934 when the Rockefeller Foundation transferred to the college land it had purchased in 1920 for the construction of a new medical school in Shanghai. With the abandonment of that project, the foundation had been holding title to this valuable property. Shanghai Medical decided to sell it, and the proceeds were used to purchase land and to construct a new campus on the western outskirts of the city. The campus housed the medical college (built with a financial subsidy from the remission of British Boxer Indemnity funds), a School of Pharmacy, a School of Nursing, and a Public Health Institute. Zhongshan Hospital, a teaching institution, was added in 1936.[31] With a strong faculty and improved facilities, the college emerged as one of the best medical institutions in the country. F. C. Yen, who had been dean of Xiangya Medical College in Changsha and vice-director of PUMC Hospital before becoming superintendent of the Red Cross Hospital and dean of Shanghai Medical College in 1928, was a prominent physician and a strong advocate of scientific medicine. He assembled in Shanghai Medical an excellent faculty that included Dr. P. V. Loh (Le Wenzhao), a Harvard graduate who headed the Department of Internal Medicine. Following closely the Johns Hopkins model of teaching and laboratory research, Yen, Loh, and their colleagues established Shanghai as a major center for diagnostic research as well as one of the country's top teaching hospitals.[32] Although its students could obtain practical training in public health at the Gaoqiao Health Demonstration Center, few chose to pursue that kind of career. Most graduates went into private practice.[33]

The separation of Shanghai Medical College from National Central University created a vacuum in medical education in the nation's capital, for now the only medical school in Nanjing was the Army Medical College. With construction of the Central Hospital in the city, the National Health Administration launched plans for a new medical college at the National Central University. Although the government initially failed to earmark funds for its operating expenses, the medical college managed to open its doors in 1935. With the support of the National Health Administration and the municipal government, a joint Hygienic Diagnostic Center was planned for 1936. The medical college offered a special course in dentistry in 1935, with a view toward establishing a full-fledged dental school by 1936–37.[34] These plans were cut short by the outbreak of the Sino-Japanese War and the National Central University was moved to Chongqing.

The fifth national medical college was the College of Medicine of National Zhongshan University in Canton. Founded in 1926, and taken over briefly by the Communists in 1927, it was reopened as a national medical school in 1928. A number of German professors were hired to reorganize the school, and both German and Chinese were used as the medium of instruction. Although proficiency in German was required for admission, many students struggled with the foreign language. Faber noted during his visit that lectures in anatomy and physiology were translated into Chinese as delivered, a cumbersome process.[35] The college did not change its curriculum from five years to six until 1933–34. It had two affiliated teaching hospitals and was generally supported by the government, which recognized the symbolic significance of a university founded by Sun Yat-sen and headed by a president, Zou Lu, who was an elder of the Guomindang.[36]

Only seven provincial medical schools had been organized by 1937. These were located in Henan, Hebei, Zhejiang, Jiangxi, Shandong, Yunnan, and Gansu. The first two were six-year medical colleges, the last a department offering a four-year course, and the rest five-year medical technical schools. The schools in Henan, Hebei, Zhejiang, and Jiangxi had existed before the founding of the Nationalist regime but they all were reorganized gradually between 1928 and 1931 to bring them into conformance with the new requirements. The schools in Shandong and Yunnan, and the medical department at Gansu College, were established after 1931. In other words, Shandong and Yunnan were the only provinces in which medical technical schools of the new type were founded after the National Health Administration adopted the policy of quickly establishing such schools in every province.[37] Lack of funds and personnel certainly contributed to the poor showing. More importantly, the idea of medical technical schools simply did not appeal to the provincial governments, the medical community, and prospective students. From the start, these schools were branded as "inferior," possessing none of the prestige accorded to medical colleges. Although both types had identical entrance requirements, graduates of medical colleges received a bachelor of medicine degree, while graduates of medical technical schools received only a diploma. Yet there was only one year's difference in the training of the graduates. Consequently, good teachers and prospective students shunned the medical technical schools and the support envisioned by the health planners never materialized. After all, even after the reorganization of 1931, the quality of some of the so-called medical colleges was hardly superior.[38] Ironically, health authorities had helped to perpetuate, and even enhance, the prestige of the few top medical colleges while undermining their scheme for solving China's health-manpower problems.

The Role of Private Medical Schools

In the past, private medical schools had made signal contributions to the development of modern education in China. In the 1930s, given the slowness and the difficulties encountered in the expansion of government institutions, they continued to play a vital role in supplying medical manpower. From the planners' point of view, the question was how to integrate these schools into the national system so that they would work together to fulfil the government's health objectives. Many private schools were genuinely concerned about their individual missions and autonomy, while attempting to contribute to China's medical reconstruction. Others were interested only in making a profit. These continued to produce poorly trained doctors despite the health administration's attempts to regulate them.

The private sector consisted of missionary and nonmissionary schools, both of which were expensive to attend. In 1933–34, PUMC and Dongnan Medical College in Shanghai had the highest combined tuition fees and student expenditures of all the medical colleges in the country ($600). St. John's University in Shanghai was second, with a combined total of $550 (tuition was $150). The distinction of charging the most tuition ($160) went to the private Guanghua Medical College in Canton. In contrast, the figures for Jiangxi Provincial Medical Technical School and National Shanghai Medical College were $120 and $320 respectively. Shanghai Medical charged only $20 for tuition, and Jiangxi Provincial was tuition free. In fact, four provincial schools did not charge any tuition at all.[39] Not surprisingly, most students attending private medical schools were from urban, and to a certain extent westernized, well-to-do families. This was especially the case with PUMC students who were largely recruited from the upper classes.[40] The quality of these schools was uneven, however. Some, like PUMC, imposed strict admissions and graduation standards, enjoyed a good reputation, and had much prestige, while others were no more than diploma mills.

In the 1930s, there were sixteen private medical schools. Seven were mission, one was Japanese-controlled (in Mukden), and the rest were independent. The seven mission schools were the College of Medicine, Aurora University (Zhendan daxue) in Shanghai; the College of Medicine, Shandong Christian, or Cheeloo, University (Qilu daxue) in Jinan; Hackett Medical College (Xiage yixueyuan) in Canton; the College of Medicine, St. John's University (Shengyuehan daxue) in Shanghai; the College of Medicine, West China Union University (Huaxi xiehe daxue) in Chengdu; Women's Christian Medical College (Shanghai nuzi yixueyuan) in Shanghai, and Mukden Medical College. The latter suspended operations after the Japanese gained control over the four northeastern provinces in 1934.[41] Although all of them qualified as medical colleges, Aurora and Hackett were the only two that offered a six-year course. The rest had seven-year programs requiring two years of premedical work. Unlike the government medical colleges, all the mission institutions except Hackett (which offered the M.B. degree) awarded Doctor of Medicine degrees, conferring upon their graduates enhanced prestige. Moreover, almost all of them were incorporated in the home countries of their controlling mission boards. This allowed their graduates the added advantage of mobility.

All the mission schools—with the exception of St. John's—registered with the Nationalist government in the early 1930s. During the tumultuous 1920s, when the Chinese had clamored to "recover educational rights," one of their demands had been control over mission educational institutions through compulsory registration with the government. Detractors of mission education denounced the "denationalization" of students in Christian schools and insisted on Chinese control of curricula and administration. In the mid-1920s, at the height of the anti-Christian movement, the warlord government in Peking had issued regulations mandating the registration of schools and colleges supported by foreign funds (including mission schools). These institutions should have Chinese presidents or principals, and their boards of directors should have a majority of Chinese. Their curricula should conform to those approved by the Ministry of Education. No compulsory religious courses would be allowed.[42]

The unsettled conditions accompanying the transition to Nationalist rule in 1926–27 made enforcement of these rules impossible. But the issue of registration and the plan to mold government and private educational institutions into one national system had come

to symbolize the assertion of China's sovereign rights. The Nationalist government continued to pursue these objectives after 1928, and
in fact it added new conditions for registration, including the introduction of courses on the Three People's Principles.[43] Negotiations
between the mission schools and the government were protracted,
but by 1934 all but one were registered (the exception, St. John's,
was not registered until 1947). By the early 1930s, the Nationalist
government also had revised its attitude toward the mission schools,
recognizing their usefulness in China's reconstruction as well as their
important links to the western powers. Mission schools now operated
with less government interference. In fact, the government began
providing financial subsidies to private, including mission, institutions, although the preference was to support education in science,
agriculture, and medicine, fields deemed vital to China's modernization. It is significant that in 1934–35 about half of all government
grants went to Christian colleges.[44]

Aurora University's College of Medicine, run by French Jesuits,
was the only Catholic institution in this group and the only one
offering a six-year course with French as the medium of instruction.
It ranked fairly high in student enrollment and in number of graduates among the Christian medical colleges. In 1932–33, it had 103
students and 12 graduates, putting it second in both categories.
Despite the fact that the length of its curriculum was the same as
that of the government medical colleges, its graduates received the
M.D. degree. Aurora also had a School of Dentistry, with a four-year
course, an important contribution to a neglected field.[45]

The other two mission schools that used a foreign language,
English, as the medium of instruction were St. John's University and
Women's Christian Medical College, both in Shanghai. The official
name of the St. John's medical college was "The Pennsylvania Medical
School, being the Medical Department of St. John's University," since
the college resulted from a merger of the Pennsylvania Medical School,
formerly of Canton, and the medical school of St. John's in 1914.
Like other seven-year mission colleges, it required two years of premedical work in a college, four years of didactic and clinical work,
and one year of internship in its two affiliated teaching hospitals.
St. John's was probably the most westernized among the mission
colleges, and for many it was a favored conduit to study abroad. With
these advantages, the fact that it did not apply for registration until
1937 (due to a dispute over the issue of religious services) was not a

liability. Many alumni returned to teach or work in the affiliated hospitals after their sojourns overseas. Others served in mission hospitals or assumed positions of influence in medical schools or the government. Dr. F. C. Yen, an alumnus, held the deanship of Xiangya Medical School for many years before becoming dean of National Shanghai Medical College. In terms of numbers of medical graduates, it ranked fairly high among the mission schools, producing 111 physicians by 1931 and 130 by the summer of 1934. Prior to 1931, except for eight who had died, all of its graduates were practicing in China.[46]

Of all the mission medical colleges, Shandong Christian (or Cheeloo), founded in 1909, emerged as one with a distinctively Chinese character. From the beginning, leaders of the college had viewed Cheeloo as an unique opportunity to "demonstrate the possibility of providing a first class medical education, using the Chinese language."[47] To this end, the school benefited from the largess of the Rockefeller Foundation, which made financial contributions from 1916 to 1936. In 1935, an additional grant was obtained from the China Foundation for the Promotion of Education and Culture, which administered the remission of the American portion of the Boxer Indemnity funds. But, unlike other mission medical colleges, the mission of Cheeloo was to serve rural China, as defined in 1928 by the China Christian Educational Association's statement that Cheeloo's programs were "designed particularly to prepare men and women to meet the needs of the rural and town populations through the training of teachers, preachers, doctors, nurses and other social and religious workers."[48] In the medical college, this rural emphasis took the form of pioneering programs that complemented the National Health Administration's work in the mid-1930s.

As early as 1927, the university had founded a Rural Institute at Longshan, a small market town east of Jinan. A rural health program gradually developed, first with a dispensary, then with the introduction of public-health initiatives, popular health education, a midwifery service, well-baby clinics, and a maternal health service. The program received a boost with the appointment of Dr. Gerald F. Winfield, a graduate of the School of Hygiene and Public Health of the Johns Hopkins University, to the Biology Department. Interested in environmental sanitation, Winfield conducted research aimed at the control of fecal-borne diseases with support from the Rockefeller Foundation. His studies resulted in a planned pilot project to compost waste in one of Longshan's villages. Unfortunately, this project never went beyond the preliminary stages as the Japanese invasion put a halt to it. Other components of Cheeloo Medical College's public-health program included school health and maternal and child welfare work in Jinan; rural health internships (one month for fourth-year medical students) at Zouping's rural health center, under the joint auspices of the National Health Administration and Cheeloo; and assistance at the nearby Jinan Leper Hospital. When the North China Council for Rural Reconstruction was launched in 1936, Cheeloo was to be partly responsible for the rural health component. Additional financial support from the Rockefeller Foundation was promised. Shandong's provincial government also granted funds to sixteen counties around the city of Jinan to help develop rural programs and train personnel.[49] Although these plans were aborted by the outbreak of war, the employment record of Cheeloo's medical graduates suggests that they would have been prominent in rural China, unlike their counterparts from St. John's. In 1930, Faber noted that of the 220 doctors graduated since 1915, the positions of 197 of them were known, and of these more than half were working in hospitals or missions in small towns.[50] Cheeloo's medical college constituted the major component of the university, and it produced the largest number of graduates among all the mission medical colleges. By the summer of 1934, 313 doctors had received their degrees from Cheeloo.

With the exception of West China Union University's College of Medicine and Dentistry in Chengdu, all the mission medical institutions were located along the eastern seaboard. The medical college of West China Union was founded in 1914, and the dentistry department, originally part of the medical faculty, in 1917. West China Union had the distinction of having launched the first modern dental school in China, awarding the degree of Doctor of Dental Surgery. The schools of medicine and dentistry were popular divisions within the university, comprising about half of total student enrollment in 1932.[51] The medical program of West China Union followed the 2–4–1 sequence of the other mission colleges. Although its official publications described its basic objective as the training of general practitioners, the college maintained after 1931 a high-quality eye, ear, nose, and throat hospital in the city, which served as the site for the teaching and clinical activities of the Department of Ophthalmology and Otolaryngology. This hospital, the only one of its kind in western China, provided valuable service to the region and helped train much-needed personnel in that specialty.[52]

Another important contribution was West China Union Medical College's involvement in public-health work. Faculty member Dr. Wallace Crawford was loaned to the West China Council on Health Education in 1929 to act as its director. The membership of the council, an organization modelled after the Joint Council on Public Health Education headed by Dr. W. W. Peters in the 1910s, included the medical college and several Christian missions working in western China. The council's activities encompassed popular health education, health campaigns, school health programs in government and mission schools, well-baby clinics, and the training of public-health workers. By 1935–36, with the National Health Administration's expansion of public-health work into Sichuan, Crawford provided valuable service in the planning of the province's health program.[53]

Christian missionaries maintained two women's medical colleges, the Hackett Medical College in Canton and the Women's Christian Medical College in Shanghai. These were the only women's medical colleges existing in China after students from the North China Union Medical College for Women (founded in 1908) were transferred to Cheeloo in 1923. Their assistance in opening the doors of other schools to women, as well as their provision of a new career choice, was immense. Medicine eventually became one of the best paid professions open to women. With the launching of large-scale medical and public-health programs by the government, they were in great demand, all the more so because most Chinese women preferred to consult female physicians. Unfortunately, the number of female medical students remained small, and they generally were drawn from the upper classes.[54] Between 1929 (when registration of physicians became mandatory) and 1937, registered Chinese male doctors outnumbered females by the ratio of 9 to 1 (8,191 to 907).[55]

Christian missionaries were pioneers in the education of Chinese women in medicine. Hackett Medical College traced its beginnings to the efforts of Dr. Mary Fulton, an American Presbyterian missionary, in 1899. After its registration with the Nationalist government in 1932, it adopted the standard six-year curriculum required of all medical colleges, and its students interned at the hundred-bed David Gregg Hospital. It enrolled 56 students in 1935–36. By the end of 1935, it had graduated altogether 240 women doctors, most of them practicing in south China.[56] Financial exigencies and the consolidation of mission activities forced the school to seek affiliation with Lingnan University and to admit men in the fall of 1933. The merger with Lingnan gave the medical school a new lease on life, and (along with the Canton Hospital) it later became part of the Dr. Sun Yat-sen Memorial Medical College of Lingnan. [57] The affiliation also led to the beginnings of a rural health program administered under Lingnan. Hackett Medical College became a cooperating unit of the Guangdong Health Center Association in 1933, and it joined in promoting such public-health activities as maternal and child welfare in nearby villages. The merger also led to the founding of a model rural health service at a branch hospital run by Lingnan, a program that anticipated the National Health Administration's move to expand rural health in Guangdong in 1935. [58]

The Women's Christian Medical College was founded in 1924 when the Methodist Episcopal Church's Women's Medical School of Suzhou moved to Shanghai to join forces with the Margaret Williamson Hospital. It had a seven-year curriculum and used only English as the medium of instruction, in contrast to Hackett Medical, which used both Chinese and English. Its annual tuition of $120 ranked (after St. John's) as the second highest among all the mission medical schools, which may partly explain its rather low enrollment—an average of twenty students per year in 1935–37. [59] Women's Christian Medical cooperated with nearby St. John's in the exchange of faculty, and students from both schools could take certain courses together. Despite financial difficulties, it continued to operate as a small women's medical college with high standards. [60]

Undoubtedly, mission medical colleges helped provide much-needed medical manpower at a time when the Nationalist government was just beginning to address this critical problem. Prior to the end of June 1934, all the Christian medical schools, including those defunct by then, had trained 969 doctors, slightly more than 15 percent of all the physicians trained in China. [61] The combined enrollment of 587 students in mission medical colleges in 1932–33 was slightly more than one-sixth of the total enrollment in all the medical colleges and medical technical schools (including the Japanese-controlled school in Manchuria and the University of Hong Kong). [62] In the 1930s, when the Nationalists began to reorganize the system and bolster enrollment in the burgeoning government institutions, the Christian colleges maintained steady enrollment, to the extent that in 1937 the percentage of medical students among Christian colleges was about the same as the national average of 6.3 percent.[63] What is more important is that conditions in mission medical colleges improved substantially in the 1920s and 1930s and several of them were recognized as high-quality institutions. It is true that by the mid-1930s national schools such as the National Shanghai Medical College and the National Zhongshan Medical College had surpassed some mission schools in the quality and quantity of personnel, equipment, and facilities, yet the mission schools continued to maintain fairly strict admissions and graduation standards, and they still trained their share of physicians for China. Most graduates served in mission hospitals or institutions, but, as devolution continued in Christian enterprises in China, more and more Chinese were assuming positions of authority. In 1930, more than 400 Chinese doctors were serving in mission hospitals compared to about 275 foreign doctors.[43] From 1926 to 1937, West China Union Medical College became increasingly reliant upon its Chinese staff of doctors and nurses in hospital and dispensary work, to the extent that the missionary medical staff was gradually reduced to the level of the early 1910s.[65] At the same time, the mission colleges' role in training pharmacists and nurses, a topic to be discussed below, should not be forgotten.

The major drawback of Christian medical education lay in its emphasis on curative medicine, despite the efforts of Cheeloo and West China Union in public-health education. This reflected the dominance of curative work in missionary medicine as a whole. Admittedly, few medical missions possessed the funds and personnel to emphasize both curative and preventive work. But preventive medicine, which took a long time to make itself felt, also did not contribute as dramatically to the evangelical goals of the missionary movement. Mission doctors employed in hospitals and colleges were recruited more for their curative skills than for their public-health expertise.[66] Also, due to budgetary constraints, the mission colleges generally failed to expand during the 1930s when the health movement was taking shape. While it is true that, as one Canadian missionary lamented, "medical missionaries soon learn that to heal China's sick millions is like trying to empty the Lake of Ontario with a dipper,"[67] it is also true that the relatively small number of mission college graduates proved to be a crucial component in the health-manpower pool during China's reconstruction.

Besides the mission institutions, there were eight private medical schools: in Peiping, PUMC and Sino-French University College of Medicine; in Shanghai, Dongnan Medical College and Tongde Medical College; in Canton, Guanghua Medical College; in Changsha, Xiangya Medical College (formerly Hunan-Yale); in Nantong (Jiangsu), Nantong University College of Medicine; and in Taiyuan (Shanxi), Chuanzhi Medical Technical School. Except for PUMC, which offered an eight-year course, and Chuanzhi, which was a medical technical school with a five-year curriculum, these colleges operated with the standard six-year curriculum. The medium of instruction was predominantly Chinese, although Xiangya used both Chinese and English, and PUMC and Sino-French used English and French, respectively.

All of these schools were expensive to attend, with tuition fees four or five times higher than those charged by the national and provincial medical colleges.[68] Except for PUMC and Xiangya (whose foreign connections and established reputations attracted contributions from government and other sources) and Sino-French (which was supported by the remission of French Boxer Indemnity funds), the private schools depended almost entirely on tuition, revenue from other fees, and local support. Consequently a large student body was essential for a school's survival. Thus, Tongde Medical College enrolled 206 students in 1935, despite the fact that it had only three laboratories, each with the capacity of about 10 students, and fifty beds for teaching purposes. Dongnan Medical College's enrollment in 1932–33 was 437, the largest of all the colleges and schools, but it had only 15 full- and 8 part-time faculty. To put these figures into perspective, in that year, Guanghua Medical College, with 155 students, also had only 7 full- and 11 part-time teachers. At the other end of the spectrum, the faculty of Xiangya Medical College, with only 61 students, consisted of 14 full- and 6 part-time members. And PUMC, with 103 students, had 116 full- and 5 part-time faculty.[69] When Faber visited some of the private colleges in 1930, he described the experience as "depressing." He found hospital facilities in Dongnan and Tongde "so dirty and badly kept that no students should be allowed to visit them." Conditions in Guanghua Medical College were better, but it lacked adequate laboratory facilities and the hospital was "badly run."[70] Conditions in these and other schools did not improve significantly in the 1930s, and the defective facilities and equipment that Faber found so alarming continued to exist despite the elevation of most of them to the status of medical colleges.

Among this group of private institutions, Xiangya (in Changsha) and, of course, PUMC were recognized as excellent schools. Their evolution illustrates how foreign philanthropists and Chinese authorities tried to adjust to the needs of state medicine. Xiangya, founded in 1913 by Dr. Edward H. Hume, a graduate of the Johns Hopkins Medical School, was the result of a cooperative effort between Hunan authorities and the College of Yale-in-China. Provincial authorities provided the site and the building, while Yale-in-China undertook to build and equip a hospital and develop a curriculum. The China Medical Board of the Rockefeller Foundation contributed funds for a science building and support from the British Boxer Indemnity funds led to the construction of an outpatient building in 1926. To further its Sinicization, in 1925 the college was reorganized under a Chinese Board of Trustees. The name was officially changed to Xiangya in both English and Chinese. After the founding of the Nationalist government, the school gradually recovered from a long series of military disruptions and won renewed support from the provincial authorities and Yale-in-China.[71]

Hume was a great advocate of scientific medicine, writing that

It would be a great mistake for medical work to be done on any but the most scientific lines. For us that means the standards of Johns Hopkins! Our medical and educational work must be carried on under the strongest Christian influence and under the highest intellectual and scientific standards of teaching and research.[72]

Under Hume and F. C. Yen, dean of the college, Xiangya emerged as a major medical center in central China, providing some training in preventive work, health education, and sanitation. In the early 1930s, the National Health Administration's plans to introduce state medicine were welcomed by the administration, which stated that the school's "greatest usefulness lies in assisting wholeheartedly the working out of a form of state medicine which shall be efficient and economical."[73] It proclaimed its willingness to modify the curriculum to accommodate the special needs of state medicine in the areas of prevention and sanitation. It would not, however, lessen its emphasis on solid scientific grounding, clinical experience, and medical research—the hallmarks of the Johns Hopkins model, elements deemed essential for a well-trained physician able to pursue postgraduate work and research. Essentially, Xiangya hoped to train sufficient numbers of physicians, researchers, and teachers to populate the burgeoning health services in the cities as well as the countryside.

The problems posed by the time and resources needed to implement such an approach plagued not only Xiangya but also PUMC and the other elite medical colleges, both public and private. All were faced with the government's demands for the rapid training of sizable numbers of doctors to meet the needs of state medicine. PUMC, with its stringent requirements (three years of college work plus five years of medical studies and internship) and its emphasis on teaching laboratories, research, and clinical practice, was reluctant to make significant changes in its training methods, which it feared would lower its standards. In his report, Faber recognized PUMC's contribution to medicine in China and noted that it was uniquely qualified to provide postgraduate training for specialists and teachers. He also suggested, however, that PUMC expand its enrollment to about fifty students per class so as to "double the chances of producing men of ability, qualified to become teachers, research workers and administrators, as well as increasing the number of competently trained teachers."[74]

While accepting the responsibility of providing postgraduate training at PUMC, Roger S. Greene, acting director of the college, was less than enthusiastic about larger classes, arguing that the facilities were equipped to accommodate only classes of thirty. At the beginning of the 1930s, the issue had not become acute, since PUMC was not being pressured by the government to expand its enrollment and the entering classes had not yet reached the maximum number of thirty.[75] But at the crux of the matter two questions remained. What role should PUMC and other private schools played in the government's medical plans? And could the government compel these institutions to do its bidding if they disagreed with the philosophy of the national health programs?

In 1929, PUMC had reorganized its Board of Trustees to include a majority of Chinese, and had named J. Heng Liu director, so as to comply with the government's requirements for registration. Registration was approved in May 1930, after PUMC changed the composition of its board again, installing a two-thirds majority of Chinese in accordance with a new ruling of early 1930.[76] The government could, in theory, revoke PUMC's approval of registration if it failed to conform to Nanjing's policies, though because of PUMC's reputation and influence that was unlikely and would be meaningless in practice. Yet, since the National Health Administration desired greater utilization of PUMC in building a national medical service, should the college be more sensitive to its goals, amending its mission to serve the government's exigent needs? For J. Heng Liu, Robert Lim, John Grant, and many other health planners, the answer was never in doubt.

The controversy over PUMC's mission involved, in fact, a debate over the role of medical schools, and in a broader sense the medical profession, in China's reconstruction. In an exchange of letters between John Grant and Dr. Alan Gregg, director of medical education of the Rockefeller Foundation, in late 1934 and early 1935, this issue was defined clearly. Selskar Gunn's report in early 1934 already had stimulated much discussion of PUMC's future, and Grant was anxious to propose a readjustment of its objectives. After consulting J. Heng Liu, Grant wrote to Gregg in December 1934 posing the question of whether PUMC should be "regarded as an end unto itself" or as "a means towards a national end."[77] There is no doubt where Grant's sympathy lay. As the first steps toward serving the "larger national demand," he suggested that government bodies, including those of the National Health Administration and the Ministry of Education, should have representation on PUMC's Board of Trustees; that salary levels of PUMC faculty and staff be adjusted downward so as to become comparable with national levels; and that language requirements be amended to allow greater usage of the college by graduates of institutions in which English was not the main medium of instruction. The ultimate objective, according to Grant, was to change PUMC into a "'national medical normal' to serve other medical colleges." In other words, PUMC's mission would be to train the teachers for the new medical schools. From the government's point of view, this should be highly desirable, he argued, because it would enable the health and education administrations "to project national plans for training of personnel based upon assurance of a 'normal' institution which is essential as a starting point in any such plan." Liu and Grant believed that the needs of the state should define the objectives of all medical schools, private and government, especially at a time when China was struggling to establish some form of state medicine.

In response, Gregg upheld the primacy of the pursuit of knowledge—in this case, medical and scientific—as a desirable goal that should not be sacrificed for nationalist purposes. "I am anxious," he wrote,

> that purely scientific standards suffer no adaptation to the exigent administration needs such as to dilute the standard. . . . Knowledge is so likely to outlive national ends and is so far more easily defined and so much more consistent than national ends, that the criticism of high standards as not serving national ends can be a boomerang.[78]

The point of reference for Gregg and others like him was the conviction that high professional standards transcend national boundaries. The objective should be to maintain those standards, a course of action, he argued, that ultimately would serve China's national interest.

Gregg's sentiment was shared by Roger Greene. Commenting on Gunn's report in 1934, he expressed skepticism about the utilization of universities to find solutions for China's reconstruction problems. He believed instead that there was "the need for a representation of the real university spirit in which knowledge is sought for its own sake, and through which severe intellectual discipline and habits of hard intellectual work can be developed." He insisted that the low standards universities would have to adopt after a shift to the practical application of medical studies would produce "still other generations of persons almost as incompetent as the leaders of today." He was much more concerned with the "upbuilding of the universities, quite apart from the immediate result to be expected in the form of men technically trained for the types of social activity" that Gunn had in mind.[79] The correct strategy, he argued, would be for PUMC to concentrate on intensive work of high quality to prepare individuals who would be "able to take the field at the right moment."[80] As for the training of teachers, he suggested in a letter to the minister of education in 1935 that National Shanghai Medical College should be asked to develop a center for that purpose.[81]

The controversy remained unresolved, despite the fact that the Rockefeller Foundation had already approved Gunn's North China program of rural reconstruction, and that the groundwork was being laid to redirect at least some of the medical resources at PUMC into social medicine. That would not come until the spring of 1936. But in mid-1935 a serious challenge arose in another quarter when a revitalized Commission on Medical Education tried to force the issue by calling for a complete overhaul of the system of training health personnel. Before addressing that development, it will be necessary to assess the training of physicians in the 1930s.

Medical Education in Nationalist China: An Assessment

It can be seen from the above discussion that, despite government attempts to enforce uniform standards and quality, the training of physicians varied greatly from school to school. The three serious problems common to most of these medical schools were finance, personnel, and facilities. Figures for 1933–34 and 1935–36 show that the annual budgets of the medical colleges and schools ranged from $48,000 to more than $3 million. Some of the university medical faculties lacked independent or fixed sources of funding and had to rely on general budgets. Most of the private schools derived the bulk of their funding from their hospitals and tuition fees.[82] Many colleges and schools also were bereft of high-quality and well-balanced teaching staffs. A study of nineteen medical colleges and schools in 1935 revealed that about half of the teachers were either foreigners or returned students from Japan, the United States, Germany, and so on. Not surprisingly, PUMC had the greatest number of its own graduates working as associates or assistants in the college. But only a few institutions (for example, PUMC and National Shanghai Medical) maintained a full-time faculty adequate to cover all essential courses. The rest depended heavily on part-time staff to teach the clinical subjects. The same study noted the meager teaching facilities in many of these schools, especially in preclinical laboratories. Some schools had to rely on charts and a few models for the teaching of anatomy, no provision being made for dissection on cadavers. The report singled out PUMC and National Zhongshan University as the only two institutions at which there were enough autopsies. Serious inadequacies also were noted in the number of hospital beds available for teaching purposes.[83]

The geographical distribution of the medical colleges and schools left much to be desired. Although they were located in thirteen of the eighteen provinces of China proper, Shanghai claimed seven of these institutions and Peiping and Canton each had two. In terms of the number of physicians trained in modern medicine who were registered with the government, from 1929 to 1937 there was a ten-fold increase (from 918 to 9,098).[84] In a survey of a sample of 5,390 physicians in 1935, 4,638 (87 percent) were Chinese. Of this Chinese group, 3,843 (83 percent) were graduates of medical schools in China.[85] Although the number of physicians graduated from Chinese medical schools was still small compared to the size of the population, it was an important beginning. The picture is not so encouraging, though, if we take into account geographical inequalities in the distribution of these physicians. In the survey of 1935, the two coastal provinces of Jiangsu and Guangdong accounted for about half of the physicians—2,010 (37.3 percent) and 606 (11.2 percent), respectively—while the percentages for interior provinces such as Hunan and Sichuan were 1 percent (56 doctors) and 1.3 percent (71 doctors), respectively. The population-per-physician ratios for the individual provinces computed from these figures are revealing. There was one physician for every 16,978 people in Jiangsu, but one for every 760,710 in Sichuan and one for every 562,522 in Hunan. Jiangsu's ratio compared favorably with the ratio of one to 81,976 recorded for the whole country.[86]

The results of the 1935 survey confirmed those of similar studies undertaken in 1932 and 1933, both of which showed the highest concentration of modern physicians to be in the provinces of Jiangsu, Guangdong, Hebei, Zhejiang, and Shandong.[87] Part of the explanation of this uneven distribution lies in the fact these provinces had the largest concentration of big cities, the political, commercial, and educational centers where medical schools and hospitals were located. Physicians congregated in such large metropolitan centers as Shanghai, Canton, Nanjing, and Peiping. In the 1935 survey, the greatest concentrations were in Shanghai, claiming 1,182, or 22 percent, of the 5,390 physicians studied; Canton, with 5.6 percent; and Nanjing, with 5.1 percent. The trend of a concentration of physicians in a small number of prosperous urban centers, even in the interior, also was evident. There were gross inequities within the cities as well. In Shanghai most doctors resided in the International Settlement and the French Concession, and very few practiced in the Chinese districts of Greater Shanghai.[88]

The tendency of physicians to cluster in the cities resulted largely from the fact that the demand for doctors was highest in those localities where modern medicine had established itself and where a larger proportion of the population could afford to pay. Hospitals, modern medical equipment, and personnel were readily available.

Metropolitan centers also provided contact with other physicians through social interactions and professional meetings. Social and cultural amenities must have been additional attractions not found in the countryside or the small towns. But in cities like Shanghai and Canton, where the concentration of physicians was greatest, competition also became fierce. Some doctors were extremely popular while others had a hard time making a living. Many resorted to questionable practices, for example, substituting common vitamin injections for other medications. It must be remembered also that in these cities trained physicians had to compete with many unqualified doctors who, because of lax government enforcement, maintained lucrative practices.[89]

The urban concentration of medical graduates reflects the fact that in China medicine was predominantly a private and individualistic profession. The training received in the medical colleges helped to shape the graduates' responses to the demands of state medicine. Curricula in the medical colleges generally aspired to follow that of PUMC, with its array of scientific subjects, although PUMC actually devoted more hours (even though they constituted a small part of the curriculum) to public-health work than did the others.[90] The efforts of John Grant and J. Heng Liu also did much to publicize the importance of public-health training. The Commission on Medical Education's revised curriculum for medical colleges, promulgated in 1935, essentially adopted the old division of subjects and the number of hours required for graduation. It continued to allot only a small portion of time for public health—3.7 percent of the total instructional hours. The percentage of public-health work in the prescribed curriculum for medical technical schools was only 4.2.[91] By 1937, most of the better schools had yet to adjust their curricula to focus on social medicine, public-health administration, epidemiology, and other kinds of courses relevant to China's needs.[92]

It is true that there was a sizable contingent of trained physicians who assumed positions in the expanding government health administrations in central or provincial political centers such as Nanjing, Peiping, and Canton. The prospect of secure government employment was a key motivation among many PUMC students who decided to specialize in public health. The public-health department, in fact, attracted the second largest number of graduates between 1924 and 1933.[93] Yet, except for a very few, the physicians in government service stayed in the cities. Other physicians became teachers and administrators in medical colleges, while many from the mission schools served in mission hospitals and institutions. But the inability of the health planners to adjust the medical curriculum to emphasize the needs of state medicine, and the slowness of the development of the public-health sector combined to make private practice an attractive choice. It has been noted that "as long as medical care was mainly for those who could pay sufficient fees to make medical practice lucrative, there were strong economic incentives to maintain private practice."[94] Ironically, it was the war that finally effected basic changes in the role of medical graduates in public service. After 1940, the government conscripted all new graduates of registered medical colleges for war service: 40 percent in the army, 30 percent in the state health services, 15 percent in the medical colleges, and 15 percent in the Red Cross.[95]

The Training of Other Health Personnel

In its plans for manpower development, Chinese health planners expended much time and effort on the training of physicians, while failing to pay enough attention to the need for pharmacists and dentists. Practitioners of indigenous medicine usually tended to the task of dispensing herbs and other medications, often with the help of apprentices. The function of modern pharmacists were generally dismissed by the public, and even by many in the medical profession, as "counting pills and pouring medicinal liquid," tasks that allegedly could be performed by nurses.[96] As a result, dispensers were trained in hospitals or through private short-term courses organized for that purpose. One of the better known schools for dispensers was the Peiping Municipal Health Bureau's Pharmacy Training Institute. Originally founded in 1929 as a private, evening, vocational school, it offered a one-year course that later was extended to two years. The Central Field Health Station also established short-term pharmacy training institutes to meet an increasing demand.[97] The number of registered dispensers rose steadily, from 839 in 1934, to 1,434 in 1935, and 2,279 in 1937.[98] College-level training of pharmacists, however, lagged behind.

The first modern pharmacy department in China was established in 1913 at the Zhejiang Medical Technical School (later the name was changed to the Zhejiang Provincial Medical and Pharmaceutical Technical School). From 1913 to 1941, this department trained 307 pharmacists, many of whom became prominent in medical circles during the Republican period.[99] Another two-year pharmacy course was offered by the pharmacy department of Cheeloo University, which founded it in 1920 as a small training program for the staff of its own and other hospitals. In 1931, it upgraded its admission requirements, accepting only graduates of senior middle schools and establishing a department of pharmacy in the medical college. The course of study lasted two years, and, because of its limited facilities, the department admitted students only every other year. The outbreak of war and Cheeloo's move to Chengdu in 1939 led to the closing of the department. By that time, 80 pharmacists, 14 of them women, had graduated from it.[100]

One pharmacy school and one university pharmacy department offered four-year courses of study: the pharmacy school of Sino-French University in Shanghai and the department of pharmacy of West China Union University. The former, established in 1929, was selective. The student body remained small, with only about twenty graduates per year. Almost all of these stayed in Shanghai, working in the many drug stores and pharmaceutical companies, or opening their own pharmacies.[101] The pharmacy department of West China Union was established in 1932 in the College of Natural Sciences. As in the case of Cheeloo, it originated as a small program supporting the work of the hospital; later it was reorganized into a full-fledged department. Enrollment was low, however, and it trained only about two hundred pharmacists from 1932 to 1949. Unlike the graduates of Sino-French University, most of West China Union's students served in hospitals and pharmacies in the interior.[102]

It is obvious that the pharmacist was not recognized as an important agent in the medical profession by either the public or the government. Not until after the Commission on Medical Education's report on health-manpower training was released in July 1935 did the government belatedly attempt to remedy the situation by establishing two pharmacy schools (in 1936). Both offered four-year courses of study, including one year of practical training in a hospital pharmacy. The National School of Pharmacy in Nanjing, opened in September, was administered directly by the Ministry of Education, which, however, failed to provide adequate facilities and teaching personnel. It managed to complete its first year before the war compelled it to move inland. Another new institution was the School of Pharmacy of the National Shanghai Medical College. When the war disrupted its operation, too, the pharmacy students first attended classes at the Sino-French Pharmacy School, and then relocated to Chongqing.[103] By the end of 1937, there were fewer than six hundred registered pharmacists in China and most of these were in urban locations.[104]

Dentistry suffered similar neglect in the prewar period. Apart from one small private school with a three-year course of study, which opened in Shanghai in 1930, the only college- level training available prior to 1936 was offered by the dental school of Aurora University, which had a four-year course, and West China Union College, which had a seven-year curriculum, including one year of internship. In fact, the excellent reputation of its dentistry school helped West China Union gain its niche among mission medical colleges. The Nationalist government, recognizing the school's contribution, provided a $7,000 grant for the purchase of dental equipment in 1934. Students, including graduates of PUMC, came from all over China as well as from other Asian countries. Enrollment averaged about thirty per year in the 1930s. In 1930, it had thirty-six students, six of them women, and in 1935 there were thirty-three men and eight women.[105] In the reorganization of health-manpower training institutions after 1935, the National Health Administration established a school of dentistry at the National Central University at Nanjing. Like other college-level institutions, it admitted only graduates of senior middle schools and offered a four-year course of study, including one year of internship.[106] For some unknown reason, dentists were not required to register with the government until 1936. Published figures at that time listed 119 registered dentists. The number increased to 258 in 1937.[107] Since essentially there were only two dental colleges, most of these must have been trained through apprenticeship in private offices. At the same time, quacks who claimed to be able to extract teeth or treat every conceivable oral problem also peddled their skills, especially in the countryside.

Nurses, Midwives, and Auxiliary Health Personnel

In the absence of a large number of physicians and other trained personnel, nurses and midwives served a most important function in health conservation and in the fight against disease. They provided primary care and, especially in rural China, often had to perform medical and surgical procedures on their own. As already noted, for a long time most nurses were trained in hospitals and did not receive the recognition they deserved. A first step toward gaining recognition of nursing as a profession was taken in 1909 when several practitioners founded the Nurses' Association of China. Several years later the association began to certify nursing schools.[108] Until the Nationalists took power, and attempts to develop central control of nursing began, the association played an important supervisory role, through the registration of approved schools, thereby helping to maintain certain standards in nursing education. When the Commission on Medical Education was established in 1929, a Committee on Nursing Education and a Committee on Midwifery Education were created to develop training guidelines.[109] But the association retained its unofficial regulatory function by administering certifying examinations to nursing graduates. The status of the association received a boost when its headquarters was moved to an office in the Ministry of Health, in February 1930, at the invitation of J. Heng Liu.[110]

The government was slow to establish uniform training and licensing procedures, however. The 1929 plan of the Ministry of Health for personnel training addressed public-health nurse and midwifery education but it did not mention registered nurses. The uncoordinated proliferation of training programs offered by private schools and government agencies created different categories of personnel performing nursing functions.[111] Not until 1932 did the National Health Administration found the Central School of Nursing in the Central Hospital in Nanjing, offering a three-year course that included public-health and midwifery training. And this school had only ninety-one students at the end of 1934.[112]

Most nurses were supplied by the numerous nursing schools located throughout the country, each with its own requirements and standards. In 1933–34, seventeen of these schools were affiliated with medical colleges and medical technical schools, twelve of them private. Shanghai had four of these schools while Canton and Peiping had two each. Their curricula ranged from two to five years, and admissions requirements varied greatly. Four admitted graduates of primary schools, ten accepted graduates of junior middle schools, and two required graduation from a senior middle school. Only one— PUMC—required two years of college. In 1933–34, these schools enrolled a total of 567 students.[113] Nursing programs below the technical-school level included about two hundred private or provincial centers, mostly affiliated with hospitals. According to data collected by the Nurses' Association of China, the number of graduates from nursing schools who had passed the certifying examination rose from 251 in 1928 to 560 in 1934. The total number of qualified nurses certified by the association was 4,143 by 1934.[114]

In an attempt to assume regulatory control over nursing educa-tion, the National Health Administration and the Ministry of Edu-cation set up a joint Commission on Nursing Education in 1934 to prepare regulations for the registration of nursing schools and their students. The new regulations, promulgated in early 1935, mandated that, to be eligible for registration, schools must admit only junior-middle-school graduates and offer a three-year course of study, in-cluding one year of public-health and practical hospital work. All schools were to be registered by June 1936.[115] Although in 1936 only 575 nurses had registered with the government, the number soared to 4,540 (949 of them men) the following year.[116]

Despite government attempts to upgrade standards and enforce compliance with the new regulations, conditions in many of the nursing schools remained unsatisfactory. After inspecting sixty-six nursing schools in 1935, the Commission on Medical Education deplored the huge gap between existing conditions and the new standards. Most serious was the lack of autonomy—financial and administrative—on the part of the schools. Since most were controlled by hospitals, students were "utilized in the hospitals without due consideration of the teaching responsibilities of the schools." Doctors and head nurses in the hospitals acted as instructors, and the curricula were designed to suit their needs and convenience. Many school adminis-trators frankly admitted that compliance with the new regulations would force them to close the schools altogether.[117]

The supply of registered nurses failed to keep up with the increase in registered physicians. In both 1936 and 1937, registered physicians outnumbered registered nurses by a ratio of two to one.[118] While a number of nurses might have been awaiting registration, clearly a way had to be found to increase the supply. Moreover, since most qualified nurses were employed in hospitals located in cities or in smaller urban centers, large parts of rural China were still bereft of the basic health care that nurses could provide.

Professional midwives, too, were important in the health-care system. Despite initial opposition by the Nurses' Association of China, which claimed midwifery to be within its proper domain, modern midwives gradually won professional recognition in the 1930s owing largely to the efforts of Dr. Marion Yang. It may be recalled that in

1929 the Ministry of Health established a National Midwifery Board to plan the development of midwifery education, and that the former Peking Midwifery School was reorganized as the First National Midwifery School. The school offered four types of study. The first was a two-year course, open to senior-middle-school graduates, for the training of "quality type" midwives. These would become teachers and supervisors, and would staff the urban and rural maternal and child-health services. The second course was a six-month supplementary training program for new graduates of provincial midwifery schools. The third was a six-month course in maternal and child health for graduate nurses, and the fourth was a regular six-month course designed to meet immediate needs by increasing the quantity of trained midwives. In 1935, these four courses graduated a total of 115 midwives, most of whom returned to their original places of employment.[119] The First National Midwifery School also trained traditional midwives in maternal and child health in Peiping and in a nearby rural health center. These courses, lasting from two weeks to two months, were designed to teach the "aseptic technique of delivery" so as to reduce the incidence of tetanus neonatorum and puerperal infection.[120]

To augment the supply of trained midwives, the Central Midwifery School, affiliated with the Central Hospital in Nanjing, was opened in 1933. It also offered a two-year course, including maternal and child care and practical training. Forty-one students were enrolled in 1934.[121] The College of Medicine of National Peiping University also operated a midwifery training institute. Apart from these, and ten other training schools administered by the provincial governments, the fifty-two midwifery schools operating in 1934 were private.[122] The registration of midwifery schools had begun in 1932, and some consolidation had been taking place. In 1935, there were thirty-eight midwifery schools, including two national and nine provincial institutions. Many of these suffered from inadequate funding and lacked proper facilities for laboratory and practical work. A survey of seventeen of these schools conducted in 1936 shows that most offered a three-year course for junior-middle-school graduates, and that they had trained 4,189 midwives by the end of the year.[123] Apparently not all midwifery-school graduates sought, or met, the criteria for registration, for government figures show only 3,174 registered midwives in 1936 and 3,694 in 1937.

A breakdown of the ages of the registered midwives in 1937 provides a significant clue to the gradual expansion of modern midwifery in China. Of the 3,694 midwives registered that year, 2,347 (64 percent) were between twenty and twenty-nine years of age, 1,058 (29 percent) were between thirty and thirty-nine, while the remaining 7 percent were above forty years of age.[124] Obviously a younger generation of midwives was being trained. Along with the retrained traditional midwives, they hopefully could begin to reverse the high rate of infant mortality caused by unsanitary practices during childbirth. But the family backgrounds of the new midwives suggests that—as in the case of women who sought modern maternal care and deliveries—most came from the middle and upper classes. An analysis of student data from the Provincial Midwifery School in Nanchang, Jiangxi, in 1931–34 reveals that the largest number of students (36.4 percent) belonged to doctors' families. Family backgrounds also included business (26.8 percent) and education (22 percent). Students from peasant families accounted for only 4.7 percent. The same study also shows that, of the sixty-two graduates whose subsequent careers were known, only one-third were working at the *xian* level. The rest were either in private practice or employed in provincial or municipal institutions.[125]

The National Health Administration and the Central Field Health Station also were assisting the provinces of Shaanxi, Jiangxi, Gansu, and Fujian to establish their own midwifery schools. The curricula would include short-term courses for traditional midwives. These courses, usually lasting for two months, also were offered in rural health centers in various parts of the country, including Tangshan, Gaoqiao, and Dingxian.[126] But, as we have seen, the retraining of traditional midwives proved to be more difficult than expected. C. C. Chen's frustration was noted in the discussion of maternal and child care in Dingxian. Li Tingan, another specialist in rural health, lamented that because of their lack of education many older midwives failed to grasp the basic concepts of modern medicine, reverting to traditional methods soon after graduating from the course. Sometimes visual reminders were used to ensure that correct procedures were followed in delivery. For example, midwives were told to put two drops of medicine from a bottle with a red label (containing silver nitrate) into the eyes of newborns to prevent blindness.[127] Still, whatever their limitations, retrained midwives provided a vital service to rural families when modern health personnel were not available.

The Training of Public-Health Personnel

While China needed a large number of physicians, nurses, midwives, and other health workers, it also required personnel with training in such public-health fields as preventive and social medicine, public-health administration, health education, sanitation, and epidemiology. Since the existing medical and nursing schools had not yet reorganized their curricula to place emphasis on such endeavors, J. Heng Liu and other health planners relied on the Central Field Health Station and some of the existing educational institutions to provide training, often in the form of special courses, in public health. These courses were designed to accomplish three things: to compensate for inadequacies in undergraduate training; to train auxiliary personnel such as school health workers and sanitary inspectors; and to provide advanced training for local administrators.[128]

The Central Field Health Station offered many such courses, including a six-month public-health-officer training course for interested physicians; a six-month public-health-nursing course for graduates certified by the Nurses' Association of China; a six-month course for sanitary inspectors open to junior-middle-school graduates; and short courses on public health for schoolteachers. By the end of 1935, graduates of these four types of courses numbered 61, 65, 118, and 119, respectively. All of them quickly found positions at various levels in the health services.[129] In addition to these courses, the Central Field Health Station cooperated with the National Central University to train specialists in health education. A two-year, college-level course of study in health education was introduced in 1931. The following year it was expanded into a full-fledged Department of Health Education, in the College of Education, with half of the four-year curriculum devoted to medical and public-health subjects. Together with the Central Hospital, the station also initiated a two-year hospital internship for medical graduates of different schools wishing to acquire practical training in public health.[130] These were viewed as temporary measures, however. The health planners' ultimate objective was to create a National Public Health Personnel Training Institute, which was not opened until 1936 in Nanjing. In addition to developing its training courses, the institute coordinated the various training programs in the country. When the war broke out, it moved to Changsha, then to Guiyang in 1938. From 1936 to 1943, 1,302 graduates received training in the institute.[131]

These activities contributed significantly to an increase in the small contingent of health workers vital to China's health reconstruction. Yet the policies adopted by Chinese planners before 1936 in fact had created a manpower hourglass. The intention of the planners had been to tackle the problem of health manpower at both the top and the bottom, in the hope of producing well-trained professionals at the top while expanding the number of auxiliaries at the bottom. But, with the expansion of the top medical colleges and the sluggish pace at which medical technical schools were being developed, the number of top-level professionals increased while the number of auxilaries did not. The prestige and power of modern medicine continued to attract China's elite. But the situation at the bottom of the health-manpower ladder was not what the health planners had envisioned. China already had large numbers of practitioners of indigenous medicine and traditional midwives who were excluded from the modern health system. In the absence of modern auxiliaries, these practitioners continued to provide medical care to most of the population. They actually constituted the bulge at the bottom of the manpower pool. The graduates of the medical technical schools and the small number of modern auxiliaries (nurses, midwives, and technical assistants) now formed a comparatively small group in the middle. In 1936, there were 8,822 registered doctors, 3,749 registered nurses and midwives, and more than a million indigenous doctors and traditional midwives.[132] The limited number of formally trained health specialists had to function as leaders and administrators. The inadequate supply of modern auxiliaries meant that modern medicine's inroads into large areas of the country were made in the main by minimally trained, local personnel.

A New Approach to Health-Manpower Training

It was recognition of this gap between the objectives of the health planners and the actual conditions in China that led to a reevaluation of health policies in late 1935 by the Commission on Medical Education. The commission, established in 1929, was reorganized in July 1935 with financial support from the Rockefeller Foundation, which at that time was readjusting its own educational policies in China. The foundation was launching at that moment its own North China Program aimed at aiding rural reconstruction through grants to the Mass Education Movement, the University of Nanjing, and

Nankai's Institute of Economics. Grants to the Commission on Medical Education were part of this movement to evaluate the future direction of China's development. Less than a year later, the North China Council for Rural Reconstruction was organized. PUMC, one of the members of the council, was made responsible for training students in social medicine. The commission's reorganization, and its attempt to reshape medical education, therefore came at a critical juncture in China's reconstruction.

The commission, with Dr. C. K. Chu as its general secretary, included representatives from the Ministry of Education and the National Health Administration. Many members, such as F. C. Yen, P. Z. King, Robert Lim, and Marion Yang, were long-time proponents of state medicine. The commission now assumed control over medical, nursing, and midwifery education, as well as health education in the primary and middle schools. It had both coordinating and executive functions in matters of medical and health education. The thrust of the first two years of the commission's new work would be to investigate and plan the improvement of the existing health-manpower training system. The third year would be devoted to effecting the actual changes.[133] Its report, issued at the end of the first year, was a bold blueprint of a new approach to the training of health personnel in China.

The commission rejected the existing system outright, judging it incapable of producing adequate medical and public-health personnel, both in quality and quantity, to meet the needs of state medicine. Instead a new system, "adjusted according to local demands in medical fields as well as according to social and economic conditions," would be established. Unlike the old system, which functioned "only for the acquisition of knowledge and not for the systematic and effective application of that knowledge," the new structure would employ the available knowledge of scientific medicine for the fullest benefit of the people. To that end, medical education must be firmly based on cooperation with organized local communities, and it must be sensitive to community needs. Drawing upon the experience of Dingxian, the authors of the report considered education of the lay public as the key factor in the new system since most of the rural medical relief that could be provided under existing economic constraints did not require the services of specialized professionals. Popular medical training and local personnel would assume much of the responsibility for health protection while higher-level professionals would attend to cases requiring specialized knowledge. This approach, according to the commission, "recognized on one hand the need of the community and on the other the limited availability of highly trained medical workers."[134]

The proposed system of training had five tiers. The lowest two levels concerned the training of the public and "village health aides." The third involved the training of intermediate professional personnel such as nurses, midwives, dentists, dispensers, and sanitary inspectors. The fourth level concerned the training of the higher-level professional personnel: physicians, pharmacists, and oral surgeons. The top level was reserved for the postgraduate training of teachers and researchers as well as specialists in public health. The first and most important level was considered to be the training of laymen through popular education aimed at imparting basic medical and public-health knowledge. Thus, every person would be able to practice personal hygiene and health protection in the community. Such education would eventually be incorporated into the schools. In the meantime, special classes conducted by nurses would be organized by the public-health services. In short, everyone would learn to "share the responsibility of protecting their own health and that of their neighbors."[135]

In rural areas, the commission recommended the systematic training of village health aides based on the model of the village health workers in Dingxian. The workers, to be recruited locally from the primary schools or adult-education classes, would be trained for no more than two years in first-aid, the treatment of simple wounds and skin diseases, the giving of vaccinations, and the recording of births and deaths. They would work in health substations under the supervision of nurses. As paramedics trained to meet the needs of the countryside they would prove to be the most valuable health workers in China. Familiar with, and responsible for the people of their own villages, the health aides would provide dependable service in the rural health program.

Moving up the health-manpower ladder, the commission recognized that intermediate health personnel would function as "interpreters" between the people and the physicians, performing the duties for which they had been trained and referring to higher professionals matters that were beyond their technical competence. Since they would be close to the people, they would understand the needs of a community, and they would respond accordingly to provide appropriate support. This was the group the health planners originally had hoped to produce in large enough numbers to replace the traditional healers. In the new scheme, the village health workers would become, to a significant extent, the huge contingent of primary-care providers positioned below intermediate personnel. They would replace, it was hoped, the traditional healers while allowing time for the intermediate group to grow. The commission recommended consolidation of the educational institutions that trained the different types of intermediate personnel. All would now receive their training in the "Medical Vocational School," or the "Medical Vocational Faculty," of a medical college. After a uniform period of initial training, the students would receive technical training and acquire practical experience in separate fields that would emphasize actual conditions. In the cases of nurses and midwives, the focus would be on the needs of the countryside. The commission did not propose to change the requirements of nursing, midwifery, or dental education, but it indicated that a two-year course following junior middle school would provide sufficient training for dispensers and sanitary inspectors.

The commission created the most controversy with a proposal to abandon the two-track system in the training of physicians in favor of the already approved six-year curriculum, including one year of internship. In doing this it not only reversed its own position but it rejected Faber's endorsement of the double standard. The failure of the two-track system over the past five years, as well as the desire to expand the pool of reasonably well-trained personnel without creating an elite corps of experts who would "monopolize" the privileges of scientific medicine, led to the decision to consolidate.[136] In their new training physicians would learn the value of community service and would come to appreciate the role of organized community effort in medicine, things that had been neglected in conventional medical education. Preventive medicine and public-health work would be emphasized in the new curriculum, which also would include subjects dealing with social reconstruction. Finally, the new system would provide for postgraduate research in various medical fields, including that of public health. The commission warned that only one or two postgraduate institutions might be necessary, since the highest-priority needs were at the more basic levels of medical care. It also identified the national government as the agency responsible for the training of postgraduate and higher professional personnel. The provinces would be responsible for the training of intermediate workers and village health aides, and the local jurisdictions would provide popular medical education to the people.

It is obvious that the commission's report incorporated C. C. Chen's concepts of lay participation and the utilization of local resources in the health-care system. The new system now hoped to train medical personnel appropriate to China's needs within the limits of available resources. In particular, the plan recognized that new types of health workers were needed, especially in the countryside. C. C. Chen had long criticized the medical profession for ignoring the basic health needs of the common people, charging that the medical colleges were producing physicians so "highly technical and specialized that their training cannot be considered as giving the essential minimum for 'a practitioner of general medicine in terms of public health.'"[137] Doctors trained under systems borrowed from the United States or Germany were divorced from China's reality, he argued. There were fourth-year medical students who could not diagnose such common diseases as trachoma, or vaccinate a patient against smallpox, "much less improve sanitary conditions in any locality."[138] In Dingxian, Chen had organized the village health workers, utilized primary-school teachers, and assembled health teams, producing a contingent of workers that took over the functions for which trained public-health personnel should have been responsible.

These were not the only possibilities in the development of new types of health-care personnel. Since 1925, the Peking First Health Station had been implementing a program of home visits by "public health visitors"—women who went from door to door to acquaint the community with hygiene and public health including maternal and child care.[139] The Nanjing municipal health bureau initiated the training of "baby carers" in June 1934 to care for babies in the city's orphanages.[140] The aim was to coordinate and develop such programs systematically so that other localities could benefit from the experience gained in these innovative efforts. Certainly, the commission's new plan did not totally abandon the Johns Hopkins model of training high-powered teachers and researchers, but planners recognized the difficulty of trying to reconcile the Johns Hopkins approach with the health-manpower needs of state medicine, and they had chosen to allocate resources to the training of intermediate and basic personnel. No mention was made of the utilization of traditional physicians whose functions were supposed to be supplanted by village health aides and the educated layman. But as long as the number of modern, basic personnel remained small the contribution of traditional healers could not be ignored or dismissed as irrelevant.

Implementing the New Plan

To gain support for the changes outlined in the report, the commission convened a conference of directors of medical colleges and technical schools in April 1936 at which the various issues of consolidation of teaching institutions, standardization of curricula, and the establishment of public-health teaching facilities were discussed. While no immediate action on consolidation was taken, the participants urged the government to move quickly to implement one of the original objectives of the Three Year Plan announced in 1931—the establishment of an experimental medical college designed specifically to train personnel for state medicine.[141] The National Zhongzheng Medical College (*Zhongzheng yixue yuan*) opened in 1937 in Nanchang, Jiangxi, only to be forced to relocate to the town of Yongxin in the southern part of the province after the war broke out. In 1938, it enrolled sixty-two students.[142]

The conference also endorsed the idea of establishing a Postgraduate Medical Institute, with departments of preclinical, clinical, and public health, to train teachers. In the meantime, the commission provided ten two-year fellowships to medical graduates to enable them to acquire additional training in such cooperating medical colleges as PUMC, National Shanghai Medical College, and National Zhongshan Medical College. Grants were given to the Central School of Nursing to support teacher-training courses, and, through the commission, the Rockefeller Foundation subsidized the training of thirteen public-health nurses at PUMC. Moreover, in the first year following its reorganization, the commission began preparing standard medical textbooks and laboratory manuals to be used in medical colleges and nursing schools.[143]

Many of the activities of the second year of the new educational plan involved continuation of the work initiated during the first. More fellowships were awarded for teacher training in special subjects and in nursing, while the commission, armed with more data on existing personnel, also proposed creation of an information bureau to monitor the supply of and demand for medical and health manpower. The most ambitious project undertaken during 1936–37 was the planning of a nationwide consolidation of existing medical, nursing, and midwifery schools on a geographical basis. The aim was to redress the maldistribution of medical institutions through the division of the country into five regions, each of which would have a "center" medical college responsible for coordinating medical education. It was hoped that this new arrangement would eliminate rivalry among schools and help standardize medical education nationwide. Nothing came out of this proposal, as war clouds began to gather in the summer of 1937.[144] By the time the Sino-Japanese War broke out in July 1937, however, some of the commission's programs had borne fruit. Several fellowship recipients were ready to return to their institutions to take up teaching positions while a number of medical textbooks were about to be published. The war not only disrupted these activities but it forced many medical schools to evacuate the war zones or Japanese-occupied areas. A number of schools, including the National Tongji Medical College and the Nantong Medical College, were destroyed. The commission suspended most of its regular functions in order to attend to emergency activities such as organizing medical corps in the medical, nursing, and midwifery schools. Its headquarters were first moved from Nanjing to Hankou, then to Changsha, and finally to Chongqing.[145] Although some consolidation occurred as a result of the relocation of many medical colleges and schools, the commission's blueprint for the reorganization of medical education in China was put on hold and faced an uncertain future.

7

Health Care in the Nationalist Decade: The Past as Prologue

The outbreak of the Sino-Japanese War in July 1937 marked the end of a chapter in the Nationalist attempt to develop a modern health-care system, which, according to its planners, would be based on scientific principles and would bring "happiness and prosperity" to the maximum number of people by improving their "mental and physical vigor."[1] This grand objective had not been realized by 1937, although the Nanjing regime had taken important and necessary steps in that direction. The war, while seriously disrupting or causing the abandonment of many of the programs introduced in the Nationalist decade, did not halt development of a national health service in unoccupied China. The exigencies of the war and massive social and economic dislocation certainly made the effort much more difficult, but the outlines of the prewar scheme remained unchanged. State medicine was still the official policy of the National Health Administration, although the Japanese occupation of most of the eastern seaboard and lower Huanghe and Yangzi provinces caused the government to shift its focus to the interior, especially to the southwestern provinces where many of the medical schools had relocated. The backwardness and poverty of much of the less-developed interior, the inflation and high cost of drugs, and the often makeshift circumstances under which health personnel had to operate created enormous hardships. As Sze Szeming of the Chinese Medical Association put it, people lived "very close to the good earth."[2]

The War Years

The war necessitated some changes in the health administration. At first, the National Military Council tried to centralize all health services by placing the National Health Administration and the Army Medical Administration under its control. But in early 1938 the National Health Administration was returned to the Ministry of the Interior with F. C. Yen as director general and P. Z. King as vice-director. Yen's appointment apparently resulted in part from lobbying by several close associates of J. Heng Liu who wanted to ensure that Liu's policies would be continued.[3] Yen stayed until April 1940 when P. Z. King, who had also served in the Central Field Health Station under Liu, took over as director general.[4] In 1941, King oversaw the merging of the Central Field Health Station and the National Public Health Personnel Training Institute to create the National Institute of Health (*Zhongyang weisheng shiyanyuan*), which combined the functions of research and field demonstrations with the training of senior public-health personnel.[5] The Central Hospital was relocated in Guiyang but the health administration opened another branch of the hospital in Chongqing in 1942. Since Gansu and the northwest emerged as a strategic region during the war, the government established the Xibei Hospital (Northwest Hospital) in Lanzhou in 1941 to act as the center of medical and health activities there.[6]

The structure of the state health system that the Nationalists tried to establish continued to be based on the prewar system: provincial and municipal health departments, *xian* health centers with hospitals, *qu* health stations, *xiang* health substations, and *bao* health workers. Not surprisingly, Gansu, Guizhou, Yunnan, and Sichuan witnessed the greatest growth in the number of health centers in 1937–41. The number of centers in Yunnan soared from 3 in 1937 to 77 in 1941, while Guizhou, literally starting from scratch in 1937, emerged with 76 centers by 1941. Official figures claimed that in 1941 there were 751 *xian* health centers in the country.[7] While this number may be an exaggeration, the important point is that, despite the disruptions of war, health work did continue.

With the quality and quantity of health services suffering as a result of the diversion of resources to war-affected areas, the training of medical and health personnel became particularly urgent. With the National Institute of Health taking over the training of senior health officers, two regional institutes (at Guiyang and Lanzhou) now trained junior personnel, including public-health nurses, midwives, sanitary inspectors, and technicians. As for the medical colleges and schools, the shortage of funds, personnel, equipment, and facilities led to a process of consolidation and merger. The Commission of Medical Education designated Kunming, Chengdu, Guiyang, and Chongqing as centers in which a number of schools would be combined into regional medical colleges. In Chengdu, the West China Union University Medical School joined forces with the newcomers, the medical schools of the National Central University and of Cheeloo University. In Guiyang, a new National Guiyang Medical College was merged with Xiangya Medical College, the Public Health Personnel Training Institute, the Central Nursing School, and the Central Hospital. The center at Kunming consisted of the National Tongji Medical College, the National Shanghai Medical College, National Zhongshan Medical College, National Zhongzheng Medical College, and the newly established Yunnan University Medical School. Yet, only the latter institution was left when Japanese bombing in 1940 forced the rest of the group to relocate again to Chongqing or other sites in Guizhou. Chongqing's group originally included only the Central Midwifery School, the National School of Pharmacy, and Jiangsu Medical College.[8] The Nationalist government tried to provide nearly free education—nominal tuition, low dormitory fees, and some subsidies. But the student attrition rate was high: 50 to 75 percent of an entering class might transfer to some other discipline.[9] Undoubtedly the uncertainly created by the war led to indecision on the part of many students. After the war, another migration took place when medical schools returned to their original locations. But much of the medical and health infrastructure created during the war years in the southwestern and northwestern provinces was retained by the provinces. The rebuilding process began in the areas vacated by the Japanese, and with American aid Nationalist health planners once again hoped to continue their efforts to establish a system of state medicine. Civil war intervened, however, and the Communist victory in 1949 marked the end of the Nationalist attempt to foster medical modernization, at least on the mainland.

The Nationalist Effort in Health: An Assessment

In trying to evaluate the Nationalist effort to build a modern healthcare system during 1928–37, it is important to review the intentions of the Nationalist leadership and the nature of the programs and methods that the health planners employed. The recognized goal was that state medicine should be introduced as quickly as possible so that modern health care could be made available to the population as a whole. But, since medical and public-health reforms were to be part of the program of national reconstruction, the objective of state medicine conformed with the avowed goals of that reconstruction—national strengthening and modernization. Unlike many other modernizing countries, which failed to incorporate health as an integral part of development, the Nationalist leadership perceived health to be part of the nation-building process. For most, the construction of a modern health-care system was not an end in itself but a means to the acquisition of power and economic prosperity. Nationalism and the social Darwinian interpretation of international relations shaped their approach. National reconstruction required a physically strong population capable of defending the motherland as well as engaging in the production processes vital to China's economic rejuvenation. Individual health concerns therefore should be subordinated to the national priorities of state building, military might, and economic development. Health planners such as J. Heng Liu certainly stressed the humanitarian side of health development, and he did not agree with the way the system had been overwhelmed by other demands of the state, but he and most of his colleagues shared a belief in the need for a politically and economically strong China. In their writings and public pronouncements they tended to reinforce the theme that the mission of modern medicine was to serve the country by protecting and improving people's health.[10]

This nationalistic bias left the health sector vulnerable, and often powerless, as it had to compete for adequate support from the central government. Politically, state building was viewed by Chiang Kai-shek in terms of political centralization and control, and in the context of the late 1920s and 1930s, when the Nationalist regime continued to be threatened by military separatism from regional militarists and the Communists, political and military priorities took precedence over other concerns. It may be recalled that military expenditures consumed a disproportionately large share of the national budget, and as long as Chiang's national unification objectives remained mired in the military phase, other sectors had to suffer the consequences. Although the shortage of resources certainly affected the entire health system, its consequences were particularly devastating in the neediest areas—in the countryside.

Despite the rhetoric of the Nationalist leaders proclaiming the need for health improvement, the importance of the health sector also paled in comparison with the emphasis placed on economic development: the modernization of the industrial and commercial sectors and the expansion of the transportation and communications systems. The technical cooperation between the Chinese National Health Administration and the Health Organization of the League of Nations was only a small part of the broad program of economic reconstruction agreed upon by the League and the National Economic Council. Areas that received much more attention and funding included fiscal reform, agriculture, cotton production, sericulture, water conservancy, education, and highway construction. As already noted, the building of a network of highways, which had strategic importance and implications for the consolidation of state power, received the largest share of funds allocated by the National Economic Council. In 1934, $6.8 million, about half of the National Economic Council's budget, was allocated to road construction, and this sum did not include a $100,000 grant to study different types of fuel for motor vehicles. Health received $500,000, the second smallest portion of the budget (the smallest being a grant for "economic research").[11]

We have also seen that health expenditures were a minuscule part of the overall budget during the Nationalist decade. Ironically, while health was seen as important to the country's economic rejuvenation, the emphasis was placed more on material and structural construction than on human capital. At the same time, it is clear that the revenue needs of the modernizing state—with its multitude of reconstruction projects, not to mention its concerns for security and military control—simply outstripped the resources that a traditional agrarian economy could provide, despite numerous increases in taxes and surcharges levied on the population.[12]

National reconstruction under the Nationalists also emphasized the establishment of central administrative organs to maintain state power and to direct the mobilization of people and resources. The desire to introduce state medicine resulted not only from the recognition that massive health problems required direct intervention but from a concern for national consolidation and the building of central power. The first moves in the creation of a national health administration focused on establishing central administrative and technical

agencies to plan and direct health policies. Given the political dis-
unity that still existed, and the fact that most provincial governments
were charged with the implementation of health policies, the goal
of a truly national health administration was not immediately realized. For the Nanjing regime, however, the central health bureaucracy—and the whole array of central agencies—were not only symbols
of its legitimacy but centers exercising administrative powers essential
to the building of state power.[13] Such a process obviously demanded
coordination among all sectors. Latitudinally, such sectoral coordination was often lacking, as we have seen, in view of the priority given
to the military and economic sectors. In fact, as Hung-mao Tien has
shown, power politics and factionalism, as well as the interference
of the party, characterized the operation of much of the central bureaucracy.[14] As we have seen, while personal connections and politics
played a role in the creation and survival of the health administration,
J. Heng Liu succeeded in establishing a relatively stable health structure. The rest of the bureaucracy, however, suffered from duplication
of functions and from rivalries that did little to help develop a
modern administrative system.

Longitudinally, health improvement, like other social programs,
needed personnel at the local levels, where the people were, to cooperate in bringing about desired changes. But there was no guarantee
that such support would be forthcoming. The Guomindang viewed
health-protection initiatives as an essential part of the seven campaigns—attempts to reach the masses, and to enrich and improve
their livelihood, but at the same time the effort to gain support for
the central government and secure control. The government's selective support of health programs was based on political necessity and
strategic calculations. The comparatively large sums allotted for the
welfare centers in Jiangxi were closely linked to the attempt to win
the hearts and minds of the populace in a former Communist stronghold. Chiang Kai-shek's interest in the programs at Dingxian and
Liang Shuming's work at Zouping in fact resulted from Chiang's
attempt to find "ways of governing the areas recently cleared of [Com-
munist] bandits."[15] Moreover, most of the health demonstration
centers and projects were located within Chiang's power base or in
the provinces of his allies. Unlike the Dingxian project, which received funding from sources outside China, it is likely that many
health programs would not have survived if there had been no central support.

Yet the success of the health programs depended on, among other factors, the mobilization of support and mass education to effect a change of attitude toward modern medicine on the part of the populace, especially in the countryside. Chiang, however, was wary of the potential of mass mobilization. Among the first actions he took after the Nationalist ascendancy were the suppression of the labor movement and the curbing of student activism. The mobilization of the people for social and health improvement was just as suspect. The Communist challenge had contributed to Nanjing's concern for security and control and reinforced its suspicions concerning non-governmental grass-roots organizations, especially if they were perceived to be potentially subversive. Chiang forcibly terminated Tao Xingzhi's Xiaozhuang rural education and health program in 1930 because of the latter's personal ties to Feng Yuxiang and the alleged radicalism of the students. He also closed down Liang Shuming's Henan Village Government Academy in the fall of 1930. Only through the support of the new governor of Shandong, Han Fuqu, was Liang able to continue his rural program at Zouping. In the spring of 1932, Chiang dispatched a military team to Dingxian to investigate rumors of subversive activities in the Mass Education Movement, though no evidence to substantiate such rumors was found.[16] To a significant extent, the introduction of experimental *xian* was another attempt to extend bureaucratic control over the countryside (as in the cases of Jiangning and Lanxi). Moreover, in Jiangxi we have seen how the government was more concerned with utilization of the *baojia* system to maintain security and control over the population than with health reforms. Although the addition of the *bao* level to the sub-*xian* health service might have been beneficial to the rural populace, the incorporation of the health service into a security system reinforced the perception that the health system was but an extension of the long arm of state control.

Certainly it should be pointed out that the strong hold of tradition and religious ideas, which, despite the introduction of modern medicine, continued to be supported by the majority of the population, proved to be a major obstacle to modern medical and health programs. But to effect fundamental attitudinal and behavioral modifications on the part of the populace required concerted efforts to educate and mobilize them so that they would actively participate in and become committed to different approaches to health amelioration. The Mass Education Movement had demonstrated the efficacy of such efforts, and the Communists had used mass education and mobilization campaigns to win the support of the people. While exhibiting ambivalence toward mass movements, the Guomindang did try to provide an ideological structure that would create oneness between the people and the government. What Chiang had to offer, however, was only a revival of certain Confucian ideas and exhortations on the value of discipline—including its importance in health betterment and personal hygiene—and these not only failed to elicit much support from intellectuals but provided little solace for those faced with the miseries of poverty, hunger, and disease. To many, the claims of a "New Life" proved in practice to be just more of the same.

Selskar Gunn, in fact, was suspicious of Chiang's motives in supporting rural reconstruction and the China Program. In 1937, he wrote to Raymond B. Fosdick, a former member of the China Medical Board and its Executive Committee: "What concerns me in terms of the China program is to arrive at a conclusion as to the real honesty of the Chinese government in connection with its National Reconstruction program." A letter from Mme. Chiang reinforced his misgivings. While applauding the China Program's rural thrust, she confided that it fit in nicely with "the spirit and aims of the New Life Movement."[17] Chiang certainly was committed to national reconstruction and serious about the various programs—including health—in the strengthening and modernization of China, but they had to be developed and carried out on his terms and based on his understanding of China's realities and needs.

Health planners in the Nationalist decade, therefore, operated with many constraints in developing a health care system that would fulfil the promise of state medicine. The approach they adopted to introduce state medicine in fact made the task more difficult. The education and training of health leaders, the tremendous influence and power of the Rockefeller Foundation (which was able to provide funds not forthcoming from the government), and the belief on the part of Chinese planners in the applicability of the advanced medical techniques of the West led to the transfer of the model of scientific medicine to China. It was, however, a model developed in the industrialized West, especially in the United States, where the pattern of disease and the priorities of health care differed radically from those of a backward, agrarian China. Scientific medicine, typified by the Johns Hopkins model, was hospital based, required the support of relatively sophisticated biomedical technology and laboratory research, and directed toward curative rather than preventive care. The development of such a system on a national scale required ample financial backing, an extensive medical-education system, and a population with some understanding of disease and modern medical practices. These conditions were almost nonexistent in China in the 1920s and 1930s. The implementation of such a model was possible, therefore, only on a restrictive scale. Urban areas where research institutions and facilities were located, and where their existence was sustained either by the volume of patient usage or by other sources of support, emerged as centers of scientific medicine. This in turn encouraged the congregation of modern physicians in the cities, to the detriment of the countryside.

We have noted the shortage and maldistribution not only of modern physicians but of other professional personnel during this period. Yet the Nationalist health planners did not intend to ignore the countryside. In their state-medicine model, modern health care was to be made available to the rural population through the hierarchy of health services developed in Dingxian, which ideally would extend downward to the lowest level of society. This rural health service was encouraged and supported by Stampar and Borcic of the League of Nations Health Organization who drew upon their experience in Eastern Europe in providing aid and advice to the Chinese. The operation of such a state system, however, required large numbers of physicians and other health personnel. Yet, because the scientific model had shaped the academic programs of most Chinese medical colleges, most graduates found themselves unable or unwilling to adapt to working in small towns and villages bereft of sophisticated equipment and financially unable to support them. Instead of laboring to meet the basic needs of China, they preferred to do the type of work for which they had been trained.

There were several ways to approach this problem. The government might have insisted on the reorganization of training institutions to deemphasize high-powered research and curative medicine, stressing instead preventive and social medicine. At the same time, it could have increased enrollments so that large numbers of medical personnel more attuned to the needs of Chinese society could be produced in a relatively short period of time. This is the solution that John Grant and J. Heng Liu urged PUMC to adopt. At the same time, the government could have tried to incorporate the huge number of existing medical practitioners—the traditional doctors—in the new health services. Unfortunately, the potential of this group was largely ignored by the health planners. Finally, lower-level, auxiliary personnel could have been trained as primary health workers to implement most preventive measures and perform medical procedures that did not require the intervention of college-trained personnel. The attempt to reorient Chinese medical education did not take place until after 1935, when the Rockefeller Foundation itself concluded that a new approach was needed. The funding for the Commission on Medical Education, which drew up the blueprint for medical-education reorganization in fact came from the Rockefeller Foundation. Medical reformers such as C. C. Chen, however, had been warning for a long time that the educational system failed to serve the needs of state medicine and that radical changes were essential. Long before such changes were initiated at the top, Chen had followed a different path in training needed health personnel, utilizing local manpower and resources to train paramedics to fill the void. Midwives, village health workers, and primary-school teachers were part of a contingent of health workers who could be trained rapidly and inexpensively to provide primary care to the neediest segment of the population. The training of these local workers also meant that the community was involved in health protection and improvement, a course of action that encouraged changes in attitudes and behavior patterns as well as a predisposition toward additional health reforms.

Still, to sustain these changes there would be required concurrent socioeconomic improvements substantial enough to allow the construction and maintenance of such simple ameliorative measures as public bath houses, latrines, and wells protected from sources of contamination. Such improvements would also enable the populace to hire and keep some modern medical personnel—nurses, technicians, and midwives—and to purchase basic drugs. Still, attitudes and behavior patterns might not change automatically. It is the combination of socioeconomic improvements with the availability of health personnel and active community involvement that spells the difference between success and failure in the development of state medicine. Thus, the Nationalist government, which failed to initiate meaningful socioeconomic reforms; the health planners, who clung to a capital-intensive-techniques approach in the development of a state health-care system; and the failure to make fundamental changes in the people's attitudes all worked against the successful implementation of a modern system of state medicine. Finally, the invasion of

China by Japan in 1937 derailed the limited programs that had been introduced by that time.

The failure of J. Heng Liu and his colleagues to establish a system of state medicine by 1937 does not mean that they made no important gains in that short period of time. They had created an infrastructure, however small and limited, that was capable of transferring and utilizing advanced medical knowledge from other countries. An organized public-health system had been initiated and the parameters of health protection had been defined. Environmental and sanitary improvements, industrial health, maternal and child care, school health, and popular health education are vital components of a modern public-health system that owe their beginnings to the efforts of the Nationalist health administration. Although there were too few trained personnel to staff the state health service, a small contingent of physicians and teachers was produced by PUMC, National Shanghai Medical College, National Zhongshan Medical College, and other medical schools. They would be instrumental in training other medical personnel in the years to come. The Nationalist health planners demonstrated the need for state medicine and initiated plans for its implementation. In particular, the hierarchy of health services that they devised and the lessons they provided in the utilization of local resources proved invaluable to the future leaders of China who eventually designed a state health service. In fact, the most important contribution of the Nationalist effort was the foundation it laid for the health planners working after 1949.

Health Care in the People's Republic

The establishment of the People's Republic in 1949 marked the beginning of another phase in China's reconstruction. As Chiang and the Nationalists had been before them, the new leaders were concerned with national strengthening and modernization. They also stressed the importance of health protection and improvement to national survival. Mao Zedong urged the people to eliminate China's "backwardness in the economic, scientific, and cultural fields," and Deng Xiaoping warned that a weak China would be vulnerable to foreign exploitation.[18] Indeed, a 1978 editorial in *Renmin ribao* (the *People's Daily*) asserted that a comparatively backward country like China could not achieve socialist modernization without the support of a healthy population.[19] Nationalism and social-Darwinian fears again helped to shape health policies the objectives of which were still the provision of modern care to the entire population. With state medicine as the recognized goal, there was much continuity in the Nationalist and Communist efforts. But there also were significant differences in the circumstances in which health policies were implemented, the methods adopted to introduce them, and the emphasis on aspects that previously had not received enough attention.

After a brief period of political consolidation, the Communist regime was in control of the entire country with the exception of Taiwan. Therefore, unlike the Nationalists in the 1930s, Communist leaders were not threatened by the consequences of political and military separatism. An external threat was posed by the outbreak of the Korean War in 1950, and China's involvement in that conflict severely drained its resources, but even the Korean conflict was adroitly manipulated by the government to propagate the virtues of health protection and the germ theory of infectious diseases. By alleging that the United States was engaging in bacteriological warfare, the government appealed to the people to protect the motherland by adopting basic sanitary measures, protecting sources of water, and obtaining vaccinations. One medical leader proclaimed that the "Anti-American Imperialism Patriotic Health Movement" not only had foiled the American conspiracy but had helped to promote the health movement.[20] National survival and health improvement went hand in hand.

Unlike the Nationalists, the Communists adopted the "mass line" in health care, which meant mass mobilization for health improvement and a stress on preventive work. The mass-line approach had been utilized in Communist-controlled areas in the 1930s and 1940s not only in health but in political, economic, and social campaigns. By actively involving the masses, Communist leaders launched nationwide "patriotic health movements" to attack specific health problems, for example, the campaign against the "four pests" (flies, mosquitoes, bedbugs, and rodents) in 1952, and the "anti-snail campaign" of 1954 initiated to eradicate schistosomiasis.[21] Such movements were intensely political in nature since the full force of the Communist party was used to ensure compliance and active participation. The Communist social restructuring, especially rural collectivization; the party's success in penetrating to the grass-roots level; and the discipline maintained by the party apparatus were important factors contributing to the relative success of these programs. At the same time, the public-health propaganda that accompanied such campaigns helped to modify people's attitudes and behavior. From the party's point of view, changes in health conduct should be integrated with all other changes required of every individual in his transformation into the new "socialist man."

This emphasis on the people's active involvement in health improvement and socialist construction underlay Mao Zedong's idea of self-reliance, a concept that often has been misinterpreted to mean the exclusion of foreign knowledge and technology. China initially adopted the Soviet medical model but abandoned it in the late 1950s as inappropriate. From then on, the leaders' emphasis was on the development of a modern but uniquely Chinese system that could meet the health needs of the huge population. According to Mao, this objective could be accomplished by learning "the good points of all countries and all nationalities" and combining them with the "concrete reality of China."[22] One important manifestation of this approach was the effort to integrate traditional Chinese medicine and western medicine. Communist policy toward indigenous medicine and its practitioners differed markedly from that of the Nationalists. Even before coming to power, the Communist leadership had urged the utilization and scientification of traditional medicine. After a period of indecision between 1949 and 1954, the government began to promote traditional medicine not only out of pragmatic considerations—its utility, low cost, and abundance of practitioners—but on the nationalistic grounds that traditional medicine represented a cultural legacy that should be studied and made available to the people.[23] Modern and traditional doctors were urged to cooperate and traditional medicine was introduced into modern medical training and practice. Research on traditional drugs was encouraged and medical schools for traditional medicine were established. Despite vicissitudes in the implementation of the policy of integration during the past forty years, traditional medicine has been preserved and utilized. Yet, the gradual accumulation of new modern-trained health personnel, the resilience of western science, and a recent stress on professionalism and technology in medicine have tended to downgrade the role of traditional medicine in the health system.[24]

There are, however, important continuities in the concept of self-reliance in health care between the 1930s and the post-1949 period. The Dingxian health program developed a new type of health worker—the village health worker—based on the training of local people, and the Nationalist health administration under J. Heng Liu tried to follow Dingxian's example by increasing the number of lower-level personnel providing primary care to the rural population. In 1935, in fact, the Commission on Medical Education recommended the institutionalization of such auxiliary personnel. After 1949, despite the expansion of rural-health manpower by the incorporation of traditional practitioners, the transfer of modern physicians to the countryside, and some tentative attempts during the Great Leap Forward of the late 1950s to train health workers in the communes, the big push for the institutionalization of new types of rural health personnel came only after 1965. Essentially, two types of personnel were trained: rural health workers trained in short-term courses of one to three months; and part-time doctors—the barefoot doctors (*chijiao yisheng*)—trained over a period of two to three years in work-study schools in *xian* hospitals or commune clinics. There were great variations in the length of training and gradually the distinction between the two types diminished. Essentially, both were products of the attempt to decentralize the health-care system so as to expand the manpower available for preventive work, environmental health, and primary medical care. The number of barefoot doctors seems to have reached a high of 1.8 million in 1975 and then declined.[25] Despite Communist claims that barefoot doctors were an innovation in health-manpower development, their lineage can be traced back to the village health workers of the 1930s.

As was also the case in the 1930s, these rural personnel were intended to supplement professional medical workers in the health system. The Communist approach to training medical workers was similar to that recommended by the Commission on Medical Education in 1935. The lower-level auxiliary personnel consisted of rural health workers, barefoot doctors, nursing aides, laboratory workers, and others. Intermediate-level personnel consisted of assistant doctors (*yishi*), nurses (*hushi*), midwives (*zhuchan shi*), pharmacists (*yaoji shi*), and laboratory technicians (*jianyan shi*). Higher-level personnel included college-educated western-style doctors (*xiyishi*), pharmacologists (*yaoshi*), and advanced laboratory technicians (*jianyan shi*).[26] There was a separate category for traditional practitioners consisting of Chinese medicine doctors (*zhongyi*) and Chinese herb specialists (*zhongyao renyuan*).

Apart from the category for practitioners of indigenous medicine, the major difference between the structures of medical training in the 1930s and the post-1949 period lie in the inclusion of assistant doctors as part of the intermediate-level medical personnel. It may be recalled that the Nationalist health administration decided on a two-track medical-education system that was later rejected by the Commission on Medical Education. The Communists revived the two-track system but shortened the assistant doctors' training in secondary medical schools to four years after junior middle school (compared to the four-year curriculum in medical-technical schools for senior-middle-school graduates in the 1930s). The assistant doctors resembled the *feldsher* of the Soviet system, and some of them later would receive training in higher medical institutions. Under the Communist regime there was a tremendous expansion of intermediate medical personnel—the least developed segment under the Nationalists—from 107,000 in 1950 to more than 1.1 million in 1980, yielding a ratio of 11.95 per 10,000 people in 1980. The number of western-style physicians also increased substantially, from about 51,000 in 1950 to 447,000 in 1980, producing a doctor-population ratio of 4.56 per 10,000 people in 1980. Although the figure was still much lower than the ratio of 202 doctors per 10,000 people found in the United States in 1980, it was an impressive improvement over the prewar situation.[27]

A brief examination of post-1949 medical leadership also reveals significant links to the 1930s. The dominance of prewar PUMC graduates in medical schools, health bureaucracies, and institutions after 1949 is remarkable. In the first year of Communist rule, twelve medical colleges in China were directed by PUMC graduates or faculty, including C. C. Chen in Chongqing.[28] In 1955, seven of the nine medical members of the Chinese Academy of Sciences in the field of biomedical science were either former PUMC faculty or graduates. So were six of the eight known directors of specialized institutes of the Chinese Academy of Medical Sciences established in 1956. Huang Chia-ssu (Huang Jaisi, PUMC '33) held the directorship of the Academy of Medical Sciences from 1958 to 1983. The Chinese Medical Association and the editorial board of its *Chinese Medical Journal* were likewise dominated by former PUMC graduates or faculty.[29] Other prominent leaders of the 1930s who continued to influence Communist medical developments included, among others, P. Z. King, F. C. Yen, and H. P. Chu (Zhu Hengbi). King, a world-renowned public-health expert who had served under J. Heng Liu, returned to China in 1950 from a post in the World Health Organization to serve in the Ministry of Health. In 1954, he became chairman of the Department of Public Health in Peking Medical College.[30] Yen, who served briefly as director general of the National Health Administration (1938–40), became vice-president and then president of Shanghai Medical College (later renamed Shanghai First Medical College) and vice-chairman of the Chinese Medical Association (1956–67).[31] H. P. Chu, one of the original founders of the Chinese Medical Association in 1932, took charge of Shanghai Medical College during the war, continued to serve there briefly after the war, and in 1955 was appointed professor and then chairman of the Department of Pharmacology in Zhejiang Medical College.[32] These and other medical leaders who stayed in China after the civil war constituted a network of experts who helped to train new doctors and researchers. Most of them suffered during the Cultural Revolution when they were denounced as elitist and inattentive to the problems of the masses.

Organizationally the Communist health structure built upon the Nationalist foundation of state medicine. Under the Ministry of Public Health were provincial and municipal health departments. As in the 1930s, the three-tiered *xian* and sub-*xian* rural health system was adopted. The *xian* maintained a health bureau (*weisheng yuan*) with a hospital, laboratory, epidemic prevention station, and maternal and child care station. These *xian*-level organizations were mostly staffed by higher- and intermediate-level medical personnel. Under the *xian* were *qu* health clinics (*weisheng suo*). But with the introduction of communes in the late 1950s *qu* health clinics became commune health clinics (*gongshe weisheng yuan*), which, until 1983, also included the former *xiang* health stations. Both intermediate- and lower-level medical personnel staffed the second-tier organizations. The third level was made up of the production brigade health stations (*shengchan dadui weisheng suo*) staffed by barefoot doctors or a combination of barefoot doctors and village doctors (*xiangcun yisheng*, in other words, those barefoot doctors who had passed a qualifying examination to meet the secondary medical-school requirements) after 1981. These were in charge of health workers and junior midwives in team health substations. Thus, the *xian*-based system of Dingxian and the Nationalists became the cornerstone of the new rural health structure of the Communists (see appendix 4). Official statistics claim that 2,123 *xian* (about 90 percent) had established health clinics by 1952. By 1982, there were 2,363 *xian* hospitals, 2,104 epidemic prevention stations, and 1,893 maternal and child care stations. In that same year, the numbers of commune/*xiang* clinics and brigade health stations were 55,496 and 608,431, respectively.[33] The expansion of the rural health service under the Communists was a noteworthy achievement, and in many ways it represented the fruition of programs initiated during the Nationalist decade.

It would be incorrect to assume that health planners in the People's Republic solved the quality-versus-quantity and urban-versus-rural dilemmas in the delivery of health care. Recent developments in medical modernization—especially the emphasis placed on the professionalization of the medical system and on biomedical technology, as well as an increasingly urban orientation—brought to the fore questions about the medical leaders' commitment to the rural areas and the possibility of a new imbalance in the health-care system.[34] It is difficult to predict the final form of the uniquely Chinese health-care system that the leaders have insisted must be developed. For one thing, China is undergoing another phase of national reconstruction based on the ideas of the Four Modernizations. Medicine, as a part of national development, will have to adjust to new demands and needs in China's development process.

Appendix 1

Organization of the Chinese National Health Administration, 1931–37

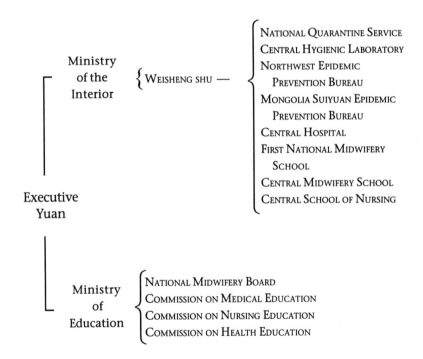

Ministry
of the   { WEISHENG SHU —
Interior

NATIONAL QUARANTINE SERVICE
CENTRAL HYGIENIC LABORATORY
NORTHWEST EPIDEMIC
    PREVENTION BUREAU
MONGOLIA SUIYUAN EPIDEMIC
    PREVENTION BUREAU
CENTRAL HOSPITAL
FIRST NATIONAL MIDWIFERY
    SCHOOL
CENTRAL MIDWIFERY SCHOOL
CENTRAL SCHOOL OF NURSING

Executive
Yuan

Ministry
of
Education

NATIONAL MIDWIFERY BOARD
COMMISSION ON MEDICAL EDUCATION
COMMISSION ON NURSING EDUCATION
COMMISSION ON HEALTH EDUCATION

National
Economic — Central Field Health Station —   NATIONAL EPIDEMIC
Council   PREVENTION BUREAU

Appendix 2

Organization of
Xian *Health Services After 1934*

Division	Population		Organization
xian	—	Health Center	⎧ Clinic and Hospital ⎨ Laboratory ⎨ Drugs and Supplies ⎨ Health Education ⎩ Administration
qu	50,000–100,000	Health Station	⎧ Clinic ⎨ Preventive Medicine ⎨ Sanitation ⎨ School Health ⎩ Health Education
xiang	5,000–10,000	Health Sub-station	⎧ Clinic ⎨ Preventive Medicine ⎨ Maternal and Child Care ⎩ Health Education
baojia	100 Households	Health Worker	

195

Appendix 3

Medical Colleges and Medical Technical Schools in China, 1936

Name	Location
1. NATIONAL	
National Peiping University, College of Medicine	Peiping
National Tongji University, College of Medicine	Shanghai
National Shanghai Medical College	Shanghai
National Central University, College of Medicine	Nanjing
National Zhongshan University, College of Medicine	Canton
Army Medical School	Nanjing
2. PROVINCIAL	
Henan Provincial University, College of Medicine	Kaifeng
Hebei Provincial Medical College	Baoding
Zhejiang Provincial Medical Technical School	Hangzhou
Jiangxi Provincial Medical Technical School	Nanchang
Shandong Provincial Medical Technical School	Jinan
Yunnan Provincial University, Medical Technical School	Kunming
Gansu College, Medical Department	Lanzhou
3. PRIVATE	
Aurora University, College of Medicine	Shanghai
Shandong Christian (Cheeloo) University, College of Medicine	Jinan
Hackett Medical College	Canton
St. John's University, College of Medicine	Shanghai
West China Union University, College of Medicine	Chengdu
Women's Christian Medical College	Shanghai
Mukden Medical College	Mukden (Shenyang)

Peiping Union Medical College	Peiping
Sino-French University, College of Medicine	Peiping
Dongnan Medical College	Shanghai
Tongde Medical College	Shanghai
Guanghua Medical College	Canton
Xiangya Medical College	Changsha
Nantong University, College of Medicine	Nantong, Jiangsu
Chuanzhi Medical Technical School	Taiyuan, Shanxi

Note: The Japanese maintained the Manchurian Medical College in Mukden.

Appendix 4

Organization of Xian Health Services in the People's Republic of China, 1982

DIVISION	ORGANIZATION	NUMBER
xian	Hospital	2,363
	Epidemic Prevention Station	2,104
	Maternal and Child Care Station	1,893
	Laboratory	823
	School of Hygiene	1,334
xiang / commune	Rural Health Clinics	55,496
cun / production brigade	Health Station	608,431

Source: Chen Haifeng, *Zhongguo weisheng baojian*, 68.

Notes

Notes to Introduction

1. Works on the Nationalist decade include Hung-mao Tien, *Government and Politics in Kuomintang China, 1927–1937* (Stanford: Stanford University Press, 1972); Lloyd E. Eastman, *The Abortive Revolution: China Under Nationalist Rule, 1927–1937* (Cambridge: Harvard University Press, 1974); William Wei, *Counterrevolution in China: The Nationalists in Jiangxi During the Soviet Period* (Ann Arbor: University of Michigan Press, 1985); Arthur N. Young, *China's Nation-Building Effort, 1927–1937: The Financial and Economic Record* (Stanford: Hoover Institution Press, 1971); Paul T. K. Sih, ed., *The Strenuous Decade: China's Nation-Building Efforts, 1927–1937* (New York: St. John's University Press, 1970); James C. Thomson, Jr., *While China Faced West: American Reformers in Nationalist China, 1928–1937* (Cambridge: Harvard University Press, 1969); Patrick Cavendish, "The 'New China' of the Kuomintang," in *Modern China's Search for a Political Form*, ed. Jack Gray, 138–86 (London: Oxford University Press, 1969); Cambridge History of China, vols. 12, 13 (Cambridge: CambridgeUniversity Press, 1983, 1986); Lloyd E. Eastman, Jerome Chen, Suzanne Pepper, and Lyman P. Van Slyke, eds., *The Nationalist Era in China, 1927–1949* (Cambridge: Cambridge University Press, 1991); and C. Martin Wilbur, "Nationalist China, 1928–1950: An Interpretation," in *China: Seventy Years After the 1911 Hsin-Hai Revolution*, ed. Hungdah Chiu and Shao-chuan Leng, 2–57 (Charlottesville: University Press of Virginia, 1984).

2. Thomson, *While China Faced West*, 8.

3. This point, often ignored in the past, is now generally recognized by

historians who may have reached different conclusions about the Nationalist decade. See Lloyd E. Eastman, "Nationalist China During the Nanking Decade, 1927–1937," in Eastman et al., Nationalist Era, 1–52; and Wilbur, "Nationalist China."

4. For an important discussion of these historiographical trends, see Paul A. Cohen, "The Post-Mao Reforms in Historical Perspective," *Journal of Asian Studies* 47, no. 3 (August 1988): 519–41.

5. Parks M. Coble, Jr., The Shanghai Capitalists and the Nationalist Government, 1927–1937 (Cambridge: Harvard University Press, 1980); Joseph Fewsmith, *Party, State, and Local Elites in Republican China: Merchant Organizations and Politics in Shanghai, 1890–1930* (Honolulu: University of Hawaii Press, 1985); Prasenjit Duara, *Culture, Power and the State: Rural North China, 1900–1942* (Stanford: Stanford University Press, 1988); Christian Henriot, "Municipal Power and Local Elites," *Republican China* 11, no. 2 (1986): 1–21.

6. James Reardon-Anderson, *The Study of Change: Chemistry in China, 1840–1949* (Cambridge: Cambridge University Press, 1991); Mary B. Bullock, *An American Transplant: The Rockefeller Foundation and Peking Union Medical College* (Berkeley: University of California Press, 1980).

7. Robert E. Bedeski, *State-Building in Modern China: The Kuomintang in the Prewar Period* (Berkeley: Center for Chinese Studies, University of California, 1981).

8. P. Cohen, "Post-Mao Reforms."

9. Arthur Kleinman, *Patients and Healers in the Context of Culture: An Exploration of the Borderland Between Anthropology, Medicine, and Psychiatry* (Berkeley: University of California Press, 1980), 25.

10. Recently, increasing attention has been paid to the study of medicine as a cultural system and the ways in which sociopolitical, economic, and cultural concerns can be brought into a coherent focus in the study of the healing process. See, e.g., Arthur Kleinman, Peter Kunstadter, E. Russell Alexander, and James L. Gale, eds., *Medicine in Chinese Cultures: Comparative Studies of Health Care in Chinese and Other Societies* (Bethesda: National Institutes of Health, 1975); and Kleinman, *Patients and Healers*. For an excellent discussion of recent trends in the study of traditional Chinese medicine, see Nathan Sivin, "Science and Medicine in Imperial China—The State of the Field," *Journal of Asian Studies* 47, no. 1 (February 1988): 41–90.

11. For discussions of Soviet base-area medicine, see Gong Chun, "Di erci guonei geming zhanzheng shiqi di hongjun weisheng gongzuo" [Health work of the Red Army during the Second Internal Revolutionary War], *Zhonghua yishi zazhi* [Journal of Chinese medical history] 14, no. 4 (1984): 226–29; Karen Minden, "The Development of Early Chinese Communist Health Policy: Health Care in the Border Region, 1936–1949," *American*

Journal of Chinese Medicine 7, no. 4 (1979): 299–315; and David M. Lampton, *The Politics of Medicine in China: The Policy Process, 1949–1977* (Boulder: Westview, 1977), 11–16. For a biography of a famous foreign doctor working with the Communists during this period, see Sydney Gordon and Ted Allan, *The Scalpel, the Sword: The Story of Doctor Norman Bethune*, rev. ed. (New York: Monthly Review Press, 1973).

Notes to Chapter 1

1. W. W. Peter, "Some Health Problems of Changing China," *Journal of the American Medical Association* 58, no. 26 (1912): 2024.

2. Association for the Advancement of Public Health in China, *Memorandum on the Need for a Public Health Organization in China: Presented to the British Boxer Indemnity Commission* (Peking: Association for the Advancement of Public Health Education in China, 1926), 4, 16–17; Hu Dingan, *Minzu jiankang zi yixue jichu* [Medical basis of the nation's health] (Chongqing: Zheng zhong shuju, 1943), 122–25. See also Tsefang Huang, "Communicable Disease Information in China," *National Medical Journal of China* 13 (1927): 92–108.

3. Marion Yang, "Midwifery Training in China," *Chinese Medical Journal* 42 (1928):769.

4. Association for the Advancement of Public Health in China, *Memorandum on the Need*, 35–37.

5. Ibid., 99–106. See also Jean Chesneaux, *The Chinese Labor Movement, 1919–1927*, trans. H. M. Wright (Stanford: Stanford University Press, 1968), 71–87.

6. J. Heng Liu and C. K. Chu, "Problems of Nutrition and Dietary Requirements in China," *Chinese Medical Journal* 61 (April–June 1943): 95–109.

7. For a discussion of the plague and its consequences, see Carl F. Nathan, *Plague Prevention and Politics in Manchuria, 1910–1931* (Cambridge: East Asian Research Center, Harvard University, 1967).

8. *New Life Centers in Rural Kiangsi* (Nanchang: Head Office of the Kiangsi Rural Welfare Centers, National Economic Council, 1936), 16.

9. Ibid., 17; *Weisheng banyue kan* [Health bimonthly] 2, no. 4 (28 February 1935): 12.

10. C. C. Chen, "Xiangcun weisheng" [Rural health], *Weisheng gongbao* [Gazette of the Ministry of Health] 2, no. 2 (1 February 1930): 187.

11. *New Life Centers in Rural Kiangsi*, 18.

12. Harold Balme, *China and Modern Medicine: A Study in Medical Missionary Development* (London: United Council for Missionary Education, 1921), 66.

13. C. Nathan, *Plague Prevention and Politics*, 61.

14. The importance of this syncretic blend of medical ideas is discussed in Kleinman, *Patients and Healers*. For an interesting discussion of the "functional complementarity" of Chinese and western medicine, see Yuet-wah Cheung, *Missionary Medicine in China: A Study of Two Canadian Protestant Missions in China Before 1937* (Lanham, Md.: University Press of America, 1988), 72–78.

15. "Plague Prevention in Tatung," *Peking Leader*, 8 March 1919, 19 March 1919, Record Group 4, Series 1, Box 8, Folder 92, Rockefeller Archive Center, North Tarrytown, New York.

16. China Medical Commission of the Rockefeller Foundation, *Medicine in China* (New York: Rockefeller Foundation, 1914), 8; *China Yearbook*, 1913, 457.

17. Balme, *China and Modern Medicine*, 181.

18. *Weisheng gongbao*, 1 April 1929.

19. K. Chimin Wong and Wu Lien-teh, *History of Chinese Medicine*, 2d ed. (Shanghai: National Quarantine Service, 1936), 787, 816. The number of nurses is given in Roger S. Greene, "Public Health and the Training of Doctors and Nurses in China," *International Review of Missions* 14 (1925): 496. As for conditions in public hospitals, a reporter described a visit to one in Peking in 1926: "The curtain at the room's entrance was very dirty; the air was putrid; and the basins at the bedside were filthy. No one seemed to look after the food for the patients, let alone give consideration to nutrition and cleanliness" (quoted in C. C. Chen, *Medicine in Rural China: A Personal Account* [Berkeley: University of California Press, 1989], 28).

20. For a discussion of the plurality of medical approaches in traditional Chinese medicine, see Paul V. Unschuld, *Medicine in China: A History of Ideas* (Berkeley: University of California Press, 1985).

21. The article was published in *Xin qingnian* [New youth] 1, no. 1 (15 September 1915): 6, translated in Ssu-yu Teng and John K. Fairbank, *China's Response to the West* (Cambridge: Harvard University Press, 1954), 245.

22. Chen Bangxian, *Zhongguo yixue shi* [A history of medicine in China], rev. ed. (Taibei: Shangwu yinshuguan, 1957), 266; Wong and Wu, *History of Chinese Medicine*, 607.

23. Ralph C. Croizier, *Traditional Medicine in Modern China: Science, Nationalism, and the Tensions of Cultural Change* (Cambridge: Harvard University Press, 1968), 81–89. The role of practitioners of traditional medicine will be discussed more fully in the following chapters.

24. Angela Ki Che Leung, "Organized Medicine in Ming-Qing China: State and Private Medical Institutions in the Lower Yangzi Region," *Late Imperial China* 8, no. 1 (June 1987): 134–66; Meng Zhaohua and Wang

Minghuan, *Zhongguo minzheng shigao* [A history of Chinese civil adminis-
tration] (Harbin: Heilongjiang renmin chubanshe, 1986), 284–88. See also
Association for the Advancement of Public Health in China, *Memorandum,*
63. For a stimulating discussion of the concept of "public vs. private," see
Mary B. Rankin, *Elite Activism and Political Transformation in China: Zhejiang
Province, 1865–1911* (Stanford: Stanford University Press, 1986).

25. During Yuan Shikai's brief tenure in office, the Sanitation Bureau
was downgraded to a division within the Bureau of Public Administration.
See Association for the Advancement of Public Health in China, *Memorandum,* 63–66.

26. Wong and Wu, *History of Chinese Medicine,* 600.

27. Association for the Advancement of Public Health in China, *Memorandum,* 66, 68.

28. Wu Lien-teh, *Plague Fighter: Autobiography of a Chinese Physician*
(Cambridge: W. Heffer and Sons, 1959), 375–402.

29. Association for the Advancement of Public Health in China, *Memorandum,* 73–74.

30. It should be pointed out that in certain foreign settlements, such as
the International Settlement in Shanghai, health departments had been
established.

31. Wong and Wu, *History of Chinese Medicine,* 596–97.

32. Li Tingan, "A Public Health Report on Canton, China," *National
Medical Journal of China* 11 (1925): 324–75.

33. Wong and Wu, *History of Chinese Medicine,* 601, 649.

34. Conrad Seipp, ed., *Health Care for the Community: Selected Papers of
Dr. John B. Grant* (Baltimore: Johns Hopkins University Press, 1963), 94.

35. For Grant's discussion of these activities, see John B. Grant, "Depart-
ment of Public Health and Preventive Medicine, Peking Union Medical
College, Peking, China," in *Methods and Problems of Medical Education* (New
York: Rockefeller Foundation, 1929), 114–16. See also "Health Station—
First Quarterly Review," Record Group 4, 2 B9, Box 66, Folder 465, Rockefeller
Archive Center.

36. M. Stauffer, ed., *The Christian Occupation of China* (Shanghai: China
Continuation Committee, 1922), 425. For the government regulations, see
B. Chen, *Zhongguo yixue shi,* 309–13.

37. Balme, *China and Modern Medicine,* 147; Wong and Wu, *History of
Chinese Medicine,* 560–62.

38. John B. Grant's Report, 10 November 1922, p. 3, Record Group 4,
Series 1, Box 78, Folder 1804, Rockefeller Archive Center.

39. Jin Lunhai, *Nongcun fuxing yu xiang jiao yundong* [Rural rejuvenation

and the rural education movement] (Shanghai: Zhonghua shuju, 1934), 160–63; C. Chen, *Medicine in Rural China*, 66–69. See also chapter 4, below.

40. James Yen, *The Ting Hsien Experiment in 1934* (Peking: Chinese National Association of the Mass Education Movement, 1934). The movement's health program will be discussed in detail in chapter 4. For its origin and early developments, see Charles W. Hayford, *To the People: James Yen and Village China* (New York: Columbia University Press, 1990), 51–53, 57–59, 88–102.

41. Henry Fowler, "Medical Mission Policy," *China Medical Journal* (1923): 253.

42. W. R. Lambuth, *Medical Missions: The Twofold Task* (New York: Student Volunteer Movement for Foreign Missions, 1920), 16, 72. See also Balme, *China and Modern Medicine*, 60–62.

43. Peter, "Health Problems," 2023.

44. Lambuth, *Medical Missions*, 226–27; Balme, *China and Modern Medicine*, 78, 1n. See also William G. Lennox, "A Self Survey of Mission Hospitals in China," *Chinese Medical Journal* 46 (1932): 484.

45. Balme, *China and Modern Medicine*, 196–97; Dugald Christie, *Medical Missions* (n.d.), Protestant Missions in China, China Pamphlet Series and China Document Series, Box 6, No. 31, United Church of Canada Archives, Toronto.

46. Balme, *China and Modern Medicine*, 188.

47. Bishop Frederick R. Graves to President Charles W. Eliot of Harvard University, 2 May 1912, quoted in Peter K. M. New and Yueh-wah Cheung, "Harvard Medical School of China, 1911–1916: An Expanded Footnote in the History of Western Medical Education in China," *Social Science and Medicine* 16 (1982): 1211.

48. Lennox, "Self Survey of Mission Hospitals," 499.

49. For a description of Dr. Peter's work, see W. W. Peter, *Broadcasting Health in China: The Field and Methods of Public Health Work in the Missionary Enterprise* (Shanghai: Presbyterian Mission Press, 1926). The quote is from page 43. For an evaluation of Peter's activities and the public-health education work of medical missionaries before 1928, see Ka-che Yip, "Health and Society in China: Public Health Education for the Community, 1917–1937," *Social Science and Medicine* 16 (1982): 1198–1200.

50. Stauffer, ed., *Christian Occupation of China*, 425. See also Ka-che Yip, "Medical Education in China: The American Connection, 1912–1937," in *Sino-American Relations Since 1900*, ed. Priscilla Roberts (Hong Kong: Center of Asian Studies, University of Hong Kong, 1991), 94–96, 99–100.

51. For a critique of the poor conditions in mission medical schools,

see China Medical Commission of the Rockefeller Foundation, *Medicine in China*, 32–34.

52. Greene's letter to Family, 9 March 1916, quoted in Warren I. Cohen, *The Chinese Connection: Roger S. Greene, Thomas W. Lamont, George E. Sokolsky, and American–East Asian Relations* (New York: Columbia University Press, 1978), 33.

53. For details of the founding of the Peking Union Medical College, see Bullock, *American Transplant*, 24–47.

54. For a discussion of the China Medical Board's activities in organizing the college and hospital, see Roger S. Greene, "China Medical Board: A Review of Its Work from 1915 to 1919," in *Fifth Annual Report, China Medical Board*, n.d., pp. 53–91, CMB, Inc., Box 23, Folder 161, Rockefeller Archive Center.

55. "The Reminiscences of Doctor John B. Grant," Oral History Research Project, Special Collections, Columbia University, conducted by Dr. Saul Benison, 1961, p. 300.

56. W. S. Carter, "The First Five Years of the Peking Union Medical College," *Chinese Medical Journal* 40 (1926): 737–38.

57. Greene, "China Medical Board," 58–63.

58. For a discussion of the China Medical Board's strategy, see Laurence A. Schneider, "The Rockefeller Foundation, the China Foundation, and the Development of Modern Science in China," *Social Science and Medicine* 16 (1982): 1217–21.

Notes to Chapter 2

1. The text of the mandate can be found in Min-ch'ien T. Z. Tyau, *Two Years of Nationalist China* (Shanghai: Kelly and Walsh, 1930), 263.

2. Benjamin Schwartz, *In Search of Wealth and Power: Yen Fu and the West* (Cambridge: Harvard University Press, 1964), 86.

3. Croizier, *Traditional Medicine in Modern China*, 59–63.

4. Ibid., 70–77.

5. Wong and Wu, *History of Chinese Medicine*, 607.

6. Ibid., 705–7.

7. C. Chen, *Medicine in Rural China*, 43–49.

8. Ibid., 50.

9. Ibid., 51.

10. Ibid., 54.

11. Ibid., 51–53.

12. Association for the Advancement of Public Health in China, *Memorandum*. In this document, the population figure for China was given as 400 million instead of 450 million.

13. Gideon Chen, "Chinese Government Economic Planning and Reconstruction," in *Problems of the Pacific, 1933* (Chicago: University of Chicago Press, 1934), 353.

14. Ibid., 358–59.

15. For a discussion of the National Reconstruction Commission and its projects, see Tyau, *Two Years of Nationalist China*, 283–96.

16. "Xunzheng shiqi jingji jianshe shishi gangyao fangzhen an" [Summary plan for the implementation of economic reconstruction in the period of tutelage], in *Geming wenxian* [Documents of the revolution], vol. 79 (Taibei: Historical Commission of the Kuomintang [Guomindang], 1979), 118–19.

17. "Report on the Work of the Preparatory Office of the National Economic Council, October 1933," in League of Nations, *Annexes to the Report to the Council of the League of Nations of its Technical Delegate on His Mission in China from Date of Appointment Until April 1, 1934* (Shanghai: *North China Daily News and Herald*, 1934), 11.

18. League of Nations, *Report of the Technical Delegate on His Mission in China from Date of Appointment Until April 1, 1934* (Geneva: League of Nations, 1934), 7.

19. Ibid., 9, 11–12.

20. For the origins of the National Economic Council and League involvement, see Gideon Chen, "Chinese Government," 361–63; Tze-hsiung Kuo, *Technical Cooperation Between China and Geneva* (Nanjing: Council of International Affairs, 1936), 1–9; and League of Nations, *Report of the Technical Delegate*, 9–10. For the strategic nature of some of the programs, see "China's Reconstruction Programme," in *Problems of the Pacific, 1933*, 181, 2n. The League's cooperation with the Nationalist government will be discussed in chapter 3.

21. Leonard S. Hsu, *A Sociological View on Rural Reconstruction* (n.p., 1935), 1, copy filed in Record Group 1, Series 601, Box 10, Folder 102, Rockefeller Archive Center. See also Lawrence M. Chen, *Public Health in National Reconstruction* (Nanjing: Council of International Affairs, 1937), 51.

22. L. Hsu, 2–3.

23. John B. Grant, "Philosophy of Rural Reconstruction in China," in *Asiatic Society of Bengal, Journal and Proceedings*, series 3: *Letters* (Calcutta: Asiatic Society of Bengal, 1940), 6:119.

24. On the developments of this belief in the West, see John Duffy, *The*

Healers: A History of American Medicine (Urbana: University of Illinois Press, 1979), 192–93.

25. L. Chen, *Public Health in National Reconstruction*, 51–52.

26. *Xin shenghuo yu jiankang* [New life and health] (Nanjing: Zheng zhong shuju, 1934), 26.

27. Wu Songshan, "Weisheng yundong it yiyi yu zhungyao" [The meaning and importance of the health movement], *Zhongyang ribao, yixue zhoukan* [Central daily, medical weekly supplement] 134 (16 February 1936); Hu Dingan, "Difang weisheng xingzheng fan lun" [General discussion of local health administration], *Jian guo yuekan* [National reconstruction monthly] 3, no. 3 (July 1930): 47.

28. Zhongguo Guomindang zhongyang xuanchuan bu [Central Propaganda Department of the Guomindang], *Weisheng yundong xuanchuan gangyao* [An outline of propaganda in the health movement] (Nanjing: Zhongyang xuanchuan bu, 1929), 4–5.

29. Zou Shuwen, *Xin shenghuo yu xiangcun jianshe* [New life and village reconstruction] (Nanjing: Zheng zhong shuju, 1934), 1.

30. *Xin shenghuo yu jiankang*, 63–85.

31. For a discussion of the state in Nationalist ideology, see John Fitzgerald, "The Misconceived Revolution: State and Society in China's Nationalist Revolution, 1923–1926," *Journal of Asian Studies* 49, no. 2 (May 1990): 323–43.

32. For Sun's plan, see Tyau, *Two Years of Nationalist China*, 439–42. For the Guomindang's plan for implementing Sun's ideas, see "Tuijin difang zizhi an" [Plan for the promotion of local self-government], in *Geming wenxian*, vol. 79, 250–57.

33. *Zhongyang dong wu yuekan* [Central party monthly], no. 5 (December 1928); no. 8 (March 1929).

34. Li Tingan, *Zhongguo xiangcun weisheng wenti* [The problem of rural health in China] (Shanghai: Shangwu yinshuguan, 1935), 1 (preface).

35. League of Nations, *Report of the Technical Delegate*, 10.

36. *Zhongyang dong wu yuekan*, no. 10 (May 1929).

37. R. K. S. Lim and C. C. Chen, "State Medicine," *Chinese Medical Journal* 51 (June 1937): 784; C. Chen, *Medicine in Rural China*, 53.

38. C. Chen, "Xiangcun weisheng," 188.

39. See, for example, Li Tingan, *Zhongguo xiangcun weisheng wenti*, 121–22; C. Chen, "Xiangcun weisheng"; Lim and Chen, "State Medicine," 780; and Mei Yilin, "Yixue shang zhi xin jianshe —gongyi" [New development in medicine—state medicine], *Zhongyang ribao* [Central daily], 1930 (no

precise date given; copy filed in the Archives of the Historical Commission of the Kuomintang, Taibei, Taiwan).

40. Ibid. It would be an oversimplification to assume that Chinese medical planners simply transferred the then current European model of state medicine to China, although they may have been influenced by such a model. See AnElissa Lucas, *Chinese Medical Modernization: Comparative Policy Continuities, 1930s–1980s* (New York: Praeger, 1982), 58–60.

41. See F. C. Yen, "Medicine of the Future in China," *Chinese Medical Journal* 50 (1936): 155–58; Lim and Chen, "State Medicine," 781–96; and Mei, "Yixue shang zhi xin jianshe—gongyi."

42. Liu's letter to the medical director of the Health Organization of the League of Nations, reproduced in "Proposals of the National Government of the Republic of China for Collaboration with the League of Nations in Health Matters," in League of Nations, *Annual Report of the Health Organization for 1929* (Geneva: League of Nations, 1930), 15.

43. Howard S. Berliner, "Philanthropic Foundation and Scientific Medicine," D.Sc. thesis, School of Hygiene and Public Health, Johns Hopkins University, 1977, 53–55, 108.

44. Barbara G. Rosenkrantz, "Cart Before Horse: Theory, Practice and Professional Image in American Public Health, 1870–1920," *Journal of the History of Medicine* 29 (1974): 55–73.

45. See chapter 6. For an interesting discussion of health-manpower planning in a developing country, see Carl E. Taylor, Rahmi Dirican, and Kurt W. Deuschle, *Health Manpower Planning in Turkey: An International Research Case Study* (Baltimore: Johns Hopkins University Press, 1968).

Notes to Chapter 3

1. "Public Health Reconstruction Under the National Government," *Chinese Medical Journal* 46 (1932): 826.

2. The Ministry of the Interior, for example, had a total of twelve ministers during the years 1928–37. See Tien, *Government and Politics in Kuomintang China*, 23.

3. Henry S. Houghton, memorandum, 18 March 1927, in CMB, Inc., Box 70, Folder 496, Rockefeller Archive Center. See also "Reminiscences of Grant," 230–31.

4. Henry S. Houghton, interview with Dr. Grant, 11 April 1927, in CMB, Inc., Record Group 4, 2 B9, Rockefeller Archive Center.

5. "Reminiscences of Grant," 261–62. Grant did not specify the time of the meeting, but based on J. Heng Liu's letter (quoted in note 7) it might have taken place in July. See also note 9; and Bullock, *American Transplant*, 152.

6. New was a Harvard Medical School graduate who had served as field director of the Red Cross Society and was the founder of the Orthopedic Hospital of Shanghai in 1928. King, a graduate of Chiba Medical College in Japan and the Johns Hopkins School of Hygiene and Public Health, had taught at Peking's National Medical College and served in the Peking First Health Station. For New's biography, see Huang Shuze, *Zhongguo xiandai ming yi zhuan* [Biographies of famous physicians in contemporary China], vol. 2 (Beijing: Kexue puji chubanshe, 1987), 16–22. For King's biography, see Li Xiangming, *Zhongguo xiandai yixuejia zhuang lue* [Short biographies of contemporary Chinese medical specialists] (Beijing: Kexue jishu wenxian chubanshe, 1984), 280–86.

7. J. Heng Liu, "Short Visit to Shanghai and Nanking," n.d., p. 1, CMB, Inc., Box 70, Folder 496, Rockefeller Archive Center.

8. "Reminiscences of Grant," 261–62.

9. Ibid., 271.

10. *Weisheng gongbao* [Gazette of the Ministry of Health], 1 January 1929, 2.; Roger S. Greene to M. K. Eggleston, 8 November 1928, in CMB, Inc., Box 70, Folder 496, Rockefeller Archive Center.

11. *Weisheng gongbao*, 1 May 1930, 1.

12. Roger S. Greene to Alan Gregg, 20 December 1934, in Roger S. Greene Papers, Houghton Library, Harvard University.

13. J. Heng Liu, "The Chinese Ministry of Health," *National Medical Journal of China* 15 (1929): 135–48.

14. Tyau, *Two Years of Nationalist China*, 270; "National Board of Health," *National Medical Journal of China* 16 (1930): 124.

15. "Public Health Reconstruction," 826.

16. "Provisional National Health Council," in Record Group 4, 2 B9, Box 75, No. 529, Rockefeller Archive Center.

17. Tien, *Government and Politics in Kuomintang China*, 15.

18. League of Nations, *Notes on Public Health and Modern Medicine in China* (Geneva: League of Nations, 1930), 13–15. This is Rajchman's report to the League.

19. *Weisheng tongji* [Health statistics] (Chongqing: Neizheng bu, 1938), 6–9.

20. League of Nations, *Notes on Public Health*, 12, 19–22.

21. J. Liu, "The Chinese Ministry of Health," 141.

22. Ibid., 138–39; "Public Health Reconstruction," 826–27.

23. *Quan guo jingji weiyuanhui choubeichu gongzuo baogao* [Work report of the Preparatory Department of the National Economic Council] (N.p., 1933), 2; "Collaboration with Governments and Public Health Administra-

tions," in League of Nations, *Minutes of 17th Session, May 4–8, 1931, League of Nations Health Organization* (Geneva: League of Nations, 1931), 14. For a constitution of the Weishengshu, see I. C. Fang, "Public Health," *China Christian Yearbook, 1932–33* (Shanghai: Christian Literature Society, 1933), 429–33.

24. Liu to Roger S. Greene, 22 November 1930, Roger S. Greene Papers.

25. Roger Greene's interview of Rajchman, 21 December 1930, p. 3, CMB, Inc., Box 22, Folder 155, Rockefeller Archive Center.

26. John Grant to Roger S. Greene, 29 August 1933, in Record Group 4, 2 B9, Box 75, No. 530, Rockefeller Archive Center; Greene to Heiser, 7 October 1933, in Record Group 4, 2 B9, Box 95, No. 682, Rockefeller Archive Center.

27. "Reminiscences of Grant," 368; Szeming Sze, *Medical Work in China, 1934–1941* (Boca Raton, Fla.: L.I.S.Z. Publications, 1984), 14.

28. Wong and Wu, *History of Chinese Medicine*, 734.

29. Ibid., 739; Fang, "Public Health," 433–37.

30. Ibid., 438; *Peipingshi zhengfu weishengchu yewu baogao* [Work report of the Peiping Health Department] (Peiping: Weisheng chu, 1934), 1.

31. R. Cecil Robertson, "Public Health," in *China Yearbook, 1938,* 131. For discussions of some aspects of this process, see "Minguo ershisan nian du Fujian sheng zheng diaocha baogao" [Investigative report of the Fujian Provincial Administration in 1934], *Neizheng tongji jikan* [Statistical quarterly of internal administration], no. 2 (January 1937): 105–30; J. Heng Liu, "San nian lai zhongyang weisheng sheshi gaikuang" [General survey of health reconstruction in the last three years], *Weisheng banyue kan* [Health bimonthly] 2, no. 1 (15 January 1935): 4–5; and *Jiangxi sheng weisheng shiye gaikuang* [A survey of health work in Jiangxi] (N.p., 1938), 1–2.

32. The rural health structure will be discussed in detail in chapter 5.

33. *Quan guo jingji weiyuanhui choubeichu gongzuo baogao,* 30–31; J. Heng Liu, "Health and Medicine," in *China Yearbook, 1935–36,* 1576–77. See also chapter 5.

34. Knud Faber, *Report on Medical Schools in China* (Geneva: League of Nations Health Organization, 1931), 9.

35. J. Heng Liu, "National Health Organization," *China Christian Yearbook, 1936–37* (Glendale, Calif.: Arthur Clark, 1937), 352–53; Szeming Sze, *China's Health Problems* (Washington, D.C.: Chinese Medical Association, 1943), 16.

36. See League of Nations, "Proposals of the National Government for Collaboration," 14–18; and Kuo, *Technical Cooperation Between China and Geneva,* 1–3.

37. Letter of J. B. Grant to J. Heng Liu, 3 December 1929, Roger S. Greene Papers.

38. League of Nations, *Report Submitted to the Secretary General by the Director of the Section for Communications and Transit, Secretary of the Council Committee, on his Mission in China, January-May 1935* (Geneva: League of Nations, 1935), 34.

39. League of Nations, "Proposals of the National Government for Collaboration," 15–18; League of Nations, *Notes on Public Health*, 43–49.

40. Kuo, *Technical Cooperation Between China and Geneva*, 5–7.

41. J. Heng Liu, "The Origin and Development of Public Health Service in China," in *Voices From Unoccupied China*, ed. Harley F. MacNair (Chicago: University of Chicago Press, 1944), 38. In 1941, the name was changed to the National Institute of Health.

42. Roger S. Greene's interview with Dr. Rajchman, 21 December 1930, p. 1, CMB, Inc., Box 22, Folder 155, Rockefeller Archive Center.

43. Ibid.

44. *Weisheng shiyan chu gongzuo baogao* [Work report of the Central Field Health Station] (Nanjing: Central Field Health Station, 1935), 2.

45. League of Nations, *Minutes of 17th Session*, 14; Brian R. Dyer, "Methods Developed at the Central Field Health Station for the Training of Sanitation Personnel," *Chinese Medical Journal* 50 (1936): 76–81.

46. Roger S. Greene's interview with Dr. Rajchman, 21 December 1930, 2.

47. League of Nations, *Report of the Health Organisation for the Period October 1932 to September 1933* (Geneva: League of Nations, 1933), 505.

48. "Report of the National Health Administration on the Three Year Plan, 1931–34," in League of Nations, *Annexes to the Report to the Council of the League of Nations of its Technical Delegate on his Mission in China from Date of Appointment Until April 1, 1934* (Shanghai: *North China Daily News and Herald*, 1934), 241.

49. The regulations governing the organization of the Central Field Health Station can be found in "Regulations Governing the Organization of the National Economic Council and of its Bureaux, Committees and Offices, 1934," in ibid., 20–22.

50. League of Nations, *Report of the Technical Delegate*, 41.

51. *Weisheng shiyan chu gongzuo baogao*, 1–3, 23–38.

52. League of Nations, *Report of the Health Organisation, 1932–33*. 509; League of Nations, *Report of the Technical Delegate*, 41.

53. For a discussion of the reorganization of medical education, see chapter 6.

54. See chapter 6. See also Roger S. Greene to Selskar M. Gunn, 12 March 1934, in Roger S. Greene Papers; and Bullock, *American Transplant*, 158.

55. These regulations are reproduced in Xue Jianwu, *Zhongguo xiangcun weisheng xingzheng* [Village health administration in China] (Shanghai: Shangwu yinshuguan, 1937), 193–99, 215–21. See also *Weisheng tongji*, 34.

56. Ibid., 184–89.

57. Wong and Wu, *History of Chinese Medicine*, 161–64.

58. "Guoyiguan di laili" [The origin of the Institute of National Medicine], *Tianwentai bao* [Observatory daily], 30 December 1968; Croizier, *Traditional Medicine in Modern China*, 134.

59. *Weisheng gongbao*, 1 December 1929, 1 January 1930; "Xianzhi zhongyi jiguo" [The process of restricting Chinese medicine], *Zhongxi yixue bao* [Journal of Chinese and western medicine] 10, no. 10 (April 1930): 33–35.

60. Xue Jianwu, *Zhonggu xiangcun weisheng xingzheng*, 190–93.

61. "Guoyiguan di laili"; "Zhongyi di hefa diwei" [The legal status of Chinese medicine], *Tianwentai bao*, n.d. Clippings of both articles are filed in the Guomindang Historical Commission Archives. Although there is no date given for the second article, it is clearly a continuation of the first, so it must have been published on 31 December 1968 or sometime in early January 1969 (see note 58). See also Wu Lien-teh, "The Rejuvenation of Medicine in China," *China Quarterly* (December 1935): 64–65; and Croizier *Traditional Medicine in Modern China*, 134–37.

62. Parks M. Coble, Jr., *The Shanghai Capitalists and the Nationalist Government, 1927–1937* (Cambridge: Harvard University Press, 1980), 67–68; Douglas S. Paauw, "Chinese National Expenditures During the Nanking Period," *Far Eastern Quarterly* 12 (November 1952): 9.

63. Ibid.

64. Coble, *Shanghai Capitalists*, 109–39. Franklin Ho, director of political affairs in the Executive Yuan in 1936, charged that "Chiang Kai-shek used the public purse as his own, though not on himself personally, but often gave orders for public funds to be used without regard to budget procedure" ("The Reminiscences of Ho Lien [Franklin L. Ho]," Oral History Research Project, Special Collections, Columbia University, 1967, 156).

65. Jia Shiyi, *Minguo xu caizheng shi* [Supplement to the fiscal history of the Republic], vol. 1 (Shanghai: Shangwu yinshuguan, 1932), 46–49. Total national expenditures in 1929 were $434 million. Assuming that the amount budgeted for health was actually spent (we do not have precise figures for health spending), the percentage was still .16. For total national expenditures in 1929, see Coble, *Shanghai Capitalists*, 68.

66. The health budget was $1.9 million, and the total of national budgeted expenditures was $893 million. See Jia Shiyi, *Minguo xu caizheng shi* (p. 50), for the total expenditures; and Wong and Wu, *History of Chinese Medicine* (pp. 735–36, 856) for the health budget. If we use the actual total national expenditures of $714 million (Coble, *Shanghai Capitalists*, 68) to calculate the percentage as in note 65, the percentage is .27.

67. Sze, *China's Health Problems*, 15. The total budget was $1,544 million and the health budget was $10.8 million.

68. For the health budget, see Wong and Wu, *History of Chinese Medicine*, 735–36. Percentages calculated in this paragraph are based on this budget.

69. *Weisheng tongji*, 22.

70. Ibid., 24–26.

71. *Jiangxi sheng weisheng shiye gaikuang*, 1; "Minguo ershisan nian du Fujian sheng zheng diaocha baogao," 118.

72. *Weisheng tongji*, 25–26.

73. Arthur Salter, *China and Silver* (New York: Economic Forum, 1934), 105.

74. *Weisheng banyue kan* 2, no. 7 (15 April 1935): 27.

75. "Reminiscences of Grant," 247, 368.

76. George E. Vincent to H. S. Houghton, 15 April 1936, Papers of Dr. J. Heng Liu, Oral History Project, Special Collections, Columbia University; H. S. Houghton to E. C. Lobenstine, 10 June 1936, CMB, Inc., Box 70, Folder 496, Rockefeller Archive Center; John Grant to SMG [*sic*], 10 April 1937, ibid. In a conversation with the author on 20 November 1993, Mrs. Irene L. Hou (daughter of Dr. J. Heng Liu) indicated that from what she had heard Dr. Liu moved funds from account to account in order to meet the immediate needs of certain projects when allocated funds were not forthcoming. He had, however, always made sure that funds were returned to the proper accounts. Dr. Liu was very upset with the accusations because they distorted his true intention, which was to establish the best possible health system in China.

Notes to Chapter 4

1. H. D. Fong, "Rural Industries in China," in *Problems of the Pacific, 1933*, 306–12.

2. Lawrence M. Chen, *Rural Rehabilitation* (Nanjing: Council of International Affairs, 1936), 8–9. Sir Arthur Salter, the League of Nations' official adviser to the National Economic Council in late 1933, had reported on this and other economic problems in *China and Silver*.

3. T'ang Leang-li, *China's New Currency System* (London: Kegan, Paul, Trench, Trubner, 1936), 56–60.

4. Chen Han-seng, "The Agrarian Problem in China," in *Problems of the Pacific, 1933*, 283–84.

5. L.Chen, *Rural Rehabilitation*, 6, 10; and Meng Zhaohua and Wang Minghuan, *Zhongguo minzheng shigao*, 256–58. Other natural disasters in this period included drought, locusts, and earthquakes.

6. *Guojia jianshe congkan* [A collection of essays on national reconstruction], vol. 2 (Taibei: Zhonghuaminguo guojia jianshe congkan bianwu weiyuanhui, 1971), 211.

7. Wong and Wu, *History of Chinese Medicine*, 856–58.

8. C. C. Chen, "A Proposed Basic Medical Curriculum," *Chinese Medical Journal* 49 (1935): 862; Li Tingan, *Zhongguo xiangcun weisheng wenti*, 5.

9. Wu Lien-teh, "Fundamentals of State Medicine," *Chinese Medical Journal* 51 (June 1937): 778.

10. C. Chen, "Proposed Basic Medical Curriculum," 862.

11. Andrija Stampar had commented on these problems in "Observations of a Rural Health Worker," *New England Journal of Medicine* 218, no. 24 (16 June 1938): 991–97.

12. C. C. Chen, "Some Problems of Medical Organization in Rural China," *Chinese Medical Journal* 51 (June 1937): 803–4.

13. Gideon Chen, "Chinese Government," 307–8; "China's Reconstruction Program," 190.

14. The Historical Commission of the Kuomintang has published four volumes of documents on the cooperative movement before the war (*Geming wenxian*, vols. 84–87). For a brief summary of the principles of the cooperative movement, see "Hezuoshe fa yuanze" [Principles of the cooperative], in ibid., 84:326–28.

15. Kuo, *Technical Cooperation Between China and Geneva*, 13–14.

16. C. Dragoni, "Report on Agricultural Reform and Development in China," in League of Nations, *Annexes*, 167–226.

17. J. Liu, "National Health Organization," 338–39.

18. C. C. Chen, "Xiangcun weisheng," 187. See also John Grant, "State Medicine: A Logical Policy for China," *National Medical Journal of China* 14 (April 1928): 73.

19. Stampar, "Observations," 995.

20. Tsefang Huang, "The Development of Health Centers," *Chinese Medical Journal* 55 (June 1939):546–60.

21. Paul Starr, *The Social Transformation of American Medicine: The Rise of*

a Sovereign Profession and the Making of a Vast Industry (New York: Basic Books, 1982), 194.

22. Ibid., 194–97. See also David A. Pearson, "The Concept of Regionalized Personal Health Services in the United States, 1920–1955," in *The Regionalization of Personal Health Services*, ed. Ernest W. Saward. Rev. ed. (New York: Prodist for the Milbank Memorial Fund, 1976), 3–60; and Victor Sidel and Ruth Sidel, *Reforming Medicine: Lessons of the Last Quarter Century* (New York: Pantheon, 1984), 16–19.

23. T. Huang, "Development of Health Centers."

24. Allan Nevins, *Study in Power: John D. Rockefeller* (New York: Charles Scribner's Sons, 1953), 324–27; Jules Abels, *The Rockefeller Billions* (New York: Macmillan, 1965), 330.

25. Lucas, *Chinese Medical Modernization*, 26–31. For a critical view of the foundation's global health programs, see E. Richard Brown, *Rockefeller Medicine Men: Medicine and Capitalism in America* (Berkeley: University of California Press, 1980), 116–17.

26. Bullock, *American Transplant*, 135–36. For the evolution and development of Grant's ideas on community health care, see also Seipp, *Health Care for the Community*.

27. Grant, "Department of Public Health," 113–16.

28. John B. Grant to Roger S. Greene, 31 October 1931, Record Group 4, 2 B9, Box 67, No. 472, Rockefeller Archive Center.

29. Li Tingan to Dr. Richard M. Pearce, 7 February 1930, Record Group 4, 2 B9, Box 76, No. 535, ibid.

30. Li Tingan, "Summary Report on Rural Public Health Practice in China," *Chinese Medical Journal* 48 (1934): 1086–90; Li Tingan, *Zhongguo xiangcun weisheng wenti*, 96–104. See also *Weisheng banyuekan*, 28 February 1935, 18–23.

31. Chen Qingzhi, *Zhongguo jiaoyu shi* [History of Chinese education] (Taibei: Shangwu yinshuguan, 1968), 785–87; Jin Lunhai, *Nongcun fuxing yu xiang jiao yundong*, 160–63.

32. C. C. Chen, interview with the author, 3 June 1985.

33. Ibid.; Guy S. Alitto, *The Last Confucian: Liang Shu-ming and the Chinese Dilemma of Modernity* (Berkeley: University of California Press, 1979), 235, 24n; Hayford, *To the People*, 64. See also C. Chen, *Medicine in Rural China*, 66–69; Ku Jinghan, "Xiaozhuang shehui weisheng diaocha" [An investigation of social medicine in Xiaozhuang], *Zhongyang ribao, yixue zhoukan* [Central daily, medical supplement], 9 February, 16 February, 23 February, and 1 March 1936.

34. J. Yen, *Ting Hsien Experiment*, 5; Hayford, *To the People*, 92–97. The

Movement had published three volumes of the survey results in Chinese. Based on these studies, Gamble later published his *Ting Hsien: A North China Rural Community* (New York: Institute of Pacific Relations, 1954).

35. *Weisheng gongbao* 2, no. 1 (1 January 1930): 57.

36. J. Yen, *Ting Hsien Experiment*, 27.

37. See Hsun-yuan Yao, "The Second Year of the Rural Health Experiment in Ting Hsien, China," *Milbank Memorial Fund Quarterly Bulletin* 10 (January 1932): 56–57.

38. John B. Grant to Roger S. Greene, 31 May 1932, with enclosure of agreement, CMB, Inc., Box 85, No. 600, Rockefeller Archive Center. See also "Reminiscences of Grant," 325B; and C. Chen, *Medicine in Rural China*, 71–72.

39. C. C. Chen, "The Rural Public Health Experiment in Ting Hsien, China," *Milbank Memorial Fund Quarterly Bulletin* 14 (January 1936): 67–70. See also Li Tingan, *Zhongguo xiangcun weisheng wenti*, 104–14.

40. C. C. Chen, "Public Health in Rural Reconstruction at Ting Hsien," *Milbank Memorial Fund Quarterly Bulletin* 12 (1934): 371, 374.

41. C. Chen, *Medicine in Rural China*, 58.

42. James Yen to Dr. Stampar, 18 May 1932, p. 3, CMB, Inc., Box 85, No. 600.1, Rockefeller Archive Center.

43. Alitto, *The Last Confucian*, 173–76, 248–64; Chen Qingzhi, *Zhongguo jiaoyu shi*, 787–88; Wang Donglin, *Liang Shuming wenda lu* [A record of questions and answers with Liang Shuming] (Changsha: Hunan renmin chubanshe, 1988), 52–53; Charles H. Corbett, *Shantung Christian University (Cheeloo)* (New York: United Board for Christian Colleges in China, 1955), 227.

44. L. Chen, *Public Health in National Reconstruction*, 80.

45. Li Tingan, *Zhongguo xiangcun weisheng wenti*, 81–85; "Report of the National Health Administration on the Three Year Plan," 259–61. The discussion of activities in Tangshan that follows is based on these sources.

46. *Weisheng shiyan chu gongzuo baogao*, 33–34; J. Liu, "National Health Organization," 339, 351–52; L. Chen, *Public Health in National Reconstruction*, 79–81. On the experimental *xian*, see "Guominzhengfu dian du Nanjing qi ershier nian zhi neizheng" [Internal administration from the founding of the national government at Nanjing to 1933]; and "Minguo ershier nian di neizheng jianshe" [Reconstruction in internal administration in 1933], both in *Geming wenxian*, 71:135–36, 145, respectively.

47. J. Heng Liu, "Some Phases of Public Health Work in China," *Chinese Medical Journal* 48 (1934): 73.

48. Ibid. See also Fang, "Public Health," 438–39; and *Weisheng tongji*, 18.

49. *Neizheng nianjian* [Yearbook of internal administration] (Shanghai:

Shangwu yinshuguan, 1935), (G)10; "Report of the National Health Administration on the Three Year Plan," 261–63.

50. *Weisheng shiyan chu gongzuo baogao*, 23–38; Stampar, "Health and Social Conditions," 132–36.

51. *Weisheng tongji*, 18; *Weisheng shiyan chu gongzuo baogao*, 33–34; J. Liu, "San nian lai zhongyang weisheng sheshi gaikuang," 5. See also J. Liu, "National Health Organization," 351.

52. "Zhongguo Guomindang di wu ci quanguo daibiao dahui neizheng-bu gongzuo baogao" [Work report of the Interior Department at the Fifth National Party Congress of the Guomindang], in *Geming wenxian*, 71:263–65; *Weisheng banyuekan* 2, no. 5 (15 March 1935): 9–11; "Public Health and Medicine," in *China Handbook, 1937–1943*, (New York: Macmillan, 1943), 673; Meng and Wang, *Zhongguo minzheng shigao*, 68–69.

53. "Guomingzhengfu diandu Nanjing qi ershier nian zhi neizheng," in *Geming wenxian*, 71:135–36; "Minguo ershier nian di neizheng jianshe," in ibid., 71:145. See also J. Xue, *Zhongguo xiangcun weisheng xingzheng*, 34–36.

54. *Neizheng nianjian*, (G)11, (G)231–32.

55. "Report of the National Health Administration on the Three Year Plan," 262.

56. The issue of popular health education and health manpower will be dealt with in the following chapters.

57. J. Liu, "National Health Organization," 351; Li Tingan, "Summary Report on Rural Public Health," 1086–90. See also Robertson, "Public Health," 132. Robertson's figures list only seventy-six health stations and substations.

58. Stampar, "Health and Social Conditions," 148–49.

59. *Xian weisheng shengzheng shishi banfa gangyao* [A summary of methods to implement county health administration] (Chongqing: Weisheng shu, 1939); Robertson, "Public Health," 132.

60. "Public Health and Medicine," 674.

61. Dr. C. C. Chen, interview with the author, 3 June 1985; J. Liu, "Health and Medicine," 1577. See also Lucas, *Chinese Medical Modernization*, 71–76.

62. Bullock, *American Transplant*, 166.

63. *New Life Centers in Rural Kiangsi*, 1–2, and chart ("The Relationship Chart of Rural Welfare Center") following p. 2. For a summary of the League experts' report, see Max Brauer, E. Briand-Clausen, and A. Stampar, "Report on a Survey of Certain Localities in Kiangsi," in League of Nations, *Annexes*, 41–69. See also William Wei, *Counterrevolution in China: The Nationalists in Jiangxi During the Soviet Period* (Ann Arbor: University of Michigan Press, 1985), 144–46.

64. *New Life Centers in Rural Kiangsi*, 1; *Jiangxi sheng weisheng shiye gaikuang*, 13–16.

65. Ibid., 9–12; Stampar, "Health and Social Conditions," 130.

66. *New Life Centers in Rural Kiangsi*, 4.

67. Ibid., 16–19.

68. Zou, *Xin shenghuo yu xiangcun jianshe*, 57–61.

69. Wei, *Counterrevolution in China*, 146.

70. *Jiangxi sheng weisheng shiye gaikuang*, 8–9.

71. For a discussion of the anti-Christian movement, see Ka-che Yip, *Religion, Nationalism and Chinese Students: The Anti-Christian Movement of 1922–1927* (Bellingham: Center for Asian Studies, Western Washington University, 1980).

72. Jessie G. Lutz, *China and the Christian Colleges, 1850–1950* (Ithaca: Cornell University Press, 1971), 283–99; *United Church of Canada Yearbook, 1932* (Toronto: United Church of Canada, 1932), 111.

73. Corbett, *Shantung Christian University (Cheeloo)*, 218.

74. *China Yearbook, 1932*, 560; *China Yearbook, 1934*, 335.

75. Thomson, *While China Faced West*, 117; *China Yearbook, 1935*, 321.

76. Ronald Rees, *China Faces the Storm: The Christian Church in China Today* (London: Edinburgh House, 1938), 60–63; *United Church of Canada Yearbook, 1936*, 86.

77. *The United Church of Canada Yearbook, 1937*, 65; Edward H. Hume, *Doctors East, Doctors West: An American Physician's Life in China* (New York: W. W. Norton, 1946), 273–75.

78. J. Liu, "National Health Organization," 355.

79. James Yen to Dr. Stampar, 18 May 1932, pp. 6–7, CMB, Inc., Box 85, No. 600.1, Rockefeller Archive Center.

80. "China Program," Record Group 1, Series 601, Box 10, Folder 108, ibid. See also Frank Ninkovich, "The Rockefeller Foundation, China, and Cultural Change," *Journal of American History* 70, no. 4 (March 1984): 809.

81. Thomson, *While China Faced West*, 140–41.

82. Bullock, *American Transplant*, 158–59.

83. "China Program."

84. Thomson, *While China Faced West*, 125–48; Bullock, *American Transplant*, 158–60.

85. Wu, "Fundamentals of State Medicine," 777.

86. "Reminiscences of Grant," 337.

87. See, for example, "Yixue jiaoyu ti wenti" [The problem of medical

education], *Zhongyang ribao, yixue zhoukan,* no. 136 (1 March 1936); and Wang Jiwen, "Zhongguo xin yixue jianshe zhi zhangai" [Obstacles to the establishment of new medicine in China], *Dagong bao* [Dagong daily] (Tianjian), 10 April 1931.

88. See, for example, *New Life Centers in Kiangsi,* 17–19; and Hu Dingan, *Xian weisheng xingzheng* [County health administration] (Chongqing: Zhong-yang zhengzhi xuexiao yanjiu bu, 1941), 2.

89. "Lun weishengbu ji yi zhuzhong yishi buxi jiaoyu" [The Ministry of Health should stress supplementary medical education], *Zhongxi yixue bao* [Journal of Chinese and western medicine] 10, no. 1 (July 1929): 1–3.

90. Chen Guofu, *Yi zheng man tan* [Random jottings on medical admin-istration] (Chongqing: Guomin chubanshe, 1941), 52; Wang Qizhang, "Hangkong jiao guo yu yiyao jiao guo" [Saving the country through aviation and saving the country through medicine], *Shenbao, yiyao zhoukan* [Shen daily, medical supplement], nos. 13, 14 (27 March 1933, 30 March 1933).

91. Li Tingan, *Zhongguo xiangcun weisheng wenti,* 113.

92. *Weisheng banyekan* 2, no. 5 (15 March 1935): 21.

93. Hayford, *To the People,* 152.

94. League of Nations, *Report Submitted to the Secretary General, 1935,* 18.

95. Alitto, *The Last Confucian,* 236–37.

96. Duara, *Culture, Power, and the State.*

97. *New Life Centers in Rural Kiangsi,* 26.

98. Stampar, "Observations," 994.

Notes to Chapter 5

1. John Duffy, *The Healers,* 196.

2. "Syllabus on Hygiene and Preventive Medicine for the Mass Educa-tion Association Institute, April 1926," p. 15, Record Group 4, 2 B9, Box 76, No. 532, Rockefeller Archive Center.

3. Ibid., 1, quoting from Winslow's "The Untilled Fields of Public Health," *Science* 51 (9 January 1920): 30.

4. For discussion of these developments, see Starr, *Social Transformation,* 189–94. See also Barbara G. Rosenkrantz, *Public Health and the State: Changing Views in Massachusetts, 1842–1936* (Cambridge: Harvard University Press, 1972).

5. Wong and Wu, *History of Chinese Medicine,* 721.

6. C. Chen, *Medicine in Rural China,* 45.

7. T. Huang, "Communicable Disease Information," 96.

8. *National Epidemic Prevention Bureau: A Report, Being a Review of its Activities from its Foundation in March 1919 to June 1934* (Peiping: Central Field Health Station, 1934), 3–4.

9. Li Tingan, "Public Health Report on Canton," 382.

10. "Regulations Governing the Public Health Experiment Station of the Police Department of the City of Peking," Record Group 4, 2 B9, Box 66, No. 465, Rockefeller Archive Center.

11. Bullock, *American Transplant*, 146.

12. T. Huang, "Communicable Disease Information," 107.

13. Chen Bangxian, *Zhongguo yixue shi*, 277–85.

14. J. Liu, "The Chinese Ministry of Health," 137, 147–48.

15. John Grant and T. M. P'eng, "Survey of Urban Public Health Practice in China," *Chinese Medical Journal* 48 (1934): 1076.

16. Li Tingan, "Summary Report of Rural Public Health," 1089.

17. *Weisheng tongji*, 71; *Weisheng shiyan chu gongzuo baogao*, 4; "Report of the National Health Administration on the Three Year Plan," 274–77.

18. *Weisheng shiyan chu gongzuo baogao*, 87–94; J. Liu, "National Health Organization," 339.

19. *Weisheng tonji*, 98.

20. For epidemiological data on these diseases at various times, see John B. Grant, "Public Health and Medical Events During 1927 and 1928," *China Yearbook, 1929–30*, 112–22 (for 1927–28); J. Liu, "Health and Medicine" (for 1934); and *Weisheng tongji*, 72–99 (for 1936).

21. *Difang weisheng xingzheng chuqi shishi fangan* [Plan for the implementation of local health administrations in the early stage] (Nanjing: Weisheng bu, 1929).

22. *Neizheng nianjian*, (G)45–(G)47; *Guojia jianshe congkan*, 2:206.

23. L. Chen, *Public Health in National Reconstruction*, 71–72; J. Liu, "Health and Medicine," 1624; Li Tingan, *Zhongguo xiangcun weisheng wenti*, 82–83.

24. *Guojia jianshe congkan*, 2:207.

25. Brauer et al., "Report on a Survey of Kiangsi," 62.

26. *Neizheng nianjian*, (G)42–(G)45.

27. J. Liu, "Health and Medicine," 1625.

28. *Zhongyang weisheng sheshi shiyan chu gongzuo baogao* [Work report of the Central Field Health Station] (Nanjing: Zhongyang weisheng sheshi shiyan chu, 1933), 28; Li Tingan, *Zhongguo xiangcun weisheng wenti*, 99; and *Quan guo jingji weiyuanhui baogao hui pian*, [A compilation of reports of the

National Economic Council], vol. 9 (Nanjing: Quan guo jingji weiyuanhui, 1936), 39.

29. "Public Health Reconstruction," 831.

30. Wong and Wu, *History of Chinese Medicine*, 802.

31. "Report of the National Health Administration on the Three Year Plan," 256–59; L. Chen, *Public Health in National Reconstruction*, 72.

32. Li Tingan, "The Campaign Against Tuberculosis," *Chinese Medical Journal* 48 (1934): 301–2.

33. Chen Bangxian, *Zhongguo yixue shi*, 283–85; *Weisheng gongbao*, 1 January 1929, 12–13.

34. L. Chen, *Public Health in National Reconstruction*, 60–61; *National Epidemic Prevention Bureau Report*, 4.

35. "Nanjingshi zhengfu ershier nian yiyue ji ershisan nian shiyue gongzuo baogao" [Work report of the municipal government of Nanjing from January 1933 to October 1934], in *Geming wenxian*, 92:370–71; *Kangjian zazhi* [Health magazine] 4, no. 3 (March 1936): 34.

36. C. C. Chen, "The Development of Systematic Training in Rural Public Health Work in China," *Milbank Memorial Fund Quarterly Bulletin* 14 (1936): 378.

37. J. Liu, "Health and Medicine," 1581.

38. Ibid., 1586–87.

39. *Quan guo jingji weiyuanhui choubeichu gongzuo baogao*, 27; and C. Chen, "Development of Systematic Training," 379. For statistics on inoculations in Anhui and Jiangxi, see *Weisheng tongji*, 101–5.

40. Nathan, *Plague Prevention and Politics*, 73.

41. L. Chen, *Public Health in National Reconstruction*, 66–68. For lists of the sera and vaccines produced by the National Epidemic Prevention Bureau, see *Neizheng nianjian*, (G)23–(G)27.

42. Ibid., (G)23.

43. "Public Health Reconstruction," 830; Kuo, *Technical Cooperation Between China and Geneva*, 11; "Report of the National Health Administration on the Three Year Plan," 246.

44. League of Nations, *Report Submitted to the Secretary General, 1935*, 38.

45. For a description of PUMC's work on kala-azar, see Bullock, *American Transplant*, 120–25.

46. *Neizheng nianjian*, (G)20–(G)21.

47. Ibid; J. Liu, "Health and Medicine," 1595–96; *Weisheng shiyan chu gongzuo baogao*, 21.

48. *Neizheng nianjian,* (G)16–(G)17; "Report of the National Health Administration on the Three Year Plan," 243.

49. Y. N. Yang, E. Landauer, C. K. Koo and P. C. Lin, "Plague Work in Fukien, China," *Chinese Medical Journal* 55 (1939): 55.

50. "Public Health Reconstruction Under the National Government," 831; "Report of the National Health Administration on the Three Year Plan," 251–53.

51. *Weisheng shiyan chu gongzuo baogao,* 8.

52. *Weisheng banyuekan,* 2 no. 2 (31 January 1935): 1–6.

53. *Weisheng tongji,* 98.

54. *Weisheng shiyan chu gongzuo baogao,* 95–96; Kuo, *Technical Cooperation Between China and Geneva,* 13.

55. For a statistical summary of the service's work in 1933 and 1934, see "Report of the National Health Administration on the Three Year Plan," 263–64; J. Liu, "Health and Medicine," 1578–79. See also League of Nations, *Report of the Health Organization, 1932–33,* 506; and F. C. Yen, "Some Problems of Public Health," *People's Tribune,* new series, 23 (1938): 113–15.

56. Tsefang Huang, "Developing a Railway Health Service," *Chinese Medical Journal* 49 (1935): 973–89.

57. *Neizheng nianjian,* (G)38–(G)39.

58. Hsun-yuan Yao, "Industrial Health Work in the Peiping Special Health Area," *China Medical Journal* 43 (1929): 379–87.

59. Wong and Wu, *History of Chinese Medicine,* 756; Li Tingan, *Zhongguo xiangcun weisheng wenti,* 103.

60. *Neizheng nianjian,* (G)38; J. Liu, "Health and Medicine," 1626.

61. Ibid.

62. For a discussion of Soong's efforts in these activities, see Y. C. Wang, *Chinese Intellectuals and the West, 1872–1949* (Chapel Hill: University of North Carolina Press, 1966), 425–32.

63. Kuo, *Technical Cooperation Between China and Geneva,* 2. See also Bullock, *American Transplant,* 139.

64. League of Nations, *Notes on Public Health,* 48.

65. League of Nations, *Annual Report of the Health Organization for 1930* (Geneva: League of Nations, 1931), 17–22.

66. J. Liu, "Health and Medicine," 1611–14; L. E. Tsao, *Quarantine Service in China* (Nanjing: Council of International Affairs, 1937), 142.

67. Kuo, *Technical Cooperation Between China and Geneva,* 10.

68. *Weisheng tongji,* 105.

69. League of Nations, *Report of the Health Organization, 1932–1933,* 509.

70. J. Liu, "Health and Medicine," 1618.

71. Tsao, *Quarantine Service,* 142–44.

72. J. Liu, "Health and Medicine," 1618, 1622–23.

73. Tsao, *Quarantine Service,* 151–56.

74. F. Yen, "Problems of Public Health," 117.

75. C. Chen,"Development of Systematic Training," 382.

76. Anne McCabe, "Maternity and Child Health Work of the First Health Station, Peiping," *Nursing Journal of China* 12, no. 4 (October 1931): 18.

77. J. Liu, "Phases of Public Health Work," 70.

78. Marion Yang, "Child Health Work in Peiping Special Health Area," *Chinese Medical Journal* 43 (1929): 920–25.

79. "Report of the National Health Administration on the Three Year Plan," 265–66.

80. J. Liu, "Phases of Public Health Work," 71.

81. Marion Yang, "Birth Control in Peiping: First Report of the Peiping Committee on Maternal Health," *Chinese Medical Journal* 48 (1934): 787.

82. Ibid., 790.

83. Li Tingan, *Zhongguo xiangcun weisheng wenti,* 63–64; P. L. Fan, "Chinese Infants and Children: A Study of the Infant and Child Mortality, Size of the Family, and Sex Ratio on 2,500 Cases," *Chinese Medical Journal* 47 (1933): 652–61. See also Bullock, *American Transplant,* 178–80.

84. *Neizheng nianjian,* (G)27–(G)28.

85. Wang Zuxiang, *Weisheng xingzheng sanshi nian suoyi* [Reminiscences of thirty years of health administration] (Taibei: Weisheng zazhi she, 1953), 21–27; "Nanjingshi zhengfu ershier nian yiyue ji ershisan nian shiyue gongzuo baogao," in *Geming wenxian* 92:324–76.

86. J. Liu, "Phases of Public Health Work," 71–72; J. Liu, "Health and Medicine," 1625.

87. *Neizheng nianjian,* (G)27.

88. Brauer et al., "Report on a Survey of Kiangsi," 60.

89. L. Chen, *Public Health in National Reconstruction,* 70; *Neizheng nianjian,* (G)28.

90. *New Life Centers in Rural Kiangsi,* 6, 19.

91. *Neizheng nianjian,* (G)28.

92. C. Chen, "Development of Systematic Training," 381–84.

93. Jin Baoshan, "Xuexiao weisheng yu qingnian jiankang" [School health and the health of youth], *Zhongyang ribao, yixue zhoukan* [Central daily, medical supplement], 19 January 1936.

94. I. C. Fang and T. A. Li, "School Health in the Peiping Special Health Area," *Chinese Medical Journal* 43 (1929): 697–706.

95. Jin Baoshan, *Xuexiao weisheng jiaoyu* [School health education] (Chongqing: Zhongyang xunlian tuan dang zheng xunlian ban, 1940), 8. Another study of school children in several cities, conducted from 1929 to 1932, confirmed these findings. See "Report of the National Health Administration on the Three Year Plan," 277.

96. For an example of Christian attempts, see *A School Health Programme: The Report of a Conference on School Health* (Shanghai: China Christian Education Association, 1925).

97. *Weisheng gongbao*, 1 July 1929, 8; Wong and Wu, *History of Chinese Medicine*, 723.

98. *Weisheng gongbao*, 1 January 1930, 121–27.

99. "Zhongguo Guomindang di si ci quanguo dibiaotahui jiaoyu gongzuo baogao" [Report on education work in the Fourth National Party Congress of the Guomindang], in *Geming wenxian*, 53:154–55. For a discussion of Three People's Principles Education, see Ka-che Yip, "Education and Political Socialization in Pre-Communist China: The Goals of San Min Chu-i Education," *Asian Profile* 9, no. 5 (October 1981): 401–13.

100. Wong and Wu, *History of Chinese Medicine*, 756; "Report of the National Health Administration on the Three Year Plan," 269.

101. *Weisheng banyuekan* 2, no. 2 (31 January 1935): 10–11; *Neizheng nianjian*, (G)28–(G)30; J. Liu, "Health and Medicine," 1627.

102. "Initial Year of the Medical Education Program," p. 55, Record Group 1, Series 601, Box 3, Folder 27, Rockefeller Archive Center.

103. Jin Baoshan, *Xuexiao weisheng jiaoyu*, 2; J. Liu, "National Health Organization," 346; "Initial Year of the Medical Education Program," 55–57.

104. *Zhongyang ribao*, 29 November 1932; *Weisheng banyukan*, 15 January 1935, 39–40, 45–46; *Weisheng banyukan*, 31 January 1935, 10–11.

105. "Report of the National Health Administration on the Three Year Plan," 270.

106. Jin Baoshan, "Xuexiao weisheng yu qingnian jiankang"; and L. Chen, *Public Health in National Reconstruction*, 71.

107. J. Bennett, "Health Education," in *Medical Care in Developing Countries*, ed. M. King (London: Oxford University Press, 1966), section 6: 2–13; R. M. Battistella and T. G. Rundall, eds., *Health Care Policy in a Changing Environment* (Berkeley: McCutchan, 1978), 224–93.

108. J. Liu, "National Health Organization," 347; *Zhongyang weisheng sheshi shiyanchu gongzuo baogao*, 35–39.

109. *Weisheng gongbao*, no. 1 (1 January 1929): 16.

110. Grant and P'eng, "Survey of Urban Public Health Practice," 1075.

111. L. Chen, *Public Health in National Reconstruction*, table 3, following p. 56.

112. C. Chen, "Rural Public Health Experiment," 70–73.

113. Li Tingan, "Campaign Against Tuberculosis," 301–3.

Notes to Chapter 6

1. The estimate of doctors and the ratio of doctors to population for England are drawn from Faber, *Medical Schools in China*, 7. The number of registered doctors is from Jin Baoshan, *Zhanshi difang weisheng xingzheng gaiyao* [Local health administration during the war] (Chongqing: Zhongyang xunlian tuan dang zheng xunlian ban, 1940), 21. The ratio of doctors to population for the United States is from Starr, *Social Transformation*, 126.

2. Faber, *Medical Schools in China*, 17–18.

3. Huang Chia-ssu, "Medical Education in China," in *Medical Education in Asia: A Symposium* (New York: China Medical Board of New York, 1981), 81.

4. The number of practitioners of native medicine is drawn from Faber, *Medical Schools in China*, 8.

5. Jin Baoshan, *Zhanshi difang weisheng xingzheng gaiyao*, 21; Bullock, *American Transplant*, 175.

6. "Initial Year of the Medical Education Program," 2.

7. Faber, *Medical Schools in China*, 5–6.

8. For these regulations, see "Daxue guicheng" [University regulations], in *Geming wenxian*, 56: 4–12.

9. T'ao Lee, "Some Statistics on Medical Schools in China for 1932–1933," *Chinese Medical Journal* 47 (1933): 1033.

10. For the reorganization of the educational ministry, see Qingzhi Chen, *Zhingguo jiaoyu shi*, 754–58.

11. Faber, *Medical Schools in China*, 8, 33.

12. Ibid., 38–39.

13. Ibid., 28.

14. Ibid., 33.

15. Ibid., 32.

16. "Law and Legislation: Establishment of Medical Schools," *Chinese Medical Journal* 46 (1932): 837–39.

17. Wong and Wu, *History of Chinese Medicine*, 791.

18. "Initial Year of the Medical Education Program," 5.

19. C. K. Chu, "The Revised Medical Curricula," *Chinese Medical Journal* 49 (1935): 837–46. This report includes tables of distribution of different subjects in the curricula of the two types of schools with total number of hours devoted to each subject.

20. S. M. Tao, "Medical Education of Chinese Women," *Chinese Medical Journal* 47 (1933): 1018–19; Lee T'ao, "Some Statistics on Medical Schools in China for the Year 1933–1934," *Chinese Medical Journal* 49 (1935): 895.

21. Lee, "Statistics on Medical Schools, 1932–1933," 1032, 1036–37.

22. "You guan gaodeng jiaoyu zhi tongji" [Statistics on higher education] in *Geming wenxian*, 56:226–27; William P. Fenn, *The Effect of the Japanese Invasion on Higher Education in China* (Hong Kong: China Institute of Pacific Relations, 1940), 20. On the whole, however, enrollment in the sciences had increased during the Nationalist decade. The table below shows the major fields of all students in institutions of higher learning during the years 1931 and 1936.

	1931		1936	
FIELD	NO.	PERCENTAGE	NO.	PERCENTAGE
Science	3,930	8.8	5,484	13.2
Agriculture	1,413	3.2	3,395	8.2
Engineering	4,084	9.3	6,987	16.8
Medicine	1,800	.1	2,590	6.2
Total	11,227	25.4	18,456	44.4

23. Faber, *Medical Schools in China*, 12–13.

24. Lee, "Statistics on Medical Schools, 1932–1933," 1031, 1035.

25. Ibid., 1037; and Lee T'ao, "Statistics on Medical Schools, 1933–34," 898.

26. "Prospectus of Medical Colleges and Schools," *Chinese Medical Journal* 49 (1935): 1017.

27. Ibid., 1018.

28. Faber, *Medical Schools in China*, 14; Dr. William Lowe, son of Dr. V. T. Loh (who was dean and professor of internal medicine of National Shanghai Medical College), interview with the author, 13–14 July 1991.

29. National Central University resulted from the merger of National Southeastern University and several technical and commercial colleges in

1927. The name of the university after the merger was Fourth Zhongshan University. It was renamed National Jiangsu University in 1928 and National Central University later the same year. See *Zhonghuaminguo daxue zhi* [General report on universities and colleges in modern China] (Taibei: China News Press, 1953), 4.

30. Faber, *Medical Schools in China*, 12.

31. *Shanghai yike daxue Huashan yiyuan bashi zhounian jinian ce* [Volume commemorating the eightieth anniversary of Huashan Hospital, Shanghai Medical College] (Shanghai: Huashan yiyuan, 1987), 1; Mary E. Ferguson, *China Medical Board and Peking Union Medical College* (New York: China Medical Board of New York, 1970), 36–37; Wong and Wu, *History of Chinese Medicine*, 695.

32. One contemporary cited National Shanghai Medical as an example of how high standards could be maintained and "meritorious work in training physicians to meet the pressing need of the country" could be carried out by a medical school despite the lack of funds and facilities. See Tao, "Medical Education of Chinese Women," 1016.

33. Dr. William Lowe, interview, 13–14 July 1991.

34. Lo Jialun, "Zhongyang daxue zhi zuijin si nian" [The last four years of Central University], in *Geming wenxian*, 65:441–57.

35. Faber, *Medical Schools in China*, 13.

36. "Guoli Zhongshan daxue xian zhuang" [Present conditions of National Zhongshan University], in *Geming wenxian*, 56:358–69.

37. "Quan guo zhuanke yishang xuexiao yilan" [A survey of institutions above the technical school level in the country], in *Geming wenxian*, 56:211–19; Lee, "Statistics on Medical Schools, 1933–1934," 898; "Initial Year of the Medical Education Program," 14–15. For descriptions of these provincial schools, see "Prospectus of Medical Colleges and Schools," 1005–7, 1009, 1012–1013, 1025, 1033–34.

38. "Initial Year of the Medical Education Program," 16–17.

39. Lee, "Statistics on Medical Schools, 1933–1934," 896.

40. Bullock, *American Transplant*, 111–14.

41. For 1933–34, published figures show that Mukden Medical College enrolled 107 students. See *China Yearbook, 1935*, 324. For the early history of the college, see S. A. Ellerbeck, "The Moukden Medical College," *China Medical Journal* 40 (1926): 743–47.

42. For the movement to recover educational rights and the issue of registration in the 1920s, see Yip, *Religion, Nationalism and Chinese Students*, 54–56; and Lutz, *China and the Christian Colleges*, 251–54.

43. Yip, *Religion, Nationalism and Chinese Students*, 74.

44. *China Christian Yearbook, 1934–35,* 273–75; Kuo, *Higher Education in China,* 38.

45. Lee, "Statistics on Medical Schools, 1932–33," 1032, 1038; "Prospectus of Medical Colleges and Schools," 999–1002.

46. Mary Lamberton, *St. John's University, Shanghai, 1879–1951* (New York: United Board for Christian Colleges in China, 1955), 145–48; 171–72; J. Liu, "Health and Medicine," 1629; "Prospectus of Medical Colleges and Schools," 1023–25; Lutz, *China and the Christian Colleges,* 277.

47. Corbett, *Shantung Christian University (Cheeloo),* 117.

48. Ibid., 216.

49. Ibid., 218–20; 226–28; "Prospectus of Medical Colleges and Schools," 1003.

50. Faber, *Medical Colleges in China,* 16.

51. *United Church of Canada Yearbook, 1932,* 114.

52. "Prospectus of Medical Colleges and Schools," 1027–28; Cheung, *Missionary Medicine,* 47.

53. *United Church of Canada Yearbook, 1932,* 114; *United Church of Canada Yearbook,* 1936, 87. See also Cheung, *Missionary Medicine,* 51–54.

54. Tao, "Medical Education of Chinese Women," 1013, 1018–19; Lang, *Chinese Family and Society,* 46, 103. Olga Lang relates the story of a village girl in Hebei in 1936. When she became ill, the family tried to help her by sending her father and uncle to Peiping to consult the doctor.

55. *Weisheng tongji,* 34. These figures include Chinese physicians trained abroad who had registered with the Chinese government.

56. *China Yearbook, 1936,* 356; "Prospectus of Medical Colleges and Schools," 1006–7; J. Allen Hofmann, "A Short Historical Sketch of Hackett Medical College and Affiliated Institutions," *China Medical Journal* 40 (1926): 776–79.

57. "Prospectus of Medical Colleges and Schools," 1006; *Report of the Commission Sent by the Rockefeller Foundation to China to Study the Problem of the Development of Medicine and Public Health, November 15, 1946,* Appendix 2, Record Group 1, Series 601, Box 2, Folder 16, Rockefeller Archive Center; William W. Cadbury and Mary H. Jones, *At the Point of a Lancet: One Hundred Years of the Canton Hospital, 1835–1935* (Shanghai: Kelly and Walsh, 1935), 246–47, 266–68.

58. Cadbury and Jones, *Point of a Lancet,* 247, 260–61.

59. *China Yearbook, 1936,* 356; Lee, "Statistics on Medical Schools, 1933–1934," 896; "Prospectus of Medical Colleges and Schools," 1031; "Quanguo zhuanke yishang xuexiao ershiwu ershiliu liang nian du xueshang renshu

beijiao biao" [Chart comparing the numbers of students in the country's schools above the technical level in 1936 and 1937], in *Geming wenxian*, 56:100. The figure for 1935 was twenty-two; for 1936, twenty-six; and for 1937, thirteen.

60. Tao, "Medical Education of Chinese Women," 1012–13.

61. J. Liu, "Health and Medicine," 1628–29. The total number of graduates from mission medical schools was 969.

62. Tao, "Medical Education of Chinese Women," 1018–19.

63. Lutz, *China and the Christian Colleges*, 303.

64. Wang Zhixin, *Zhongguo jidujiao shi gang* [A brief historical survey of Christianity in China] (Hong Kong: Jidujiao wenyi chubanshe, 1959), 340.

65. Cheung, *Missionary Medicine*, 47.

66. Ibid., 114.

67. Ibid., 108–9.

68. Lee, "Statistics on Medical Schools, 1933–1934," 896.

69. "Prospectus of Medical Colleges and Schools," 1026; Lee, "Statistics on Medical Schools, 1932–1933," 1037.

70. Faber, *Medical Schools in China*, 16–17.

71. Hume had written about his experience in his book, *Doctors East, Doctors West*. See also "Prospectus of Medical Colleges and Schools," 1010–12; and Jonathan Spence, *To Change China: Western Advisers in China, 1620–1960* (Boston: Little, Brown, 1969), 161–83.

72. Quoted in William Reeves, Jr., "Sino-American Cooperation in Medicine: The Origins of Hsiang-Ya (1902–1914)," in *American Missionaries in China: Papers from Harvard Seminars*, ed. Liu Kwang-ching (Cambridge: East Asian Research Center, Harvard University), 139.

73. "Prospectus of Medical Colleges and Schools," 1012.

74. Faber, *Medical Schools in China*, 31.

75. Roger S. Greene to Dr. Mason, 1 January, 1931, CMB, Inc., Box 22, Folder 155, Rockefeller Archive Center.

76. Ferguson, *China Medical Board and Peking Union Medical College*, 62–66. J. Heng Liu continued in his position at the Ministry of Health while on leave from PUMC.

77. Grant to Gregg, 4 December 1934, CMB, Inc., Box 29, Folder 203, Rockefeller Archive Center.

78. Gregg to Grant, 8 January 1935, ibid.

79. Greene to Gunn, 12 January 1934, Roger S. Greene Papers.

80. Green to Gunn, 12 March 1934, ibid.

81. Greene to Shih-chieh Wang, Minister of Education, 4 August 1935, ibid.

82. "Initial Year of the Medical Education Program," 17–18; Lee, "Statistics on Medical Schools, 1933–1934," 898–99.

83. "Initial Year of the Medical Education Program," 18–19; Lee, "Statistics on Medical Schools, 1933–1934," 898–901; Tao, "Medical Education of Chinese Women," 1021.

84. Jin Baoshan, *Zhanshi difang weisheng xingzheng gaiyao*, 21; *Weisheng tongji*, 34. The number for 1937 would be 9,584 if we add the 486 foreign doctors registered with the government.

85. Hsi-ju Chu and Daniel G. Lai, "Distribution of Modern-Trained Physicians in China," *Chinese Medical Journal* 49 (1935): 544.

86. Ibid., 544–46. The distribution of physicians by provinces is as follows.

PROVINCE	NUMBER	PERCENTAGE
Jiangsu	2,010	37.3
Guangdong	606	11.2
Hebei	387	7.2
Zhejiang	350	6.5
Liaoning	352	6.5
Shandong	244	4.5
Hubei	192	3.6
Fujian	153	2.8
Jiangxi	85	1.6
Sichuan	71	1.3
Anhui	63	1.2
Hunan	56	1.0
The rest of China	284	5.3
Unknown	537	10.0

87. William G. Lennox, "The Distribution of Medical School Graduates in China," *Chinese Medical Journal* 46 (1932): 406; Zhongguo Guomindang zhongyang tongjichu [Central Statistical Bureau of the Guomindang], *Minguo ershier nian zhi jianshe* [Reconstruction in 1933] (Nanjing: Central Statistical Bureau of the Guomindang, 1934), 68–69.

88. Chu and Lai, "Distribution of Modern-Trained Physicians," 547–50.

89. Dr. William Lowe, interview, 13–14 July 1991. See also Lennox, "Distribution of Medical School Graduates," 409.

90. For the required courses in medical colleges and the number of hours devoted to public health, see Lee, "Statistics on Medical Schools, 1932–1933," 1034.

91. For required course hours in the commission's revised curricula, see Chu, "Revised Medical Curricula," 838–39, 942–43.

92. L. Chen, *Public Health in National Reconstruction*, 76–77.

93. Bullock, *American Transplant*, 126; "Reminiscences of Grant," 300–301.

94. Taylor et al., *Health Manpower Planning in Turkey*, 64.

95. Sze, *Chinea's Health Problems*, 25.

96. Xue Yu, ed., *Zhongguo yaoxue shi liao* [Historical materials on Chinese medicine and pharmacology] (Beijing: Renmin weisheng chubanshe, 1984), 381–82.

97. Ibid., 380.

98. Jin Baoshan, *Zhanshi difang weisheng xingzheng gaiyao*, 21.

99. Xue Yu, *Zhongguo yaoxue shi liao*, 358–59.

100. Ibid., 360–61.

101. Ibid., 362–64; Wong and Wu, *History of Chinese Medicine*, 805.

102. Ibid., 367–69; William Band, *Science in the Christian Universities at Chengtu, China*, n.d., 7–9, pamphlet filed in United Church of Canada Archives, China Pamphlet Series and China Document Series.

103. Xue Yu, *Zhongguo yaoxue shi liao*, 369–72; L. Chen, *Public Health in National Reconstruction*, 75–76.

104. Jin Baoshan, *Zhanshi difang weisheng xingzheng gaiyao*, 21.

105. Cheung, *Missionary Medicine*, 50; "Prospectus of Medical Colleges and Schools," 1028; Wong and Wu, *History of Chinese Medicine*, 803.

106. L. Chen, *Public Health in National Reconstruction*, 75.

107. Jin Baoshan, *Zhanshi difang weisheng xingzheng gaiyao*, 21.

108. Wong and Wu, *History of Chinese Medicine*, 560–62.

109. *Guojia jianshe congkan*, 2:184.

110. Wong and Wu, *History of Chinese Medicine*, 562.

111. J. Liu, "Chinese Ministry of Health," 140.

112. J. Liu, "San nian lai zhongyang weisheng sheshi gaikuang," 7. For a list of the courses in the curriculum, see *Neizheng nianjian*, (G)202–(G)203.

113. Lee, "Statistics on Medical Schools, 1933–1934," 897.

114. *Neizheng nianjian*, (G)203–(G)206.

115. Chen Bangxian, *Zhongguo yixue shi*, 319; L. Chen, *Public Health in National Reconstruction*, 75.

116. Jin Baoshan, *Zhanshi difang weisheng xingzheng gaiyao*, 21; *Weisheng tongji*, 41–42.

117. "Initial Year of the Medical Education Program," 21–22.

118. Jin Baoshan, *Zhanshi difang weisheng xingzheng gaiyao*, 21.

119. *Neizheng nianjian*, (G)206–(G)208; "Report of the National Health Administration on the Three Year Plan," 265–66.

120. Ibid., 266.

121. *Neizheng nianjian*, (G)209.

122. Ibid., (G)209–(G)211.

123. "Initial Year of the Medical Education Program," 23–24.

124. *Weisheng tongji*, 40; Jin Baoshan, *Zhanshi difang weisheng xingzheng gaiyao*, 21.

125. "Report on a Survey in Kiangsi," 60.

126. *Weisheng shiyanchu gongzuo baogao*, 23–31; Li Tingan, *Zhongguo xiangcun weisheng wenti*, 66, 86, 102; C. Chen, "Development of Systematic Training," 381–84.

127. Li Tingan, *Zhongguo xiangcun weisheng wenti*, 66; Y. C. Mei, "Government Health Work," *China Christian Yearbook, 1929*, 367.

128. J. Heng Liu, "The Central Field Health Station as a Training Center for Public Health Workers," *Chinese Medical Journal* 49 (1935): 943.

129. Ibid., 944; J. Liu "Health and Medicine," 1627–28.

130. Ibid., 1628; "Report of the National Health Administration on the Three Year Plan," 270.

131. *Weishengshu gonggong weisheng renyuan xunliansuo gaikuang* [General survey of the National Public Health Training Institute] (Chongqing: Weisheng renyuan xunlian suo, 1943), 1.

132. Jin Baoshan, *Zhanshi difang weisheng xingzheng gaiyao*, 21.

133. "Initial Year of the Medical Education Program," 2, 9–12, 58, 77–80; Commission on Medical Education of the Ministry of Education, "Annual Report for Year July 1938 to June 1939," p.1, Record Group 1, Series 601, Box 3, Folder 28, Rockefeller Archive Center.

134. "Initial Year of the Medical Education Program," 25–27.

135. Ibid., 27.

136. The report was quite harsh in its treatment of the "scientists" and "experts" who failed to perform their duty to serve the people (see pp. 25, 34).

137. C. Chen, "Rural Public Health Experiment," 79.

138. C. Chen, "State Medicine and Medical Education," *Chinese Medical Journal* 49 (1935): 954.

139. McCabe, "Maternity and Child Health Work," 14–18.

140. "Nanjingshi zhengfu ershier nian yiyue ji ershisan nian shiyue gongzuo baogao," 372.

141. "Initial Year of the Medical Education Program," 43–45.

142. Commission on Education, "Medical Education in 1937 (the Year Ending June 1938)," p. 2, Record Group 1, Series 601, Box 3, Folder 28, Rockefeller Archive Center; "Quanguo zhuanke yishang xuexiao ershiwu ershiliu liang nian du xueshang renshu beijiao biao," in *Geming wenxian,* 56:111.

143. "Initial Year of the Medical Education Program," 46–53, 63.

144. Ministry of Education,"Second Year Program," 1–7.

145. Commission on Education "Medical Education in 1937," 1–4.

Notes to Chapter 7

1. J. Liu, "Some Phases of Public Health Work," 70.

2. Sze, *Medical Work in China,* 41.

3. Ibid., 17–18.

4. Li Xiangming, *Zhongguo xiandai yixuejia zhuan lue,* 281.

5. "Public Health and Medicine," *China Yearbook, 1942,* 671.

6. *Guojia jianshe congkan,* 2:181–82.

7. "Public Health and Medicine," *China Yearbook, 1942,* 674.

8. Commission on Medical Education, "Annual Report, 1938–39," 1–3.

9. *Report of the Commission Sent by the Rockefeller Foundation, 1946.*

10. See, for example, the prefaces Liu wrote for Li Tingan, *Zhongguo xiangcun weisheng wenti;* and Hu Dingan, *Hu Dingan gongzhong weisheng yanlun ji* [A collection of Hu Dingan's public speeches and writings on public health] (Shanghai: Dadong shuju, 1930).

11. "The National Economic Council Project and Allocation of Funds for 1934," in League of Nations, *Annexes,* 31–40.

12. Prasenjit Duara's study of rural north China discusses the failure of the Nationalist government to expand its revenue base during this period (Duara, *Culture, Power and the State*).

13. Bedeski, *State-Building in Modern China,* 82–89.

14. Tien, *Government and Politics in Kuomintang China,* 18–26.

15. Alitto, *The Last Confucian,* 233.

16. Hayford, *To the People,* 119.

17. Quoted in Ninkovich, "The Rockefeller Foundation, China, and Cultural Change," 812.

18. Mao's speech of 25 January 1956, quoted in John M. H. Lindbeck, "Organization and Development of Science," in *Sciences in Communist China*, ed., Sidney H. Gould (Washington, D.C.: American Association for the Advancement of Science, 1961), 3. Deng's speech to the National Science Conference, delivered on 18 March 1978, is reproduced in *Peking Review*, 24 March 1978, 10.

19. *Renmin ribao*, 8 April 1978.

20. Fu Lien-chang, "Summing Up Report on the Activities of the Chinese Medical Association Since the Eighth General Conference," *Chinese Medical Journal* 71 (May-June 1953): 233.

21. For an interesting account of the mass line in health campaigns, see Joshua S. Horn, *Away With All Pests: An English Surgeon in People's China, 1954–1969* (New York: Monthly Review Press, 1971), 94–106.

22. Stuart R. Schram, ed., *Chairman Mao Talks to the People* (New York: Random House, 1974), 81–82.

23. Fu Lien-chang, "Why Our Western-trained Doctors Should Learn Traditional Chinese Medicine," *Chinese Medical Journal* 5 (September-October 1955): 366–67.

24. For discussions of traditional medicine in the People's Republic, see Croizier, *Traditional Medicine in Modern China*; David M. Lampton, *The Politics of Medicine in China: The Policy Process, 1949–1977* (Boulder, Colo.: Westview, 1977); S. M. Hillier and J. A. Jewell, *Health Care and Traditional Medicine in China, 1800–1982* (London: Routledge and Kegan Paul, 1983); and Ka-che Yip, "Medicine and Nationalism in the People's Republic of China, 1949–1980," *Canadian Review of Studies in Nationalism* 10, no. 2 (Fall 1983): 175–87. For interesting observations and comments on the current status of traditional medicine based on recent study tours to China, see Marilynn M. Rosenthal, *Health Care in the People's Republic of China: Moving Toward Modernization* (Boulder, Colo.: Westview, 1987), 35–73.

25. "Facts and Figures on China's Medical Work," *China Reconstructs* 30 (April 1981): 69–70; Chen Haifeng, *Zhongguo weisheng baojian* [Hygiene and health protection in China] (Beijing: Renmin weisheng chubanshe, 1985), 72–73.

26. The categories are based on those used by the Ministry of Public Health. See Chen Haifeng, *Zhongguo weisheng baojian*, 56; and Ruth Sidel and Victor W. Sidel, *The Health of China* (Boston: Beacon, 1982), 208–9. See also Lucas, *Chinese Medical Modernization*, 156.

27. Sidel and Sidel, *The Health of China*, 30, 208–9. The ratio for the United States is taken from Starr, *Social Transformation*, 422.

28. Huang Chia-ssu, "Medical Education in China," 82.

29. Bullock, *American Transplant*, 215–16. For the career of Huang Jiasi after 1949, see S. Huang, *Zhongguo xiandai ming yi zhuan*, 236–42.

30. Li Xiangming, *Zhongguo xiandai yixuejia zhuan lue*, 280–86.

31. Lucas, Chinese Medical Modernization, 98.

32. Huang Shuze, *Zhongguo xiandai ming yi zhuan*, 7–15.

33. Chen Haifeng, *Zhongguo weisheng baojian*, 38, 44–46, 67–77; *Dangdai Zhongguo di weisheng shiye* [Health enterprise in contemporary China] (Beijing: Zhongguo shehui kexue chubanshe, 1986), 42–49.

34. For a discussion of some of these problems, see Ka-che Yip, "Medical Modernization in the People's Republic of China," in *Proceedings of the Sixth International Symposium on Asian Studies* (Hong Kong: Asian Research Service, 1984), 529–37.

Glossary

Andong 安東

bao 保
baojia 保甲
Binying (Binyin) 丙寅

Cai, Yuanpei 蔡元培
Chen bao 晨報
Chen, Duxiu 陳獨秀
Chen, Guofu 陳果夫
Chen, Zhiqian (C. C. Chen) 陳志潛
chijiao yisheng 赤腳醫生
Chuanzhi 川至
cun 村

Dagong bao 大公報
daxue qu 大學區
Dingxian 定縣
Dongnan 東南

Fang, Shishan 方石珊
Feng, Yuxiang 馮玉祥

Gaoqiao 高橋
gongshe weisheng yuan 公社衛生院
Gongyi 公醫
Guanghua 光華
Guanyin 觀音
Guiyang 貴陽

239

Guomindang　國民黨
Guoyiguan　國醫館

Han, Fuqu　韓復渠
Heze xian　菏澤縣
Hu, Xuanming (S. M. Woo)　胡宣明
Huang, Jaisi (Huang Chia-ssu)　黃家駟
Huang, Zifang (T. F. Huang)　黃子方
Huaxi xiehe daxue　華西協合大學
hushi　護士

Jiang, Menglin (Chiang Monlin)　蔣夢麟
Jiangning xian　江寧縣
jianyan shi　檢驗師, 檢驗士
jiesheng po　接生婆
Jin, Baoshan (P. Z. King)　金寶善
Jining　濟寧
Jintangqin　津塘秦

Kang, Youwei　康有爲
Kong, Xiangxi (H. H. Kung)　孔祥熙

Lanzhou　蘭州
Le, Wenzhao (P. V. Loh)　樂文照
li　禮
Li, Shufen　李樹芬
Li, Tingan　李廷安
Lian　廉
Liang, Qichao　梁啓超
Liang, Shuming　梁漱溟
Lichuan　黎川
Lingnan　嶺南
Lin, Kesheng (Robert K. S. Lim)　林可勝
Liu, Ruiheng (J. Heng Liu)　劉瑞恆
Longshan　龍山

Longyan　龍巖
Lu Xun　魯迅

Nantong　南通
Niu, Huisheng (New Way-sung)　牛惠生

qi　恥
Qilu daxue (Cheeloo)　齊魯大學
Qinhuangdao　秦皇島
qu　區
Quanguo jingji weiyuanhui　全國經濟委員會
quanxisuo　傳習所
Qingjiangpu　清江浦

Remin ribao　人民日報

San min zhuyi　三民主義
Shanghai nüzi yixueyuan　上海女子醫學院
Shen bao　申報
shengchan dadui weisheng suo　生產大隊衛生所
Sipailou　四牌樓
Shengyuehan daxue　聖約翰大學
Song, Ziwen (T. V. Soong)　宋子文
Sun, Fo　孫科

Tanggu　塘沽
Tangshan　湯山
Tao, Xingzhi　陶行知
Tai xian　泰縣
Tongde　同德
Tongji　同濟

Wang, Jingwei　汪精衛
Wang, Zuxiang　王祖祥
weisheng　衛生

Weisheng shiyan chu　衛生實驗處
Weisheng shu　衛生署
weisheng suo　衛生所
weisheng yuan　衛生院
Wu, Liande (Wu Lien-teh)　伍連德
Wusong　吳淞

Xiyishi　西醫師
Xiage yixueyuan　夏葛醫學院
xian　縣
xiang　鄉
Xian zheng jianshe shiyan qu　縣政建設實驗區
xiangcun yisheng　鄉村醫生
Xiangya　湘雅
Xiaozhuang　曉莊
Xie, Yuanfu (George Y. Char)　謝元甫
Xue, Dubi　薛篤弼

Yan, Xishan　閻錫山
Yan, Yangchu (James Y. C. Yen)　晏陽初
Yan, Fu　嚴復
Yan, Fuqing (F. C. Yen)　顏福慶
Yancheng xian　鹽城縣
yaoji shi　藥劑士
yaoshi　藥師
Yang, Chongrui (Marion Yang)　楊崇瑞
yi　義
Yingkou　營口
yin yang　陰陽
yishi　醫士
yixue zhuanke xuexiao　醫學專科學校
Yongxin　永新
yuan　院

Zhang, Fuliang　張福良
Zhang, Xueliang　張學良

Zhendan daxue　震旦大學
Zhenjiang　鎮江
Zhongshan　中山
Zhongyang fang yi chu　中央防疫處
Zhongyang ribao　中央日報
Zhongyang weisheng shiyan suo　中央衛生試驗所
Zhongyang weisheng shiyan yuan　中央衛生實驗院
zhongyao renyuan　中藥人員
zhongyi　中醫
Zhongzheng　中正
zhuanmen　專門
zhuchan shi　助產士
Zhu, Hengbi (H. P. Chu)　朱恆壁
Zhu, Zhanggeng (C. K. Zhu)　朱章賡
Zou, Lu　鄒魯
Zouping　鄒平

Bibliography

Archives and Manuscript Collections

Archives of the Historical Commission of the Kuomintang [Guomin-dang]. Taibei, Taiwan.
"The Reminiscences of Dr. John B. Grant" (1961), Oral History Research Project, Special Collections, Columbia University.
"The Reminiscences of Ho Lien (Franklin L. Ho)" (1967), Oral History Research Project, Special Collections, Columbia University.
Papers of Dr. J. Heng Liu, Oral History Project, Special Collections, Columbia University.
Rockefeller Archive Center, North Tarrytown, New York.
Roger S. Greene Papers, Houghton Library, Harvard University.
United Church of Canada Archives, Toronto, Canada.

Interviews

Dr. C. C. Chen, 10 December 1979, Johns Hopkins University; and 3 June 1985, University of California, Berkeley.
Dr. William Lowe, 13–14 July 1991, Short Hills, New Jersey.

Books and Articles

Abels, Jules. *The Rockefeller Billions*. New York: Macmillan, 1965.
Alitto, Guy. *The Last Confucian: Liang Shu-ming and the Chinese Dilemma of Modernity*. Berkeley: University of California Press, 1979.
Association for the Advancement of Public Health in China. *Memorandum on the Need for a Public Health Organization in China, Presented to the British Boxer Indemnity Commission*. Peking: Association for the Advancement of Public Health in China, 1926.

Averiel, Stephen C. "The New Life in Action: The Nationalist Government in South Jiangxi, 1934–1937" *China Quarterly* 88 (1981): 594–628.

Baker, Timothy, and Mark Perlman. *Health Manpower in a Developing Economy: Taiwan, a Case Study in Planning.* Baltimore: Johns Hopkins University Press, 1967.

Balfour, Marshall C., Roger F. Evans, Frank W. Notestein, and Irene B. Taeuber. *Public Health and Demography in the Far East: Report of a Survey Trip, September 13-December 13,* 1948. New York: Rockefeller Foundation, 1950.

Balme, Harold. *China and Modern Medicine: A Study in Medical Missionary Education.* London: United Council for Missionary Education, 1921.

Band, William. *Science in the Christian Universities at Chengtu, China.* N.d. Pamphlet filed in the United Church of Canada Archives, China Pamphlet Series and China Document Series.

Battistella, R. M., and T. G. Rundall, eds. *Health Care Policy in a Changing Environment.* Berkeley: McCutchan, 1978.

Bedeski, Robert E. *State-Building in Modern China: The Kuomintang in the Prewar Period.* Berkeley: Center for Chinese Studies, University of California, 1981.

Beijing Zhongyixue yuan, ed. 北京中醫學院. *Zhongguo yixue shi jiangyi* 中國醫學史講義 [Lectures on the history of medicine in China]. Hong Kong: Yiyao weisheng chubanshe, 1974.

Bennett, J. "Health Education." In *Medical Care in Developing Countries,* ed. M. King. London: Oxford University Press, 1966.

Berliner, Howard S. "Philanthropic Foundations and Scientific Medicine." D.Sc. thesis, School of Hygiene and Public Health, Johns Hopkins University, 1977.

Boorman, Howard L., ed. *Biographical Dictionary of Republican China.* 2 vols. New York: Columbia University Press, 1967.

Bowers, John Z. "The Founding of Peking Union Medical College: Policies and Personalities," parts I and II, *Bulletin of the History of Medicine* 45 (1971): 305–21, 409–29.

———. *Western Medicine in a Chinese Palace.* New York: Josiah Macy Foundation, 1972.

———. "Imperialism and Medical Education in China" *Bulletin of the History of Medicine* 48 (1974): 449–64.

———, ed. Medicine and Society in China. New York: Josiah Macy Foundation, 1974.

Bowers, John Z., J. William Hess, and Nathan Sivin, eds. *Science and*

Medicine in Twentieth Century China: Research and Education. Ann Arbor: Center for Chinese Studies, University of Michigan, 1988.

Brauer, Max, E. Briand-Clausen, and A. Stampar. "Report on a Survey of Certain Localities in Kiangsi." In League of Nations, *Annexes to the Report to the Council of the League of Nations of its Technical Delegate on his Mission in China from Date of Appointment Until April 1, 1934*, 41–69. Shanghai: *North China Daily News and Herald*, 1934.

Brown, E. Richard. *Rockefeller Medicine Men: Medicine and Capitalism in America*. Berkeley: University of California Press, 1980.

Buck, John L. *Land Utilization in China*. Chicago: University of Chicago Press, 1937.

Buck, Peter. *American Science and Modern China, 1876–1936*. Cambridge: Cambridge University Press, 1980.

Bullock, Mary B. *An American Transplant: The Rockefeller Foundation and Peking Union Medical College*. Berkeley: University of California Press, 1980.

Cadbury, William W., and Mary H. Jones. *At the Point of a Lancet: One Hundred Years of the Canton Hospital, 1835–1935*. Shanghai: Kelly and Walsh, 1935.

Cambridge History of China. Vols. 12, 13. Cambridge: Cambridge University Press, 1983, 1986.

Carter, W. S. "The First Five Years of the Peking Union Medical College" *Chinese Medical Journal*, 40 (1926): 726–43.

Cavendish, Patrick. "The 'New China' of the Kuomintang" In *Modern China's Search for a Political Form*, ed. Jack Gray, 138–86. London: Oxford University Press, 1969.

Chen, Bangxian 陳邦賢. *Zhongguo yixue shi* 中國醫學史 [A history of medicine in China]. Rev. ed. Taibei: Shangwu yinshuguan, 1957. Originally published in 1937.

Chen, C. C. [Chen Zhiqian]. "Xiangcun weisheng" 鄉村衛生 [Rural health]. *Weisheng gongbao* 衛生公報 [Gazette of the Ministry of Health] 2, no. 2 (1 February 1930).

————. "A Practical Survey of Rural Health." *Chinese Medical Journal* 47 (1933): 680–88.

————. "Scientific Medicine as Applied in Ting Hsien." *Milbank Memorial Fund Quarterly Bulletin* 11 (1933): 97–129.

————. "An Experiment in Health Education in Chinese Country Schools." *Milbank Memorial Fund Quarterly Bulletin* 12 (1934): 232–47.

———. "Public Health in Rural Reconstruction at Ting Hsien." *Milbank Memorial Fund Quarterly Bulletin* 12 (1934):370–78.

———. "A Proposed Basic Medical Curriculum." *Chinese Medical Journal* 49 (1935): 861–67.

———. "State Medicine and Medical Education." *Chinese Medical Journal* 49 (1935): 951–54.

———. "The Development of Systematic Training in Rural Public Health Work in China." *Milbank Memorial Fund Quarterly Bulletin* 14 (1936):370–87.

———. "The Rural Public Health Experiment in Ting Hsien, China," *Milbank Memorial Fund Quarterly Bulletin* 14 (1936): 66–80.

———. "Some Problems of Medical Organization in Rural China." *Chinese Medical Journal* 51 (1937): 803–14.

———. "Ting Hsien and the Public Health Movement in China." *Milbank Memorial Fund Quarterly Bulletin* 15 (1937): 380–90.

———. "Xingban weisheng shiye shi zhengfu di zeren" 興辦衛生事業是政府的責任 [It is the government's duty to establish health enterprises]. *Yiqiao* 醫潮 [Tides of medicine] 1, no. 6 (October 1947): 1–2.

———. *Medicine in Rural China: A Personal Account.* Berkeley: University of California Press, 1989.

Chen, Gideon. "Chinese Government Economic Planning and Reconstruction." In *Problems of the Pacific, 1933,* 352–82. Chicago: University of Chicago Press, 1934.

Chen, Guofu 陳果夫. *Yi zheng man tan* 醫政漫譚 [Random jottings on medical administration]. Chongqing: Guomin chubanshe, 1941.

Chen, Haifeng 陳海峰. *Zhongguo weisheng baojian* 中國衛生保健 [Hygiene and health protection in China]. Beijing: Renmin weisheng chubanshe, 1985.

Chen, Han-seng. "The Agrarian Problem in China." In *Problems of the Pacific, 1933,* 271–97. Chicago: University of Chicago Press, 1934.

Chen, Jerome. *China and the West: Society and Culture, 1815–1937.* Bloomington: Indiana University Press, 1979.

Chen, Lawrence M. The Co-operative Movement in China. Nanjing: Council of International Affairs, 1936.

———. *Rural Rehabilitation.* Nanjing: Council of International Affairs, 1936.

————. *Chinese National Railways and Reconstruction*. Nanjing: Council of International Affairs, 1936.

————. *Public Health in National Reconstruction*. Nanjing: Council of International Affairs, 1937.

Chen, Qingzhi 陳青之. *Zhongguo jiaoyu shi* 中國教育史 [History of Chinese education]. Taibei: Shangwu yinshuguan, 1968.

Chen, Qitian 陳啓天. *Jindai Zhongguo jiaoyu shi* 近代中國教育史 [History of education in modern China]. Taibei: Zhonghua shuju, 1967.

Chen, Shengkun 陳勝崑. *Jindai yixue zai Zhongguo* 近代醫學在中國 [Modern medicine in China]. Taibei: Dangdai yixue zazhi she, 1978.

————. *Zhongguo jibing shi* 中國疾病史 [History of diseases in China]. Taibei: Ziran kexue wenhua shiye gongsi, 1981.

Cheng, Chu-yuan. *Scientific and Engineering Manpower in Communist China, 1949–1963*. Washington, D.C.: National Science Foundation, 1965.

Cheng, Mei Yu. "An Investigation of Infant Mortality and its Causes in Chengtu." *Chinese Medical Journal* 62 (1944): 47–54.

Chesneaux, Jean. *The Chinese Labor Movement, 1919–1927*, trans. H. M. Wright. Stanford: Stanford University Press, 1968.

Cheung, Yuet-wah. *Missionary Medicine in China: A Study of Two Canadian Protestant Missions in China Before 1937*. Lanham, Md.: University Press of America, 1988.

Ch'i, Hsi-sheng. *Nationalist China at War: Military Defeats and Political Collapse, 1937–45*. Ann Arbor: University of Michigan Press, 1982.

Chiang, Monlin. *Tides From the West: A Chinese Autobiography*. New Haven: Yale University Press, 1947.

Ch'ien Tuan-sheng. *The Government and Politics of China, 1912–1949*. Stanford: Stanford University Press, 1970.

Chin, Ping-sheng. *Ding Xian (Ting Hsien): Where IIRR Has its Roots*. New York: International Institute of Rural Reconstruction, 1984.

China Christian Yearbook. Shanghai: Christian Literature Society. Various issues.

China Handbook, 1937–1943. New York: Macmillan, 1943.

China Medical Commission, Rockefeller Foundation. *Medicine in China*. New York: Rockefeller Foundation, 1914.

"China Program." Record Group 1, Series 601, Box 10, Folder 108, Rockefeller Archive Center.

China Yearbook. Tianjin and Shanghai: Tianjin Press and the *North China Daily News.* Various issues, 1913–37.

Chinese Medical Association. *The Chinese Medical Directory,* 1932, 1936, 1939.

"China's Reconstruction Program." In *Problems of the Pacific, 1933,* 178–200. Chicago: University of Chicago Press, 1934.

Christie, Dugald. *Thirty Years in Moukden.* New York: McBride, Nast, 1914.

———. *Medical Missions.* N.d. United Church of Canada Archives, Toronto, Protestant Missions in China, China Pamphlet Series and China Document Series, Box 6, no. 31.

Chu, C. K. [Zhu Zhanggeng] 朱章賡. "The Revised Medical Curricula." *Chinese Medical Journal* 49 (1935):837–46.

———. "The Training of Personnel for State Medicine." *Chinese Medical Journal* 51 (1937): 373–80.

Chu, Hsi-ju, and Daniel G. Lai. "Distribution of Modern-Trained Physicians in China." *Chinese Medical Journal* 49 (1935): 542–52.

Coble, Parks M., Jr. *The Shanghai Capitalists and the Nationalist Government, 1927–1937.* Cambridge: Harvard University Press, 1980.

Cohen, Paul A. "The Post-Mao Reforms in Historical Perspective." *Journal of Asian Studies* 47, no. 3 (August 1988): 519–41.

Cohen, Warren I. *The Chinese Connection: Roger S. Greene, Thomas W. Lamont, George E. Sokolsky, and American–East Asian Relations.* New York: Columbia University Press, 1978.

Commission on Medical Education, Ministry of Education. "Initial Year of the Medical Education Program." Record Group 1, Series 601, Box 3, Folder 27, Rockefeller Archive Center.

———. "The Second Year Program in Medical Education (July 1936–June 1937)." Record Group 1, Series 601, Box 3, Folder 28, Rockefeller Archive Center.

———. "Medical Education in 1937 (the Year Ending June 1938)." Record Group 1, Series 601, Box 3, Folder 28, Rockefeller Archive Center.

———. "Annual Report for Year July 1938 to June 1939." Record Group 1, Series 601, Box 3, Folder 28, Rockefeller Archive Center.

Corbett, Charles H. *Shantung Christian University (Cheeloo).* New York: United Board for Christian Colleges in China, 1955.

———. *Lingnan University.* New York: United Board for Christian Colleges in China, 1955.

Croizier, Ralph C. *Traditional Medicine in Modern China: Science,*

Nationalism, and the Tensions of Cultural Change. Cambridge: Harvard University Press, 1968.

———. "Medicine, Modernization, and Cultural Crisis in China and India." *Comparative Studies in Society and History* 12, no. 3 (July 1970): 275–91.

Dangdai Zhongguo di weisheng shiye 當代中國的衛生事業 [Health enterprise in contemporary China]. Beijing: Zhongguo shehui kexue chubanshe, 1986.

Dean, Genevieve C. *Science and Technology in the Development of Modern China.* London: Mansell, 1974.

Difang weisheng xingzheng chuqi shishi fangan 地方衛生行政初期實施方案 [Plan for the implementation of local health administration in the early stage]. Nanjing: Weisheng bu, 1929. Copy filed in Archives of the Historical Commission of the Kuomintang.

Dirlik, Arif. "The Ideological Foundations of the New Life Movement: A Study in Counterrevolution." *Journal of Asian Studies* 34, no. 4 (August 1975): 945–80.

Djukanovic, V., and E. P. Mach, eds. *Alternative Approaches to Meeting Basic Health Needs in Developing Countries.* Geneva: World Health Organization, 1975.

Dolan, John P., and William N. Adams-Smith. *Health and Society: A Documentary History of Medicine.* New York: Seabury Press, 1978.

Dragoni, C. "Report on Agricultural Reform and Development in China." In League of Nations, *Annexes to the Report to the Council of the League of Nations of its Technical Delegate on His Mission in China from Date of Appointment Until April 1, 1934,* 167–226. Shanghai: *North China Daily News and Herald,* 1934.

Duara, Prasenjit. *Culture, Power and the State: Rural North China, 1900–1942.* Stanford: Stanford University Press, 1988.

Duffy, John. *The Healers: A History of American Medicine.* Urbana: University of Illinois Press, 1979.

Dyer, Brian R. "Methods Developed at the Central Field Health Station for the Training of Sanitation Personnel." *Chinese Medical Journal* 50 (1936): 76–81.

Eastman, Lloyd E. *The Abortive Revolution: China Under Nationalist Rule, 1927–1937.* Cambridge: Harvard University Press, 1974.

———. "Nationalist China During the Nanking Decade." In *The Nationalist Era in China, 1927–1949,* ed. Lloyd E. Eastman, Jerome Chen, Suzanne Pepper, and Lyman P. Van Slyke, 1–52. Cambridge: Cambridge University Press, 1991.

Eastman, Lloyd E., Jerome Chen, Suzanne Pepper, and Lyman P. Van Slyke, eds. *The Nationalist Era in China, 1927–1949*. Cambridge: Cambridge University Press, 1991.

Edwards, Dwight W. *Yenching University*. New York: United Board for Christian Colleges in China, 1959.

Ellerbeck, S. A. "The Moudken Medical College." *Chinese Medical Journal* 40 (1926): 743–47.

Ewen, Jean. *China Nurse, 1932–1939*. Toronto: McClelland and Steward, 1981.

Faber, Knud. *Report on Medical Schools in China*. Geneva: League of Nations Health Organization, 1931.

"Facts and Figures on China's Medical Work." *China Reconstructs* 30 (April 1981).

Fan, Xingzhun 范行准. *Zhongguo yixue shi lue* 中國醫學史略 [A short history of medicine in China]. Beijing: Zhong yi gu ji chubanshe, 1986.

Fan, P. L. "Chinese Infants and Children: A Study of the Infant and Child Mortality, Size of the Family, and Sex Ratio on 2,500 Cases." *Chinese Medical Journal* 47 (1933):652–61.

Fang, I. C. "Public Health." In *China Christian Yearbook, 1932–33*, 429–44. Shanghai: Christian Literature Society, 1933.

Fang I. C., and T. A. Li. "School Health in the Peiping Special Health Area." *Chinese Medical Journal* 43 (1929):697–706.

Faure, David. *The Rural Economy of Pre-Liberation China: Trade Expansion and Peasant Livelihood in Jiangsu and Guangdong, 1870–1937*. New York: Oxford University Press, 1989.

Fenn, William P. *The Effect of the Japanese Invasion on Higher Education in China*. Hong Kong: China Institute of Pacific Relations, 1940.

Ferguson, Mary E. *China Medical Board and Peking Union Medical College*. New York: China Medical Board of New York, 1970.

Fewsmith, Joseph. *Party, State, and Local Elites in Republican China: Merchant Organizations and Politics in Shanghai, 1890–1930*. Honolulu: University of Hawaii Press, 1985.

Fitzgerald, John. "The Misconceived Revolution: State and Society in China's Nationalist Revolution, 1923–1926." *Journal of Asian Studies* 49, no. 2 (May 1990): 323–43.

Fong, H. D. "Rural Industries in China." *In Problems of the Pacific, 1933*, 306–12. Chicago: University of Chicago Press, 1934.

Foster, W. D. *The Early History of Scientific Medicine in Uganda*. Nairobi: East African Literature Bureau, 1970.

Fowler, Henry. "Medical Mission Policy." *China Medical Journal* (1923): 246–55.

Fu Lien-chang. "Summing Up Report on the Activities of the Chinese Medical Association Since the Eigth General Conference," *Chinese Medical Journal* 71 (May-June 1953).

———. "Why Our Western-trained Doctors Should Learn Traditional Chinese Medicine." *Chinese Medical Journal* 5 (September-October 1955).

Fujiansheng weisheng jianshe jingguo 福建省衛生建設經過 [The process of health reconstruction in Fujian]. N.p., 1939.

Furth, Charlotte, ed. *The Limits of Change: Essays on Conservative Alternatives in Republican China.* Cambridge: Harvard University Press, 1976.

Gamble, Sidney. *Ting Hsien: A North China Rural Community.* New York: Institute of Pacific Relations, 1954.

Gao, Yinzu 高蔭祖. *Zhonghuaminguo dashi ji* 中華民國大事記 [A record of major events of the Chinese Republic]. Taibei: Shijie she, 1957.

Geming wenxian 革命文獻 [Documents of the revolution]. Taibei: Historical Commission of the Kuomintang, 1970–1982.

Volume 53: *Kangzhan qian jiaoyu yu xueshu* 抗戰前教育與學術 [Education and scholarship before the War of Resistance].

Volume 54: *Kangzhan qian jiaoyu zhengce yu gaige* 抗戰前教育政策與改革 [Educational policy and reform before the War of Resistance].

Volume 55: *Kangzhan qian jiaoyu kaikuang yu jiantao* 抗戰前教育概況與檢討 [General conditions of education before the War of Resistance and an evaluation].

Volume 56: *Kangzhan qian zhi gaodeng jiaoyu* 抗戰前之高等教育 [Higher education before the War of Resistance].

Volume 71: *Kangzhan qian guojia jianshe shiliao—neizheng fangmian* 抗戰前國家建設史料 —— 內政方面 [Historical materials on national reconstruction before the War of Resistance—internal administration].

Volume 73: *Kangzhan qian guojia jianshe shiliao—caizheng fangmian* 抗戰前國家建設史料 —— 財政方面 [Historical materials on national reconstruction before the War of Resistance—fiscal developments].

Volumes 79–80: *Zhongguo Guomindang lijie lici zhongzhuanhui zhongyao jueyian huipian* 中國國民黨歷屆歷次中全會重要決議案彙編 [Compilations of important resolutions in all plenary sessions of the Central Committees of the Guomindang].

Volumes 84–87: *Kangzhan qian guojia jianshe shiliao—hezuo yundong* 抗戰前國家建設史料 —— 合作運動 [Historical materials on national reconstruction before the War of Resistance—the cooperative movement].

Volumes 91–93: *Kangzhan qian guojia jianshe shiliao—shoudao jianshe* 抗戰前國家建設史料 —— 首都建設 [Historical materials on national reconstruction before the War of Resistance—reconstruction in the nation's capital].

Gervais, A. *Medicine Man in China*. New York: Frederick A. Stokes, 1934.

Gong, Chun 龔純. "Di erci guonei geming zhanzheng shiqi di hongjun weisheng gongzuo" 第二次國內革命戰爭時期的紅軍衛生工作 [Health work of the Red Army during the Second Internal Revolutionary War], *Zhonghua yishi zazhi* 中華醫史雜誌 [Journal of Chinese medical history] 14, no. 4 (1984): 226–29.

Gordon, Sydney, and Ted Allan. *The Scalpel, the Sword: The Story of Doctor Norman Bethune*. New York: Monthly Review Press, 1973.

Gould, Sidney H., ed. *Sciences in Communist China*. Washington, D.C.: American Association for the Advancement of Science, 1961.

Grant, John B. "Public Health Work in China." *Chinese Medical Journal* 37 (1923): 677–78.

――――. "State Medicine: A Logical Policy for China." *National Medical Journal of China* 14 (April 1928): 65–80.

――――. "Public Health and Medical Events During 1927 and 1928." In *China Yearbook, 1929–30*, 112–22.

――――. "Department of Public Health and Preventive Medicine, Peking Union Medical College, Peking, China." In *Methods and Problems of Medical Education*. New York: Rockefeller Foundation, 1929.

――――. "Philosophy of Rural Reconstruction in China." In *Asiatic Society of Bengal Journal and Proceedings*. Series 3, vol. 4: *Letters*, Calcutta: Asiatic Society of Bengal, 1940, 6: 119–38.

――――. "Western Medicine in Pre-Communist China." *American Journal of Public Health*, special supplement, 50, no. 6 (1960):36–39.

Grant, John B., and T. M. P'eng. "Survey of Urban Public Health Practice in China." *Chinese Medical Journal* 48 (1934): 1074–79.

Greene, Roger S. "Public Health and the Training of Doctors and Nurses in China." *International Review of Missions* 14 (1925): 481–98.

――――. "China Medical Board: A Review of its Work from 1915 to 1919." Fifth Annual Report, China Medical Board (n.d.), pp. 53–91, CMB, Inc., Box 23, Folder 161, Rockefeller Archive Center.

Gregg, Alice H. *China and Educational Autonomy: The Changing Role of the Protestant Educational Missionary in China, 1807–1937.* Syracuse: Syracuse University Press, 1946.

Guangdongsheng zhengfu minzhengteng 廣東省政府民政廳 [Department of Civil Affairs, Guangdong Province], comp. *Yinian lai di Guangdong weisheng xingzheng* 一年來的廣東衛生行政 [Health administration of Guangdong in the past year]. Guangzhou: Minzhengteng, 1940.

Guangzhoushi zhengfu 廣州市政府 [Municipal government of Guangzhou]. *Weisheng nianbao* 衛生年報 [Yearbook of health]. Guangzhou: Weisheng chu, 1925–28.

Guojia jianshe congkan 國家建設叢刊 [A collection of essays on national reconstruction]. Vol. 2. Taibei: Zhonghuaminguo guojia jianshe congkan bianwu weiyuanhui, 1971.

"Guoyiguan di laili" 國醫館的來歷 [The origin of the Institute of National Medicine]. *Tianwentai bao* 天文台報 [Observatory daily], 30 December 1968. Copy filed in the Archives of the Historical Commission of the Kuomintang.

Hayford, Charles W. *To the People: James Yen and Village China.* New York: Columbia University Press, 1990.

"Health Station—First Quarterly Review." Record Group 4, 2 B9, Box 66, Folder 465, Rockefeller Archive Center.

Hemenway, Ruth V. *A Memoir of Revolutionary China, 1924–1941.* Amherst: University of Massachusetts Press, 1977.

Henriot, Christian. "Municipal Power and Local Elites." *Republican China* 11, no. 2 (1986): 1–21.

Hillier, S. M., and J. A. Jewell. *Health Care and Traditional Medicine in China, 1800–1982.* London: Routledge and Kegan Paul, 1983.

Hofmann, Allen. "A Short Historical Sketch of Hackett Medical College and Affiliated Institutions." *China Medical Journal* 40 (1926): 776–79.

Holden, Reuben. *Yale-in-China: The Mainland Years, 1901–1951.* New Haven: Yale-in-China Association, 1964.

Horn, Joshua S. *Away With All Pests: An English Surgeon in People's China, 1954–1969.* New York: Monthly Review Press, 1971.

Hsu, Leonard S. *A Sociological View on Rural Reconstruction.* N.p., 1935. Copy filed in Record Group 1, Series 601, Box 10, Folder 102, Rockefeller Archive Center.

Hsu, Kang-liang, and Fu-tang Chu. "Statistics Concerning Births and Deaths in the Children of 2,168 Chinese Families." *National Medical Journal of China* 16 (1930): 744–55.

Hu, Dingan 胡定安 [Hu, T. A.]. *Xian weisheng xingzheng* 縣衛生行政 [County health administration]. Chongqing: Zhongyang zhengzhi xuexiao yanjiu bu, 1941. Copy filed in Archives of the Historical Commission of the Kuomintang.

——— . *Minzu jiankang zi yixue jichu* 民族健康之醫學基礎 [Medical basis of the nation's health]. Chongqing: Zheng zhong shuju, 1943.

——— . "Difang weisheng xingzheng fan lun" 地方衛生行政汎論 [General discussion of local health administration]. *Jian guo yuekan* 建國月刊 [National reconstruction monthly] 3, no. 3 (July 1930): 47–50.

——— . *Hu Dingan gongzhong weisheng yanlun ji* 胡定安公眾衛生言論集 [A collection of Hu Dingan's public speeches and writings on public health]. Shanghai: Dadong shuju, 1930.

Hu, Xuanming [S. M. Woo] 胡宣明. "Weisheng dangqu ying juyi xia ceng di gongzuo" 衛生當局應注意下層的工作 [The health authorities should pay attention to the work at the basic levels]. *Kangjian zazhi* 康健雜誌 [Health magazine] 2, no. 6 (15 June 1934).

Huang Chia-ssu [Huang Jiasi]. "Medical Education in China." In *Medical Education in Asia: A Symposium*. New York: China Medical Board of New York, 1981.

Huang, Shuze, ed. 黃樹則. *Zhongguo xiandai ming yi zhuan* 中國現代名醫傳 [Biographies of famous physicians in contemporary China] Vol. 2. Beijing: Kexue puji chubanshe, 1987.

Huang, Tsefang [Huang Zifang] 黃子方. "Communicable Disease Information in China." *National Medical Journal of China* 13 (1927): 92–108.

——— . "Developing a Railway Health Service." *Chinese Medical Journal* 49 (1935): 973–89.

——— . "The Development of Health Centers." *Chinese Medical Journal* 55 (June 1939): 546–60.

Huard, Pierre, and Wong Ming. *Chinese Medicine*, trans. Bernard Fielding. New York: McGraw-Hill, 1968.

Hume, Edward H. "Medical Education in China, 1916." In *China Mission Yearbook, 1917*, 422–29 Shanghai: Christian Literature Society, 1918.

——— . "Relationships in Medicine Between China and the Western World," *China Medical Journal* 39 (1925): 185–98.

——— . *Doctors East, Doctors West: An American Physician's Life in China*. New York: W. W. Norton, 1946.

Hymes, Robert. "Not Quite Gentlemen? Doctors in Sung and Yuan." *Chinese Science* 8 (1987): 9–76.

"Initial Year of the Medical Education Program," Record Group 1, Series 601, Box 3, Folder 27, Rockefeller Archive Center.

Israel, John. *Student Nationalism in China, 1927–1937.* Stanford: Stanford University Press, 1966.

Jeffery, Roger. *The Politics of Health in India.* Berkeley: University of California Press, 1988.

Jia, Dedao 賈得道. *Zhongguo yixue shi lue* 中國醫學史略 [A short history of medicine in China]. Taiyuan: Shanxi renmin chuban-she, 1979.

Jia, Shiyi 賈士貽. *Minguo xu caizheng shi* 民國續財政史 [Supplement to the fiscal history of the Republic]. Vol. 1. Shanghai: Shangwu yinshuguan, 1932.

Jiangxi sheng weisheng shiye gaikuang 江西省衛生事業概況 [A survey of health work in Jiangxi]. Nanchang: N.p., 1938. Copy filed in the Archives of the Historical Commission of the Kuomintang.

Jiaoyubu gaodeng jiaoyusi 教育部高等教育司 [Department of Higher Education, Ministry of Education]. *Ershiniandu zhuanguo gaodeng jiaoyu tongji* 二十年度全國高等教育統計 [Statistics of the country's higher education in 1931]. Nanjing: Jiaoyu bu, 1933.

Jin, Baoshan [P. Z. King] 金寶善. "Xuexiao weisheng yu qingnian jiankang" 學校衛生與青年健康 [School health and the health of youth]. *Zhongyang ribao, yixue zhoukan* 中央日報醫學周刊 [Central daily, medical supplement], 19 January 1936.

——— . *Xuexiao weisheng jiaoyu* 學校衛生教育 [School health education]. Chongqing: Zhongyang xunlian tuan dang zheng xunlian ban, 1940. Copy filed in the Archives of the Historical Commission of the Kuomintang.

——— . *Zhanshi difang weisheng xingzheng gaiyao* 戰時地方衛生行政概要 [Local health administration during the war]. Chongqing: Zhongyang xunlian tuan dang zheng xunlian ban, 1940. Copy filed in the Archives of the Historical Commission of the Kuomintang.

——— . *Weisheng xingzheng wenti* 衛生行政問題 [The problem of health administration]. Chongqing: Zhongyang xunlian tuan dang zheng gaoji xunlian ban, 1944. Copy filed in the Archives of the Historical Commission of the Kuomintang.

Jin, Lunhai 金輪海. *Nongcun fuxing yu xiang jiao yundong* 農村復興與鄉教運動 [Rural rejuvenation and the rural education movement]. Shanghai: Zhonghua shuju, 1934.

Kerr, L. White, Donald O. Anderson, Esko Kalimo, and Bogdan M. Kleczkowski. *Health Services: Concepts and Information for National Planning and Management.* Geneva: World Health Organization, 1977.

Kim, C. S. "A Brief Survey of the Public Health Activities in Shanghai." *China Medical Journal* 42 (1928):162–80.

King. M., ed. *Medical Care in Developing Countries.* London: Oxford University Press, 1966.

Kleinman, Arthur. *Patients and Healers in the Context of Culture: an Exploration of the Borderland Between Anthropology, Medicine, and Psychiatry.* Berkeley: University of California Press, 1980.

Kleinman, Arthur, Peter Kunstadter, E. Russell Alexander, and James L. Gale, eds. *Medicine in Chinese Cultures: Comparative Studies of Health Care in China and Other Societies.* Bethesda: National Institutes of Health, 1975.

Kong, Songling 孔松齡. *Zhongguo yixue yanjin* 中國醫學演進 [The progress of medicine in China]. Taibei: Xidai chuban youxian gongsi, 1976.

Kotenev, Anatol M. *New Lamps for Old: An Interpretation of Events in Modern China and Whither They Lead.* Shanghai: *North China Daily News and Herald,* 1931.

Ku, Jinghan 顧景漢. "Xiaozhuang shehui weisheng diaocha" 曉莊社會衛生調查 [An investigation of social medicine in Xiaozhuang]. *Zhongyang ribao, yixue zhoukan* 中央日報醫學周刊 [Central daily, medical supplement], 9 February 1936, 16 February 1936, 23 February 1936, 1 March 1936.

Kuhn, Philip A. "Local Self-government Under the Republic: Problems of Control, Autonomy, and Mobilization." In *Conflict and Control in Late Imperial China,* ed. Frederic Wakeman, Jr., and Carolyn Grant. Berkeley: University of California Press, 1975.

Kuo, Tze-hsiung. *Higher Education in China.* Nanjing: Council of International Affairs, 1937.

――――. *Technical Cooperation Between China and Geneva.* Nanjing: Council of International Affairs, 1936.

Kwok, D. W. Y. *Scientism in Chinese Thought, 1900–1950.* New Haven: Yale University Press, 1965.

Lamberton, Mary. *St. John's University, Shanghai, 1879–1951.* New York: United Board for Christian Colleges in China, 1955.

Lambuth, Walter R. *Medical Missions: The Twofold Task.* New York: Student Volunteer Movement for Foreign Missions, 1920.

Lampton, David M. *The Politics of Medicine in China: The Policy Process, 1949–1977.* Boulder, Colo.: Westview, 1977.

Lamson, H. D. *Social Pathology in China: A Source Book for the Study of Problems of Livelihood, Health and the Family.* Shanghai: Commercial Press, 1935.

Lang, Olga. *Chinese Family and Society.* New Haven: Yale University Press, 1946.

"Law and Legislation: Establishment of Medical Schools." *Chinese Medical Journal* 46 (1932): 837–39.

League of Nations. *Report Submitted to the Secretary General by the Director of the Section for Communications and Transit, Secretary of the Council Committee, on his Mission in China, January-May 1935.* Geneva: League of Nations, 1935.

———. *Annexes to the Report to the Council of the League of Nations of its Technical Delegate on his Mission in China from Date of Appointment Until April 1, 1934.* Shanghai: *North China Daily News and Herald,* 1934.

———. *Minutes of 17th Session, May 4–8, 1931, League of Nations Health Organization.* Geneva: League of Nations, 1931.

———. *Annual Report of the Health Organization for 1930.* Geneva: League of Nations, 1931.

———. *Report of the Health Organization for the Period October 1932 to September 1933.* Geneva: League of Nations, 1933.

———. "Proposals of the National Government of the Republic of China for Collaboration with the League of Nations in Health Matters." In *Annual Report of the Health Organization for 1929.* Geneva: League of Nations, 1930.

———. *Notes on Public Health and Modern Medicine in China.* Geneva: League of Nations, 1930.

———. Council Committee on Technical Cooperation Between League of Nations and China. *Report of the Technical Delegate on his Mission in China from Date of Appointment Until April 1, 1934.* Geneva: League of Nations, 1934.

———. Mission of Educational Experts. *The Reorganization of Education in China.* Paris: League of Nations Institute of Intellectual Cooperation, 1932.

Lee, T'ao. "Some Statistics on Medical Schools in China for 1932–1933." *Chinese Medical Journal* 47 (1933): 1029–39.

———. "Some Statistics on Medical Schools in China for the Year 1933–1934," *Chinese Medical Journal* 49 (1935): 894–902.

Lennox, William G. "The Distribution of Medical School Graduates in China." *Chinese Medical Journal* 46 (1932): 404–11.

————. "A Self Survey of Mission Hospitals in China." *Chinese Medical Journal* 46 (1932): 484–534.

Leung, Angela Ki Che. "Organized Medicine in Ming-Qing China: State and Private Medical Institutions in the Lower Yangzi Region." *Late Imperial China* 8, no. 1 (June 1987): 134–66.

Leslie, Charles. "The Modernization of Asian Medical Systems." In *Rethinking Modernization: Anthropological Perspectives*, ed. J. J. Poggie and R. Lynch. Westport: Greenwood, 1974.

————, ed. *Asian Medical Systems: A Comparative Study*. Berkeley: University of California Press, 1976.

Li, Tingan 李廷安. "A Public Health Report on Canton, China." *National Medical Journal of China* 11 (1925): 324–75.

————. "The Campaign Against Tuberculosis." *Chinese Medical Journal* 48 (1934): 301–3.

————. *Zhongguo xiangcun weisheng wenti* 中國鄉村衛生問題 [The problem of rural health in China]. Shanghai: Shangwu yinshuguan, 1935.

————. "Summary Report on Rural Public Health Practice in China." *Chinese Medical Journal* 48 (1934): 1086–90.

————. *Guo li yu jiankang* 國力與健康 [Health and national strength]. Chengdu: Zhongxi shuju, 1943.

————. *Zhong wai yixue shi gailun* 中外醫學概論 [A general discussion of Chinese and foreign medical history]. Shanghai: Shangwu yinshuguan, 1944.

————. "Jibing baoxian yu gongyi zhidu" 疾病保險與公醫制度 [Health insurance and state medicine]. *Huaxi yi xun* 華西醫訊 [Medical news of west China] 1, no. 4 (15 December 1944): 153–57.

Li, Xiangming 李向明. *Zhongguo xiandai yixuejia zhuan lue* 中國現代醫學家傳略 [Short biographies of contemporary Chinese medical specialists]. Beijing: Kexue jishu wenxian chubanshe, 1984.

Lim, Robert K. S., and C. C. Chen. "State Medicine." *Chinese Medical Journal* 51 (1937): 781–96.

Lindbeck, M. H. "Organization and Development of Science." In *Sciences in Communist China*, ed. Sidney H. Gould, 3–58. Washington, D.C: American Association for the Advancement of Science, 1961.

Liu, J. Heng [Liu Ruiheng] 劉瑞恆. "Short Visit to Shanghai and Nanking," n.d., p. 1 CMB, Inc., Box 70, Folder 496, Rockefeller Archive Center.

———. "The Chinese Ministry of Health." *National Medical Journal of China* 15 (1929): 135–48.

———. "Some Phases of Public Health Work in China." *Chinese Medical Journal* 48 (1934): 70–73.

———. "San nian lai zhongyang weisheng sheshi gaikuang" 三年來中央衛生設施概況 [General survey of health reconstruction in the last three years]. *Weisheng banyue kan* 衛生半月刊 [Health bimonthly] 2, no. 1 (15 January 1935): 1–12.

———. "The Central Field Health Station as a Training Center for Public Health Workers." *Chinese Medical Journal* 49 (1935): 942–45.

———. "Health and Medicine." In *China Yearbook, 1935–36*, 1567–1642. Shanghai: *North China Daily News*, 1936.

———. "National Health Organization." In *China Christian Yearbook, 1936–37*, 336–55. Glendale, Calif.: Arthur Clark, 1937.

———. "The Origin and Development of Public Health Service in China." In *Voices from Unoccupied China*, ed. Harley F. MacNair, 36–45. Chicago: University of Chicago Press, 1944.

Liu, J. Heng, and C. K. Chu. "Problems of Nutrition and Dietary Requirements in China." *Chinese Medical Journal* 61 (1943): 95–109.

Liu, Sijin ed. 劉似錦 . *Liu Ruiheng boshi yu Zhongguo yiyao ji weisheng shiye* 劉瑞恆博士與中國醫藥及衛生事業 [Dr. J. Heng Liu and medical and health development in China]. Taibei: Shangwu yinshuguan, 1989.

Lock, Margaret M. *East Asian Medicine in Urban Japan*. Berkeley: University of California Press, 1980.

Lu, Albert T. *Renaissance of Rural Kiangsi*. Nanjing: Council of International Affairs, 1936.

Lucas, AnElissa. *Chinese Medical Modernization: Comparative Policy Continuities, 1930s–1980s*. New York: Praeger, 1982.

"Lun weishengbu ji ying zhuzhong yishi buxi jiaoyu" 論衛生部亟應注重醫事補習教育 [The Ministry of Health should stress supplementary medical education]. *Zhongxi yixue bao* 中西醫學報 [Journal of Chinese and western medicine] 10, no. 1 (July 1929): 1–3.

Lutz, Jessie G. *China and the Christian Colleges, 1850–1950*. Ithaca: Cornell University Press, 1971.

MacNair, Harley F., ed. *Voices From Unoccupied China*. Chicago: University of Chicago Press, 1944.

McCabe, Anne. "Maternity and Child Health Work of the First Health

Station, Peiping." *Nursing Journal of China* 12, no. 4 (October 1931): 14–18.

McNeill, William H. *Plagues and Peoples.* Garden City, N.Y.: Doubleday, 1977.

Mei, Y. C. "Government Health Work." In *China Christian Yearbook.* 1929, 361–78.

Mei, Yilin 梅貽林. "Yixue shang zhi xin jianshe—gongyi" 醫學上之 新建設 —— 公醫 [New development in medicine—state medicine]. *Zhongyang ribao* [Central daily], 1930. No precise date given. Copy filed in the Archives of the Historical Commission of the Kuomintang.

Meng Zhaohua 孟昭華 and Wang Minghuan 王明寰. *Zhongguo minzheng shigao* 中國民政史稿 [A history of Chinese civil administration]. Harbin: Heilongjiang renmin chubanshe, 1986.

Minden, Karen. "The Development of Early Chinese Communist Health Policy: Health Care in the Border Region, 1936–1949." *American Journal of Chinese Medicine* 7, no. 4 (1979): 299–315.

Miner, Noel R. "Chekiang: The Nationalist's Effort in Agrarian Reform and Construction." Ph.D. diss., Stanford University, 1973.

"Minguo ershisan nian du Fujian sheng zheng diaocha baogao" 民 國二十三年度福建省政調查報告 [Investigative report of the Fujian Provincial Administration in 1934]. *Neizheng tongji jikan* 內政統計季刊 [Statistical quarterly of internal administration], no. 2 (January 1937): 105–30.

Morgan, L. G. *The Teaching of Science to the Chinese.* Hong Kong: Kelly and Walsh, 1933.

Mullan, Fitzhugh. *Plague and Politics: The Story of the United States Public Health Service.* New York: Basic Books, 1989.

Myers, Ramon. *The Chinese Peasant Economy: Agricultural Developments in Hopei and Shantung, 1890–1940.* Cambridge: Harvard University Press, 1970.

Nathan, Andrew J. *A History of the Chinese International Famine Relief Commission.* Cambridge: Harvard University Press, 1965.

Nathan, Carl F. *Plague Prevention and Politics in Manchuria, 1910–1931.* Cambridge: East Asian Research Center, Harvard University, 1967.

"National Board of Health." *National Medical Journal of China* 16 (1930): 124.

"The National Economic Council Project and Allocation of Funds for 1934." In League of Nations, *Annexes to the Report to the Council of the League of Nations of its Technical Delegate on His Mission in*

China from Date of Appointment Until April 1, 1934. Shanghai: *North China Daily News and Herald,* 1934.

National Economic Council. *Rural Reconstruction in Kiangsi.* Nanchang: National Economic Council, 1935.

National Epidemic Prevention Bureau: A Report, Being a Review of its Activities from its Foundation in March 1919 to June 1934. Peiping: Central Field Health Station, 1934.

Needham, Joseph. *Clerks and Craftsmen in China and the West: Lectures and Addresses on the History of Science and Technology.* Cambridge: Cambridge University Press, 1970.

Neizheng nianjian 內政年鑒 [Yearbook of internal administration]. Shanghai: Shangwu yinshuguan, 1935.

Neizhengbu ershiyi nian liuyue fan gongzuo baogao 內政部二十一年六月份工作報告 [Work report of the Ministry of the Interior in June 1932]. Nanjing: Neizhengbu, 1932. Copy filed in the Archives of the Historical Commission of the Kuomintang.

Nevins, Allan. *Study in Power: John D. Rockefeller.* New York: Charles Scribner's Sons, 1953.

New Life Centers in Rural Kiangsi. Nanchang: Head Office of Kiangsi Rural Welfare Centers, National Economic Council, 1936.

New, Peter, and Yueh-wah Cheung. "Harvard Medical School of China, 1911–1916: An Expanded Footnote in the History of Western Medical Education in China," *Social Science and Medicine* 16 (1982): 1207–15.

Ninkovich, Frank. "The Rockefeller Foundation, China, and Cultural Change." *Journal of American History* 70, no. 4 (March 1984): 799–820.

Ohnuki-Tierney, Emiko. *Illness and Culture in Contemporary Japan.* Cambridge: Cambridge University Press, 1984.

Oksenberg, Michel, ed. *China's Developmental Experience.* New York: Praeger, 1973.

Oldt, F. "State Medicine Problems." *Chinese Medical Journal* 51 (1937): 797–802.

Orleans, Leo A. *Health Policies and Services in China, 1974.* Washington, D.C.: Government Printing Office, 1974.

Paauw, Douglas S. "Chinese National Expenditures During the Nanking Period." *Far Eastern Quarterly* 12 (November 1952): 3–26.

Parmelee, Donna E., Gail Henderson, and Myron S. Cohen. "Medicine Under Socialism: Some Observations on Yugoslavia and China." *Social Science and Medicine* 16 (1982): 1389–96.

Payer, Cheryl A. "Western Economic Assistance to Nationalist China, 1927–1937: A Comparison with Postwar Aid Programs." Ph.D. diss., Harvard University, 1972.

Paywes, Moshe and A. Michael Davis, eds. *Health Problems in Developing States.* New York: Grune and Stratton, 1968.

Pearson, David A. "The Concept of Regionalized Personal Health Services in the United States, 1920–1955." In *The Regionalization of Personal Health Services,* ed. Ernest W. Saward, 3–60. Rev. ed. New York: Prodist for the Milbank Memorial Fund, 1976.

Peipingshi zhengfu weishengchu yewu baogao 北平市政府衛生處業務報告 [Work report of the Peiping Health Department]. Peiping: Weisheng chu, 1934.

Peter, W. W. "Some Health Problems of Changing China." *Journal of the American Medical Association* 58, no. 26 (1912): 2023–24.

———. *Broadcasting Health in China: The Field and Methods of Public Health Work in the Missionary Enterprise.* Shanghai: Presbyterian Mission Press, 1926.

"Plague Prevention in Tatung." *Peking Leader,* 8 March 1919, and 19 March 1919. Record Group 4, Series 1, Box 8, Folder 92, Rockefeller Archive Center.

Presbyterian Church in the U.S.A., Board of Foreign Missions. *Report on Japan and China of the Deputation Sent by the Board of Foreign Missions of the Presbyterian Church in the U.S.A. to Visit These Fields and to Attend a Series of Evaluation Conferences in China in 1926.* New York: Board of Foreign Missions of the Presbyterian Church in the U.S.A., 1927.

Problems of the Pacific, 1933. Chicago: University of Chicago Press, 1934.

"Prospectus of Medical Colleges and Schools." *Chinese Medical Journal* 49 (1935): 998–1034.

"Provisional National Health Council." Record Group 4, 2 B9, Box 75, No. 529, Rockefeller Archive Center.

Pruitt, Ida. "Medical Social Workers: Their Work and Training." *Chinese Medical Journal* 49 (1935): 909–16.

"Public Health and Medicine." In *China Yearbook, 1942,* 665–95.

"Public Health Reconstruction Under the National Government." *Chinese Medical Journal* 46 (1932): 826–34.

Qian, Shipu 錢實甫. *Beiyang zhengfu shiqi di zhengzhi zhidu* 北洋政府時期的政治制度 [The political system during the Beiyang government period]. Vols. 1, 2. Beijing: Zhonghua shuju, 1984.

Quan guo jingji weiyuanhui choubeichu gongzuo baogao 全國經濟委員會籌備處工作報告 [Work report of the Preparatory Department of the National Economic Council]. Nanjing: N.p., 1933.

Quan guo jingji weiyuanhui baogao hui pian 全國經濟委員會報告彙編 [Compilation of reports of the National Economic Council]. Vol. 9. Nanjing: Quan guo jingji weiyuanhui, 1936.

Rankin, Mary B. *Elite Activism and Political Transformation in China: Zhejiang Province, 1865–1911*. Stanford: Stanford University Press, 1986.

Reardon-Anderson, James. *The Study of Change: Chemistry in China, 1840–1949*. Cambridge: Cambridge University Press, 1991.

Rees, Ronald. *China Faces the Storm: The Christian Church in China Today*. London: Edinburgh House, 1938.

Reeves, William, Jr. "Sino-American Cooperation in Medicine: The Origins of Hsiang-ya (1902–1914)." In *American Missionaries in China: Papers from Harvard Seminars*, ed. Kwang-ching Liu, 129–82. Cambridge: East Asian Research Center, Harvard University, 1966,

"Regulations Governing the Public Health Experiment Station of the Police Department of the City of Peking." Record Group 4, 2 B9, Box 66, Folder 465, Rockefeller Archive Center.

"Regulations Governing the Organization of the National Economic Council and of its Bureaux, Committees and Offices, 1934." In League of Nations, *Annexes to the Report to the Council of the League of Nations of its Technical Delegate on his Mission in China from Date of Appointment Until April 1, 1934*. Shanghai: *North China Daily News and Herald*, 1934.

Ren, Mianzhi 任勉芝. *Zhongguo yiyao shi dagang* 中國醫藥史大綱 [An outline history of medicine and pharmacology in China]. Hong Kong: Xinya yixue chubanshe, 1976.

Report of the Commission Sent by the Rockefeller Foundation to China to Study the Problem of the Development of Medicine and Public Health, November 15, 1946. Record Group 1, Series 601, Box 2, Folder 16, Rockefeller Archive Center.

"Report of the National Health Administration on the Three Year Plan, 1931–34." In League of Nations, *Annexes to the Report to the Council of the League of Nations of its Technical Delegate on his Mission in China from Date of Appointment Until April 1, 1934*. Shanghai: *North China Daily News and Herald*, 1934.

"Report on the Work of the Preparatory Office of the National

Economic Council, 1933." In League of Nations, *Annexes to the Report to the Council of the League of Nations of its Technical Delegate on his Mission in China from Date of Appointment Until April 1, 1934.* Shanghai: *North China Daily News and Herald*, 1934.

Risse, Guenter B., ed. *Modern China and Traditional Chinese Medicine.* Springfield, Ill.: Charles C. Thomas, 1973.

Robertson, R. Cecil. "Public Health." In *China Yearbook, 1938*, 128–41.

Rosen, George. *A History of Public Health.* New York: MD Publications, 1958.

Rosenkrantz, Barbara G. *Public Health and the State: Changing Views in Massachusetts, 1842–1936.* Cambridge: Harvard University Press, 1972.

———. "Cart Before Horse: Theory, Practice and Professional Image in American Public Health, 1870–1920." *Journal of the History of Medicine* 29 (1974): 55–73.

Rosenthal, Marilynn M. *Health Care in the People's Republic of China: Moving Toward Modernization.* Boulder, Colo.: Westview, 1987.

Salter, Arthur. *China and Silver.* New York: Economic Forum, 1934.

Schneider, Laurence A. "The Rockefeller Foundation, the China Foundation, and the Development of Modern Science in China." *Social Science and Medicine* 16 (1982): 1217–21.

A School Health Programme: The Report of a Conference on School Health. Shanghai: China Christian Education Association, 1925. Copy filed in United Church of Canada Archives.

Schram, Stuart R., ed. *Chairman Mao Talks to the People.* New York: Random House, 1974.

———. ed. *The Scope of State Power in China.* Hong Kong: Chinese University of Hong Kong, 1985.

Schwartz, Benjamin. *In Search of Wealth and Power: Yen Fu and the West.* Cambridge: Harvard University Press, 1964.

Science Society of China. *The Science Society of China: Its History, Organization and Activities.* Shanghai: Science Society of China, 1931.

Scott, Munroe. *McClue: The China Years.* Toronto: Penguin, 1979.

Seipp, Conrad, ed. *Health Care for the Community: Selected Papers of Dr. John B. Grant.* Baltimore: Johns Hopkins University Press, 1963.

Selden, Mark. *The Yenan Way in Revolutionary China.* Cambridge: Harvard University Press, 1971.

Shanghai yike daxue huashan yiyuan bashi zhounian jinian ce 上海醫科大學華山醫院八十周年紀念冊 [Volume commemorating the eightieth anniversary of Huashan Hospital, Shanghai Medical College]. Shanghai: Huashan yiyuan, 1987.

Shen, Tsung-han. *The Sino-American Joint Commission in Rural Reconstruction: Twenty Years of Cooperation for Agricultural Development.* Ithaca: Cornell University Press, 1970.

Sheridan, James E. *China in Disintegration: The Republican Era in Chinese History, 1912–1949.* New York: Free Press, 1975.

Si, Yuanyi 姒元翼. *Zhongguo yixue shi* 中國醫學史 [History of medicine in China]. Beijing: Renmin weisheng chubanshe, 1984.

Sidel, Victor, and Ruth Sidel. *The Health of China.* Boston: Beacon, 1982.

————. *Reforming Medicine: Lessons of the Last Quarter Century.* New York: Pantheon, 1984.

Sih, Paul T. K., ed. *The Strenuous Decade: China's Nation Building Efforts, 1927–1937.* New York: St. John's University Press, 1970.

Sivin, Nathan, ed. *Science and Technology in East Asia.* New York: Science History Publications, 1977.

————. *Traditional Medicine in Contemporary China: A Partial Translation of Revised Outline of Chinese Medicine (1972) with an Introductory Study on Change in Present-day and Early Medicine.* Ann Arbor: University of Michigan, Center for Chinese Studies, 1987.

————. "Science and Medicine in Imperial China—the State of the Field." *Journal of Asian Studies* 47, no. 1 (February 1988):41–90.

Skocpol, Theda. *States and Social Revolution: A Comparative Analysis of France, Russia and China.* Cambridge: Cambridge University Press, 1979.

Spence, Jonathan. *To Change China: Western Advisers in China, 1620–1960.* Boston: Little, Brown, 1969.

————. *The Search for Modern China.* New York: W. W. Norton, 1990.

Stampar, Andrija. "Observations of a Rural Health Worker." *New England Journal of Medicine* 218, no. 24 (16 June 1938), 991–97.

————. "Health and Social Conditions in China." In *Serving the Course of Public Health: Selected Papers of Andrija Stampar,* ed. M. D. Grmek, 123–51. Zagreb: Andrija Stampar School of Public Health, 1966.

Starr, Paul. *The Social Transformation of American Medicine: The Rise of a Sovereign Profession and the Making of a Vast Industry.* New York: Basic Books, 1982.

Stauffer, M., ed. *The Christian Occupation of China.* Shanghai: China Continuation Committee, 1922.

Struthers, E. B. "The Relation of Medical School to the Rural Health Program." *Chinese Medical Journal* 52 (1937): 447–49.

"Syllabus on Hygiene and Preventive Medicine for the Mass Education Association Institute, April 1926." Record Group 4, 2 B9, Box 76, Folder 532, Rockefeller Archive Center.

Sze, Szeming. *China's Health Problems.* Washington, D.C.: Chinese Medical Association, 1943.

———. *Medical Work in China, 1934–1941.* Boca Raton, Fla: L.I.S.Z. Publications, 1984.

T'ang, Leang-li. *China's New Currency System.* London: Kegan, Paul, Trench, Trubner, 1936.

Tao, S. M. "Medical Education of Chinese Women." *Chinese Medical Journal* 47 (1933): 1010–28.

Tawney, R. H. *Land and Labor in China.* London: Allen and Unwin, 1932.

Taylor, Carl E., Rahmi Dirican, and Kurt W. Deuschle. *Health Manpower Planning in Turkey: An International Research Case Study.* Baltimore: Johns Hopkins University Press, 1968.

Teng, Ssu-yu, and John K. Fairbank. *China's Response to the West.* Cambridge: Harvard University Press, 1954.

Thomson, James C., Jr. *While China Faced West: American Reformers in Nationalist China, 1928–1937.* Cambridge: Harvard University Press, 1969.

Tien, Hung-mao. *Government and Politics in Kuomintang China, 1927–1937.* Stanford: Stanford University Press, 1972.

Tongrenhui, ed. 同仁會. *Zhonghuaminguo yishi zonglan* 中華民國醫事綜覽 [A Comprehensive view of Chinese medical affairs]. Tokyo: Tongrenhui, 1935.

Tsao, L. E. *Quarantine Service in China.* Nanjing: Council of International Affairs, 1937.

Tseng, Lily. "Midwifery." *China Medical Journal* 44 (1930): 431–45.

Twiss, George. *Science and Education in China.* Shanghai: Commercial Press, 1925.

Tyau, Min-ch'ien T. Z. *Two Years of Nationalist China.* Shanghai: Kelly and Walsh, 1930.

United Church of Canada, issues of *United Church of Canada Yearbook,* Toronto. 1932, 1936, 1937.

Unschuld, Paul V. *Medicine in China: A History of Ideas.* Berkeley: University of California Press, 1985.

"A Visit to the Health Administration of the National Government at Nanking." *Chinese Medical Journal* 46 (1932): 834–36.

Wang Donglin 汪東林. *Liang Shuming wenda lu*. 梁漱溟問答錄 [A record of questions and answers with Liang Shuming]. Changsha: Hunan renmin chubanshe, 1988.

Wang Jiwen 汪緝文. "Zhongguo xin yixue jianshe zhi zhangai" 中國新醫學建設之障礙 [Obstacles to the establishment of new medicine in China]. *Dagong bao* [Dagong daily] (Tianjian), 10 April 1931.

Wang, Qizhang 汪企張. "Hangkong jiao guo yu yiyao jiao guo" 航空救國與醫藥救國 [Saving the country through aviation and saving the country through medicine], *Shenbao, yiyao zhoukan* 申報醫藥周刊 [Shen daily, medical supplement], 27 March 1933, and 30 March 1933.

Wang, Y. C. *Chinese Intellectuals and the West, 1872–1949*. Chapel Hill: University of North Carolina Press, 1966.

Wang, Zhixin 王治心. *Zhongguo jidujiao shi gang* 中國基督教史綱 [A brief historical survey of Christianity in China]. Hong Kong: Jidujiao wenyi chubanshe, 1959.

Wang, Zuxiang 王祖祥. *Weisheng xingzheng sanshi nian suoyi* 衛生行政三十年瑣憶 [Reminiscences of thirty years of health administration]. Taibei: Weisheng zazhi she, 1953.

Weeks, Lewis E., and Howard J. Berman. *Shapers of American Health Care Policy: An Oral History*. Ann Arbor: Health Administration Press, 1985.

Wegman, Myron E., Lin Tsung-yi, and Elizabeth F. Purcell. *Public Health in the People's Republic of China*. New York: Josiah Macy, Jr., Foundation, 1973.

Wei, William. *Counterrevolution in China: The Nationalists in Jiangxi During the Soviet Period*. Ann Arbor: University of Michigan Press, 1985.

Weisheng banyue kan 衛生半月刊 [Health bimonthly]. Various issues, 1935.

Weisheng gongbao 衛生公報 [Gazette of the Ministry of Health]. Various issues, 1929–30.

Weisheng shiyan chu gongzuo baogao 衛生實驗處工作報告 [Work report of the Central Field Health Station]. Nanjing: Central Field Health Station, 1935.

Weishengshu gonggong weisheng renyuan xunliansuo gaikuang 衛生署公

共衛生人員訓練所概況 [General survey of the National Public Health Personnel Training Institute]. Chongqing: Weisheng ren-yuan xunlian suo, 1943. Copy filed in the Archives of the Historical Commission of the Kuomintang.

Weishengshu, Guominzhengfu 國民政府衛生署 [National Health Administration]. *Weisheng fagui* 衛生法規 [Health regulations]. Nanjing: Weisheng shu, 1936.

——— . *Zhongyang weisheng sheshi gaikuang yingji* 中央衛生設施概況 影集 [National public health activities, a pictorial survey]. Nanjing: Weisheng shu, 1934.

Weisheng tongji 衛生統計 [Health statistics]. Chongqing: Neizheng bu, 1938. Copy filed in the Archives of the Historical Commission of the Kuomintang.

Weisheng xingzheng jiangyi 衛生行政講義 [Lectures on health administration]. Shanghai: Dadong shuju, 1925.

Whitmore, Clara B. "A History of the Development of Western Medicine in China." Ph.D. diss., University of Southern California, 1934.

Wilbur, C. Martin. *The Nationalist Revolution in China, 1923–1928.* Cambridge: Cambridge University Press, 1983.

——— . "Nationalist China, 1928–1950: An Interpretation." In *China: Seventy Years After the 1911 Hsin-Hai Revolution,* ed. Hungdah Chiu and Shao-chuan Leng, 2–57. Charlottesville: University Press of Virginia, 1984.

Wilenski, Peter. *The Delivery of Health Services in the People's Republic of China.* Ottawa: International Development Research Center, 1976.

Wong, K. Chimin, and Wu Lien-teh. *History of Chinese Medicine.* 2d ed. Shanghai: National Quarantine Service, 1936.

Woo, G. H. "Medical Progress in China." *Asiatic Review* 38 (1942): 179–87.

Wu Lien-teh. "Modern Chinese Physicians and Practice." In *China Mission Yearbook, 1926,* 355–63.

——— . "The Rejuvenation of Medicine in China." *China Quarterly* (December 1935): 55–66.

——— . "A Hundred Years of Modern Medicine in China." *Chinese Medical Journal* 50 (1936): 152–54.

——— . "Public Hospitals in China." *China Quarterly* (Summer 1936): 1–11.

——— . "Fundamentals of State Medicine," *Chinese Medical Journal* 51 (1937): 773–80.

———. *Plague Fighter: Autobiography of a Chinese Physician*. Cambridge: W. Heffer and Sons, 1959.

Wu, Songshan 吳嵩山 "Weisheng yundong ti yaoyi yu zhungyao" 衛生運動的要義與重要 [The meaning and importance of the health movement] *Zhongyang ribao, yixue zhoukan*, 中央日報醫學周刊 [Central daily, medical supplement] no. 134, 16 February 1936.

Xian weisheng xingzheng shishi banfa gangyao 縣衛生行政實施辦法綱要 [A summary of methods to implement county health administration]. Chongqing: Weisheng shu, 1939.

"Xianzhi zhongyi jingguo" 限制中醫經過 [The process of restricting Chinese medicine]. *Zhongxi yixue bao* 中西醫學報 [Journal of Chinese and western medicine] 10, no. 10 (April 1930): 33–35.

Xin shenghuo yu jiankang 新生活與健康. [New life and health]. Nanjing: Zheng zhong shuju, 1934.

Xu, Xingding 徐興鼎. "Woguo lidai yaoshi guanli gaishu" 我國歷代藥事管理概述 [A general discussion of medical administrations throughout the dynasties in our country], *Zhonghua yishi zazhi* 中華醫史雜誌 [Journal of Chinese medical history] 14, no. 2 (1984):117–20.

Xue, Jianwu 薛建吾. *Zhongguo xiangcun weisheng xingzheng* 中國鄉村衛生行政 [Village health administration in China]. Shanghai: Shengwu yinshuguan, 1937.

Xue, Yu 薛愚, ed. *Zhongguo yaoxue shi liao* 中國藥學史料 [Historical materials on Chinese medicine and pharmacology]. Beijing: Renmin weisheng chubanshe, 1984.

Yang, Marion. "Midwifery Training in China." *Chinese Medical Journal* 42 (1928): 768–75.

———. "Child Health Work in the Peiping Special Health Area." *Chinese Medical Journal* 43 (1929): 920–25.

———. "Birth Control in Peiping: First Report of the Peiping Committee on Maternal Health." *Chinese Medical Journal* 48 (1934): 786–91.

Yang, Y. N., E. Landauer, C. K. Koo, and P. C. Lin. "Plague Work in Fukien. China," *Chinese Medical Journal* 55 (1939): 55–73.

Yao, Hsun-yuan. "Industrial Health Work in the Peiping Special Health Area." *Chinese Medical Journal* 43 (1929): 379–87.

———. "The Second Year of the Rural Health Experiment in Ting Hsien, China." *Milbank Memorial Fund Quarterly Bulletin* 10 (January 1932): 55–66.

Ye, Shu 葉曙. *Bingli sanshisan nian.* 病理三十年 [Thirty-three years of medicine]. Taibei: Chuanji wenxue chubanshe, 1982.

Yen, F.C. [Yan Fuqing]. "An Example of Cooperation with the Chinese in Medical Education." *Journal of the American Medical Association* 4, no. 17 (24 April 1915): 1385–87.

——. "The Hsiang-Ya Medical College." *China Medical Journal* 15 (1926): 776–79.

——. "Medicine of the Future in China." *Chinese Medical Journal* 50 (1936): 155–58.

——. "Some Problems of Public Health." *People's Tribune,* new series, 23 (1938): 113–19.

Yen, James. *The Ting Hsien Experiment in 1934.* Beijing: Chinese National Association of the Mass Education Movement, 1934.

"Yixue jiaoyu ti wenti" 醫學教育的問題 [The problem of medical education], *Zhongyang ribao, yixue zhoukan* 中央日報醫學周刊 [Central daily, medical supplement], no. 136 (1 March 1936).

Yip, Ka-che. *Religion, Nationalism, and Chinese Students: The Anti-Christian Movement of 1922–1927.* Bellingham: Center for Asian Studies, Western Washington University, 1980.

——. "Health Policy in the Kuomintang Period, 1927–1937." In *Proceedings of the Second International Symposium on Asian Studies,* 205–13. Hong Kong: Asian Research Service, 1980.

——. "Education and Political Socialization in Pre-Communist China: The Goals of San Min Chu-i Education." *Asian Profile* 9, no. 5 (October 1981): 401–13.

——. "Health and Society in China: Public Health Education for the Community, 1917–1937." *Social Science and Medicine* 16 (1982): 1197–1205.

——. "Medicine and Nationalism in the People's Republic of China, 1949–1980," *Canadian Review of Studies in Nationalism* 10, no. 2 (1983): 175–87.

——. "Medical Modernization in the People's Republic of China." In *Proceedings of the Sixth International Symposium on Asian Studies,* 529–37. Hong Kong: Asian Research Service, 1984.

——. "Minkoku-ki Chugoku ni okeru Rokkufera—zaidan no iryo, shakai katsudo" 民国期中国におけるロツクフエラ——財団の医療社会活動 [Medical and social activities of the Rockefeller Foundation in Republican China]. In *Bei-chu kyoiku bunryu no kiseki—kokusai bunka kyoryoku no rekishiteki kyokun* 米中教育交流の軌跡——国際文化協力の歴史的教訓 [U.S–China educational exchange: Historical lessons in international cultural co-operation], ed. Abe Hiroshi 阿部洋, trans. Gary Tsuchimochi, 206–22. Tokyo: Kanzankai, 1985.

————. "Medical Education in China: The American Connection, 1912–1937." In *Sino-American Relations Since 1900*, ed. Priscilla Roberts, 94–105. Hong Kong, Center of Asian Studies, University of Hong Kong, 1991.

————. "Health and Nationalist Reconstruction: Rural Health in Nationalist China 1928–1937." *Modern Asian Studies* 26, no. 2 (1992): 395–415.

Yiyao weisheng ti mofan 醫藥衛生的模範 [The model of medicine and health]. Yanan: Shanganning bianchu zhengfu, 1944.

Young, Arthur N. *China's Nation-Building Effort, 1927–1937: The Financial and Economic Record*. Stanford: Hoover Institution Press, 1971.

Yu, Shenchu 俞慎初. *Zhongguo yixue jian shi* 中國醫學簡史 [A brief history of medicine in China]. Fuzhou: Fujian kexue jishu chubanshe, 1983.

Yung, W. W. "Child Health Work in Peiping First Health Area, 1925–1935." *Chinese Medical Journal* 50 (1936): 562–72.

Zen, Sophia H., ed. *Symposium on Chinese Culture*. Shanghai: Commercial Press, 1931.

Zhen, Zhiya 甄志亞, ed. *Zhongguo yixue shi* 中國醫學史 [History of medicine in China]. Shanghai: Shanghai kexue jishu chubanshe, 1984.

Zheng, Manqing 鄭曼青. *Zhongguo yiyaoxue shi* 中國醫藥學史 [History of medicine and pharmacology in China]. Taibei: Shangwu yinshuguan, 1982.

Zhongguo Guomindang zhongyang tongjichu 中國國民黨中央統計處 [Central Statistical Bureau of the Guomindang]. *Minguo ershier nian zhi jianshe* 民國二十二年之建設 [Reconstruction in 1933]. Nanjing: Central Statistical Bureau of the Guomindang, 1934.

————. *Minguo ershisan nian zhi jianshe* 民國二十年三年之建設 [Reconstruction in 1934]. Nanjing: Central Statistical Bureau of the Guomindang, 1935.

Zhongguo Guomindang zhongyang xuanchuan bu 中國國民黨中央宣傳部 [Central Propaganda Department of the Guomindang]. *Weisheng yundong xuanchuan gangyao* 衛生運動宣傳綱要 [An outline of propaganda in the health movement]. Nanjing: Zhongyang xuanchuan bu, 1929.

———. *Qi xiang yundong xuanchuan gangyao* 七項運動宣傳綱要 [An outline of the propaganda in the seven campaigns]. Nanjing: Zhongyang xuanchuan bu, 1929.

Zhonghuaminguo daxue zhi 中華民國大學誌 [General report on universities and colleges in modern China]. Taibei: China News Press, 1953.

Zhongyang dang wu yuekan 中央黨務月刊 [Central party monthly]. Various issues, 1928–29.

Zhongyang weisheng sheshi shiyan chu gongzuo baogao 中央衛生設施實驗處工作報告 [Work report of the Central Field Health Station]. Nanjing: Zhongyang weisheng sheshi shiyan chu, 1933.

"Zhongyi di hefa diwei" 中醫的合法地位. *Tianwentai bao* 天文台報 [Observatory daily], n.d. [31 December 1968?]. Copy filed in the Archives of the Historical Commission of the Kuomintang.

Zou, Shuwen 鄒樹文. *Xin shenghuo yu xiangcun jianshe* 新生活與鄉村建設 [New life and village reconstruction]. Nanjing: Zheng zhong shuju, 1934.

Zhu, Zishuang 朱子爽. *Zhongguo guomindang jiaoyu zhengce* 中國國民黨教育政策 [The educational policy of the Guomindang]. Chongqing: Guomin tushu gongsi, 1941.

Index

275

health programs, 126; and popular health education, 129; and pharmacy education, 161; and midwifery education, 167; and training of public health personnel, 168; merged with National Public Health Personnel Training Institute, 177

Central Hospital: 52, 55, 143, 193; founding of, 58; funding of, 63, 65; work in maternal and child health, 121; and nursing education, 164; and midwifery education, 166; public health training in, 168; relocation of, 177–178

Central Hygienic Laboratory: 50, 52, 193; funding of 63; work of, 109

Central Midwifery School: 52, 193; founding of 58, 121; midwifery work of, 123; curriculum of, 166; relocation of, 178

Central School Health Service: 126

Central School of Nursing: 52, 58, 193; midwifery work of, 123; founding of, 164; teacher-training courses in, 174; relocation of, 178

Changsha: 45; school health services in, 126

Char, George Y.: *see* Xie Yuanfu

Chen bao: 28

Chen, Duxiu: 14, 27

Chen, Guofu: 51

Chen, Zhiqian (C. C. Chen): vii, 94, 101; at Xiaozhuang, 18, 76; as editor of Binying Weekly, 28–29; on state medicine, 39–40, 185; at Dingxian, 77–79, 96, 173; on developing maternal health programs, 124; on traditional midwives, 167; Commission on Medical Education influenced by, 173; post-1949 career of, 190

Chengdu: wartime medical schools in, 178

Chiang, Kai-shek: 1–4, 34, 45–46, 49, 51, 71, 79; and New Life Movement, 36–37, 89–90, 97, 183; and national budget, 62, 214n.64; closed down Xiaozhuang project, 77, 182; and political objective in rural programs, 181; and view of mass movements, 182

Chiang, Kai-shek, Mme.: 48, 64; and Christian participation in rural reconstruction, 91–92; on the China Program, 183

Chiang, Monlin (Jiang Menglin): 136

China Christian Educational Association: 148; and mission of Shandong Christian Medical College, 148

China Foundation for the Promotion of Education and Culture: 148

China Medical Board of the Rockefeller Foundation: 22, 183; grants to colleges, 24–25; supported Xiangya Medical College, 154

China Program of the Rockefeller Foundation: 94–95; Mme. Chiang Kai-shek's view of, 183

Chinese Academy of Medical Sciences: 190

Chinese Academy of Sciences: 190

Chinese Drug Research Institute: 63

Chinese Maritime Customs: 116

Chinese Medical Association: 28, 92, 176, 190

Chinese Medical Journal: 190

Chinese Medical Missionary Association: 21

Chinese Red Cross: 161

Cholera: 10, 12, 16, 57, 69, 75, 104, 108, 110

Monographs of the
Association for Asian Studies

1. *Money Economy of Medieval Japan: A Study in the Use of Coins*, by Delmer M. Brown. 1951
2. *China's Management of the American Barbarians: A Study of Sino-American Relations, 1841–1861, with Documents*, by Earl Swisher. 1951.
3. *Leadership and Power in the Chinese Community of Thailand*, by G. William Skinner. 1958.
4. *Siam Under Rama III, 1824–1851*, by Walter F. Vella. 1957.
5. *The Rise of the Merchant Class in Tokugawa Japan: 1600–1868*, by Charles David Sheldon. 1958.
6. *Chinese Secret Societies in Malaya*, by L. F. Comber. 1959.
7. *The Traditional Chinese Clan Rules*, by Hui-Chen Wang Liu. 1959.
8. *A Comparative Analysis of the Jajmani System*, by Thomas O. Beidelman. 1959.
9. *Colonial Labour Policy and Administration 1910–1941*, by J. Norman Parmer. 1959.
10. *Bankguad—A Community Study in Thailand*, by Howard Keva Kaufman. 1959.
11. *Agricultural Involution: The Processes of Ecological Change in Indonesia*, by Clifford Geertz. 1963.
12. *Maharashta Purana*, By Edward C. Dimock, Jr., and Pratul Chandra Gupta. 1964.
13. *Conciliation in Japanese Legal Practice*, by Dan Fenno Henderson. 1964.
14. *The Malayan Tin Industry to 1914*, by Wong Lin Ken. 1965.
*15. *Reform, Rebellion, and the Heavenly Way*, by Benjamin F. Weems. 1964.
16. *Korean Literature: Topics and Themes*, by Peter H. Lee. 1965.
17. *Ch'oe Pu's Diary: A Record of Drifting Across the Sea*, by John Meskill. 1965.
18. *The British in Malaya: The First Forty Years*, by K. G. Tregonning. 1965.
19. *Chiaraijima Village: Land Tenure, Taxation, and Local Trade*, by William Chambliss. 1965.

*20. *Shinran's Gospel of Pure Grace,* by Alfred Bloom. 1965.
21. *Before Aggression: Europeans Prepare the Japanese Army,* by Ernst L. Presseisen. 1965.
*22. *A Documentary Chronicle of Sino-Western Relations: 1644–1820,* by Lo-shu Fu. 1966.
23. *K'ang Yu-wei: A Biography and a Symposium,* trans. and ed. by Jung-pang Lo. 1967
24. *The Restoration of Thailand Under Rama I: 1782–1809,* by Klaus Wenk. 1968.
*25. *Political Centers and Cultural Regions in Early Bengal,* by Barrie M. Morrison. 1969.
*26. *The Peasant Rebellions of the Late Ming Dynasty,* by James Bunyan Parsons. 1969.
27. *Politics and Nationalist Awakening in South India: 1852–1891,* by R. Suntharalingam. 1974.
28. *Masks of Fiction in Dream of the Red Chamber: Myth, Mimesis, and Persona,* by Lucien Miller. 1975.
29. *Dogen Kigen—Mystical Realist,* by Hee-Jin Kim. 1975.
*30. *The New Jerusalem: Aspects of Utopianism in the Thought of Kagawa Toyohiko,* by George B. Bikle, Jr. 1976.
*31. *Big City Government in India: Councilor, Administrator, and Citizen in Delhi,* by Philip Oldenburg. 1976.
*32. *Political Behavior of Adolescents in China: The Cultural Revolution in Kwangchow,* by David M. Raddock. 1977.
*33. *Philippine Policy Toward Sabah: A Claim to Independence,* by Lela Garner Noble. 1977.
34. *Code and Custom in a Thai Provincial Court,* by David M. Engel. 1978.
*35. *Robe and Plough: Monasticism and Economic Interest in Early Medieval Sri Lanka,* by R. A. L. H. Gunawardana. 1979.
*36. *Burmese Sit-tans, 1764–1826: Records of Rural Life and Administration,* by Frank N. Trager and William J. Koenig. 1979.
*37. *An Introduction to Javanese Law: A Translation of and Commentary on the Agama,* by M. C. Hoadley and M. B. Hooker. 1980.
*38. *An Anthology of Modern Writing from Sri Lanka,* by Ranjini Obeyesekere and Chitra Fernando, eds. 1981.
*39. *Academies in Ming China: An Historical Essay,* by John Meskill. 1982.
*40. *Kerajaan: Malay Political Culture on the Eve of Colonial Rule,* by A. C. Milner. 1982.
*41. *Chinese Religion in Western Languages: A Comprehensive and Classified Bibliography of Publications in English, French and German through 1980,* by Laurence G. Thompson. 1984.

*42. *Crime and Criminality in British India*, by Anand A. Yang. 1985.
*43. *Social Protest and Popular Culture in Eighteenth-Century Japan*, by Anne Walthall. 1986.
*44. *Shaohsing: Competition and Cooperation in Nineteenth-Century China*, by James H. Cole. 1986.
*45. *Islam in Java: Normative Piety and Mysticism in the Sultanate of Yogyakarta*, by Mark R. Woodward. 1989.
*46. *The Textual History of the Huai-nan Tzu*, by Harold D. Roth. 1992.
*47. *Chinese Religion: Publications in Western Languages, 1981 through 1990*, by Thompson and Seaman. 1993.
*48. *Indigenous People of Asia*, by R. H. Barnes, Andrew Gray, and Benedict Kingsbury, eds. 1995.
*49. *Gentlemanly Interests and Wealth on the Yangtze Delta*, by John Meskill. 1995.
*50. *Health and National Reconstruction in Nationalist China: The Development of Modern Health Services, 1928–1937*, by Ka-che Yip, 1995.

* Indicates publication is available from the Association for Asian Studies, 1 Lane Hall, University of Michigan, Ann Arbor, MI 48109.